For Gina:
I couldn't have done it without you.

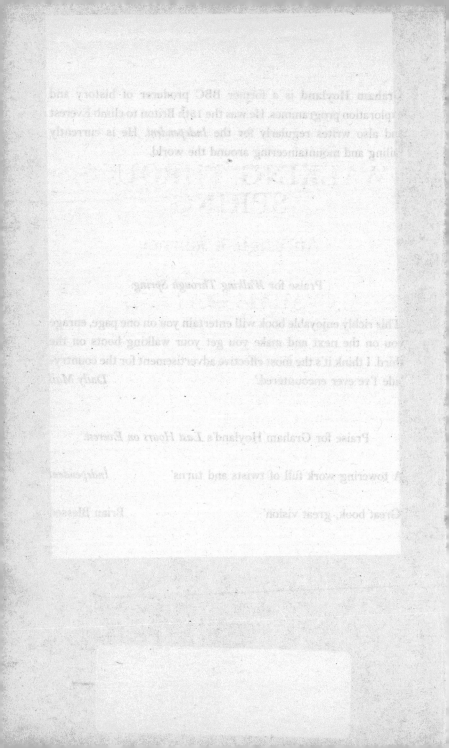

Graham Hoyland is a former BBC producer of history and exploration programmes. He was the 15th Briton to climb Everest and also writes regularly for the Independent. He is currently sailing and mountaineering around the world.

A WALKING YEAR

SPRING

GRAHAM K. HOYLAND

WALKING THROUGH SPRING

An English Journey

GRAHAM HOYLAND

WILLIAM
COLLINS

William Collins
An imprint of HarperCollins*Publishers*
1 London Bridge Street
London SE1 9GF

WilliamCollinsBooks.com

This William Collins paperback edition published in 2017

22 21 20 19 18 17
10 9 8 7 6 5 4 3 2 1

First published in the United Kingdom by William Collins in 2016

Text © Graham Hoyland, 2016
Frontispiece map created by Martin Brown

Graham Hoyland asserts his moral right to be identified as the author of this work.

A catalogue record for this book is available from the British Library.

ISBN 978-0-00-815614-5

Typeset by Palimpsest Book Production Ltd, Falkirk, Stirlingshire
Printed and bound in Great Britain by Clays Ltd, St Ives plc

MIX
Paper from
responsible sources
FSC® C007454

FSC™ is a non-profit international organisation established to promote
the responsible management of the world's forests. Products carrying the
FSC label are independently certified to assure consumers that they come
from forests that are managed to meet the social, economic and ecological needs
of present and future generations, and other controlled sources.

Find out more about HarperCollins and the environment at
www.harpercollins.co.uk/green

INTRODUCTION

The English spring appears in the southern counties sometime in March, then moves north, travelling at much the same speed as a walking man. It gets to the border with Scotland in a few weeks. On the way it loosens winter's grip with tiny shoots of green, a haze of leaves on a distant wood, a breath of warm wind in the night. Spring is an indefinite event, but has to do with the appearance of certain flowers, birds and insects. It is a feeling as much as a happening.

This book is about a journey through England, walking with the spring, taking the whole season to complete. It documents my journey as I walked from the south coast on 20 March 2015, the first day of the season, up to the border with Scotland, which was reached on the last full day of spring: 20 June. Following Richard Jefferies, Edward Thomas and Robert Macfarlane into the wilder parts of our country, *Walking through Spring* is a book in the English pastoral tradition.

I connected a labyrinth of ancient footpaths into a new English trail running from south to north, marking each mile travelled by planting an acorn in hedgerows of blackthorn, hawthorn, dogwood and hazel, thus drawing a line of oak trees that stretched through the English countryside.

On the way many aspects of spring were explored: how does the Earth's angle to the Sun make the seasons change? Which plants start blooming first? Which birds survive the bitter winter in our hedgerows and which arrive in spring after over-wintering overseas? The joy of the natural world was seen, smelled and experienced as the season unfolded – from dairy cows cantering and kicking their heels when released into lush meadows, to galloping bands of lambs in the Peak District. England's unique botanical, geographical and social landscape was mapped as spring unfolded across the country.

We crunched through the leftover leaves of autumn, waded through a haze of bluebells in the woods, and examined the snowdrops, crocuses, catkins, primroses and daffodils which chart the progress of the season. I walked with people who know about walking, who observe nature and understand it deeply. We saw wide views of the great estuaries from the ridgeways and gazed up at the night sky from beside a campfire. On the way we read some of England's best nature writers, trying to grasp the essence of the country.

Avoiding roads with their narrow streams of gleaming cars, *Walking through Spring* began on the seashore at Christchurch, Dorset, passed beside the New Forest, followed the old ways to Salisbury and Bath, then headed north along the Cotswold escarpment. I visited Slad, home of Laurie Lee's *Cider with Rosie.* Then through secret green ways almost to the centre of Birmingham, and then along canal towpaths up the Derwent Valley. We stamped through the Yorkshire Dales, sailed a dinghy through the Lake District with *Swallows and Amazons*, and then took in an otter's point of view down the River Eden to the Scottish border.

My journey also engaged with England's rural characters: farmers, beekeepers, pub landlords and narrowboat owners. What does spring mean to them? Is the season really getting earlier every year? Away from the cars and motorways, can walking through a season help us reconnect with the old England of Wildwood and Pan?

I had missed more than a dozen English springs in recent years. Nine were lost on Mount Everest, where I went time after time in the March climbing season. Hunched in a tent on the Tibetan plateau, where the dry wind never stops, I dreamed of water meadows and wildflowers in the west of England. Searching amongst the icy blocks of the north side of Everest for something I never found, I longed to be back in England. Later, I turned to sailing in the tropics, where the turquoise seas and garish slashes of colour in the jungle could never compare with England's subdued palette of greens. Another five springs were lost in that way.

The child is father of the man, and I had a happy boyhood in the fields and streams of the county of Rutland. Dad, an artist and nature-poet, fed me on a diet of writers who have sustained me ever since. First was 'BB', or Denys Watkins-Pitchford. His stories of gnome-like little men living in the roots of an oak next to a stream might sound fey, but these were rough-living little people, spearing sticklebacks and brewing elderberry wine in tiny wooden barrels. In spring they build a boat and set off downstream to search for Cloudberry, their missing brother. BB's descriptions of the birds, animals and plants fascinated me, and I would creep amongst the sedges and shallows of our local streams, imagining that I, too, was living off the country.

Later I was given *Bevis: The Story of a Boy*, by one of our finest nature writers, Richard Jefferies. Bevis built a gun and made gunpowder, then shot, cooked and ate wildlife, and he sailed his homemade boat on a great lake. Again, the characters are unsentimental and nature is red in tooth and claw.

Edward Thomas was the next author I was given, and his *Pursuit of Spring* brings us to the season. His journey to find new life in the country after winter was the germ of the idea that grew into this book. These pastoral writers shared a view of the English countryside which always seemed to have a sense of loss and imminent doom hanging over it. For Thomas Hardy it was the railways that destroyed the countryside; for Jefferies industrialisation and the steam-plough; by my boyhood in the 1960s the fields around our village were being steadily raped by agri-business. Centuries-old hedgerows were dug out, trees cut down; ancient footpaths became notional lines across vast, prairie-like fields. Pesticides decimated songbird populations and Rachel Carson's seminal *Silent Spring* was published in the US, documenting the abuse of DDT and the resultant death of the bird populations, and forecasting the death of nature.

During my lifetime I have heard fewer and fewer songbirds in the countryside. Urban sprawl continues, and by the time my father died at the end of the century his predictions seemed to have become true. Our old village in Rutland is now surrounded by giant corduroy fields packed with subsidised wheat. Butterfly Lane and Cannonball Lane have been dug up or built over. The place looks like a service station car park. But it was the lack of trees that was most distressing – the lovely willows by the stream have been grubbed up to make money, all for a few more square metres of cash crop. As soon as I had a home of my own I planted an orchard, and now fifteen apple trees stand in full blossom every spring below Wavering Down in Somerset.

That is why I want to walk through England and plant trees, and find an answer to the question: does spring still come to England's green and pleasant land?

CHAPTER ONE

*Starting from the Dorset seashore – why we have spring – trees full
of rooks, building their nests – a hare –* Masquerade *– Admiral
Collingwood planting oaks for the navy – collecting acorns – taking
old paths through a New Forest – the Knightwood Oak –* Alice in
Wonderland *– Salisbury Cathedral, which took a thousand oaks to
build – a meeting with William Golding –* The Spire *– paganism –
signs of spring in literature – apple blossom – spring cleaning*

Our old van was struggling up the long incline towards
the summit of Shap Fell on the A6. It was Easter. I
could just see out of the window and felt awed by the
bleak moorland. Back home in the south the daffodils were out,
but up here the winter still gripped the countryside. 'The spring
starts in England in the southern counties in March, then moves
north, travelling at walking speed,' said my dad, 'but it'll get to
Scotland in a few weeks.' Shortly afterwards we breasted Shap
Summit with a cheer from the family, and the fuming old van
started a long, relieved descent towards Scotland.

Somewhere in my five-year-old brain the thought lodged
that a season could travel north through a country and appear
later in another one. Warmth and life would start in the south
and move north; start in the valleys and move to the mountain-
tops. I stored away the thought: one day I will walk with the
spring.

That impulse re-emerged much later in life. After years

spent abroad I felt a need to re-immerse myself in England
and the long-forgotten childhood memory from Shap Summit
returned. First I had to find out if Dad was right. The English
spring does indeed start in the far south and travels northwards. But why do we have spring? Why do we have seasons
at all? I started asking people these questions and got a
surprising range of answers. The most popular was 'the Earth
must be closer to the Sun in summer'. This is a clever answer,
because the Earth's orbit is indeed slightly elliptical. However,
England in the Northern Hemisphere has winter when the
Earth is closest to the Sun, the perihelion, and summer when
it is furthest from the Sun, the aphelion. The Sun is 91,400,000
miles away in January and 94,500,000 miles away in July. So
that can't be the answer.

It took the Ancient Greeks to figure out the reason why
there are seasons, and modern scientists to find the reason for
the reason. The simple answer is that the Earth is tilted on its
axis at 23.4 degrees. As it makes its year-long journey around
the Sun, England in the Northern Hemisphere is leaning
towards the Sun for half the year, and leaning away from it for
the other half. Although the strength of the Sun remains
constant, it falls on a greater area in the winter than in the
summer. This varying relative strength of the sunlight on
Earth and length of the days brings longer, hotter days in
summer and shorter, colder days in winter. Increasing day
length and temperature initiate most of the changes we call
spring. If all of this is hard to visualise, walking around a
standard lamp (the Sun) with a tilted revolving globe (the
Earth) may make it all clear.

Why is the Earth tilted? It seems that early in the Solar
System's history something very big hit the Earth and whacked
it out of kilter. The bits that flew off whirled around, collected

together and became the Moon. Put like that it sounds about as likely as any other creation myth, but that is the accepted theory. What interests me is how contingent it all is: without that collision there would not only be no seasons, but possibly no living creatures either. Our disproportionally large moon drove tides which are now thought to have provided the conditions that gave rise to life. With these thoughts in mind I decided: let's do it. Let's go and find the English spring.

As I walk out of the sea that fine March morning I meet a young man carrying a boa constrictor draped around his neck. 'He loves the spring,' he says in reply to my question, stroking the creature. 'He wakes up from hibernation and lies under the sunlamp. Then I take him for walks.' The glittering eyes regard me balefully. The tattooed mid-section looks as thick as a man's thigh. 'He's never squeezed me yet,' he murmurs fondly, walking off, 'and I've had him since this big.' He waggles his little finger, partly by way of explanation, partly in farewell.

But the animals that stick in my mind on the first day of our walk were two roe deer that I met on the New Forest road when driving over from Lymington. It was very early, their time of day, and they were crossing a minor road in woodland. I stopped the car and let them stalk across in front of me. A bounce into the undergrowth, and then they turned to watch me with that relaxed attentiveness possessed by wild animals. They seemed at home in the woods. I want to join them, to learn how to watch like that.

Starting from the south coast seems a logical thing to do. Spring progresses through England from south to north, and the spring equinox is a good time to begin, when the days start becoming longer than the nights. We start our journey at the seaside town of Christchurch in Dorset on the 20th day of March, tramp past the priory, and set off up the Avon Valley. This footpath will take us north to Salisbury, and Christchurch is conveniently placed on the sea at the mouth of the Avon river.

With me is my girlfriend Gina, who is planning the route and organising the logistics. We have returned early from our main occupation, which is a slow journey around the world in an old boat, trying to sail across each of the seven oceans and climb the highest mountain in each continent. We have both missed England, and soft green countryside, and the idea of walking with the spring seems very appealing. Instead of big expeditions we want a mini-expedition, to return from the exotic to the domestic, to reconnect with our homeland, to find the wilderness in England.

The first thing we notice as we set out is that the Dorset verges are well-tended. This county is something of a botanical garden, with a warm coastline, lowland heath, chalk land and sandy land, too. The council has been experimenting with methods to reduce soil fertility on the road verges which helps to reduce grass growth and thus the expense of mowing. One technique is to remove the topsoil to reveal the subsoil, another is to plant yellow rattle to reduce the grass. This semi-parasitic plant used to be a problem for farmers as it reduces hay yields by up to 50 per cent, but it's an attractive yellow-flowered plant with a bladder containing the seeds. When this dries out and becomes papery the seeds will rattle when shaken. In the past this would mean it was time to cut the hay, giving its other name: hay rattle. Also, twenty sheep have been recruited by

Dorset council to graze the verges along the A354 near Weymouth. This will make sure there's just enough grass to let the wildflowers come up again next year. Fences keep the sheep safe from cars, and I hope they'll be wearing the English national costume: fluorescent jacket and trousers.

After a mile of walking we're out of the town and beside the Avon Valley lakes. Winter is still here, with the grass still dry, light-brown and sere. The hedges thin out and so I bend over to plant the first acorn. A man walking a black-and-white terrier stops to talk. I ask him what signs of spring he had noticed. 'The swans are chasing their last year's young away.' He pointed at a huge nest in the distance, with a swan sitting on it somewhat self-consciously. She looked like a collapsed ballerina. 'That means the new cygnets will hatch in a few weeks.' He ponders a moment. 'I think it's the male that chases them away.' I suggest that this fact might interest human parents of stay-at-home children. He grunts and then strolls on, the terrier snuffling in the verge beside him.

Great oaks from little acorns grow – in this case *Quercus robur*. My plan is to leave a line of oaks through England, an average of one a mile, to help in a small way to fill the gaps in the country's hedgerows. Not all the seedlings will grow to maturity, but by way-pointing each site by GPS we hope to return over the years and replant those that are missing. My sister Vhairi has a huge oak in her garden in Lymington, and it was this tree that gave me the idea. I had hoped to gather enough acorns from it to plant a line through England, but in the end her oak had an unproductive autumn and so I had to order 500 acorns from a professional nursery.

In spring, oaks flower as they come into leaf. They are beneficial trees, they support more wildlife than any other British tree, including over 280 species of insects, and their harvest of acorns can provide an autumnal feast for pigs, badgers, squirrels, pigeons, ducks, jays, mice, deer and even wild boar. They are large, beautiful and particularly enduring trees, living as long as a thousand years. A medieval knight, granted three crops on a tract of land by a grateful king, asked for the crop to be oak trees, thus providing his descendants with nearly three thousand years of ownership. John Dryden wrote this:

> Three centuries he grows, and three he stays
> supreme in state; and in three more decays.[1]

A lifespan of nearly a thousand years is on a different time-scale to ours. A mature oak can eventually grow more than 130 feet high (40 metres) and weigh over 14 tons. It doesn't matter to me that I'll never see these trees full-grown. The idea that one day they might stand in our landscape is enough.

I'm not alone in this oak-planting activity. Captain Cuthbert Collingwood, later Vice-Admiral, friend and comrade of Nelson at Trafalgar, knew that it took 2,000 to 3,000 oaks to build a Royal Navy ship such as HMS *Victory*. He was concerned that there were insufficient trees to build a future navy, so whenever he visited landed friends he would take his dog Bounce for a walk with a pocketful of acorns and plant one wherever he saw a space.

He didn't see the ironclads coming. HMS *Warrior*, an all-iron ship, was launched in 1860, and the Admiralty

---

[1] John Dryden, *Palamon and Arcite*, Book III (1700)

immediately stopped the construction of all-wooden ships of the line shortly afterwards. Oaks all over England presumably breathed a collective sigh of relief.

The first sign of spring around here is trees full of rooks' nests. They nest high and in colonies. By now, in late March, the eggs are laid and the air is full of their cries: *Kaah! Kaah!* They fan their tails and bow at every call. We see them strutting around the fields, probing for earthworms and insect larvae with their strong bills. They eat acorns, too. There are lots of waterfowl on these lakes, and we see more swans on the nest. Many of the hedges have been grubbed out here, but there are signs of some being replanted. I make a mental note to find a farmer somewhere to explain which way the trend is going.

At this early stage Gina and I are wearing rubber wellington boots, not knowing how wet the Avon Valley trail would be. In fact, the path turns out to be well drained and the wellies too hot, so we revert to our Italian leather walking boots. These wonderful contraptions, still made out of real cow, have taken us many miles in comfort. I wear plastic boots on ice and snow, and I've tried Goretex footwear once or twice, but for a good all-rounder, traditional leather boots with woollen socks are hard to beat. Plus you can eat them if rations run short, as Captain John Franklin did in the Arctic in 1822: 'the man who ate his boots'. Marinate overnight, boil vigorously and serve. As A.A. Milne wrote in *Winnie the Pooh*: 'When you see someone putting on his Big Boots, you can be pretty sure that an Adventure is going to happen.'

Elsewhere on our bodies are a variety of sailing clothes made by Henri Lloyd and waterproof jackets and leggings made by Berghaus – as are our rucksacks. Thanks to all this kit, we kept dry and warm throughout the 500 miles of walking, with no serious blisters.

I've just seen a hare. Climbing over a stile he explodes away from under me, long legs and forked ears looking strangely like a deer. 'Stubble-stag!' I suddenly understand what the name means. My heart is hammering with the shock.

Seamus Heaney's translation of the Middle English text 'Names of the Hare' lists seventy-two different names for the hare. Here are just some of them:

> The stubble-stag, the long lugs,
> the stook-deer, the frisky legs,
> the wild one, the skipper,
> the hug-the-ground, the lurker.[1]

He's always been considered a magical beast, hard to pin down. This is my first close sighting. I've been on the lookout but only caught a brief glimpse of one far away in a ploughed field with a rainbow arching over it.

Hares are very fast, running at up to 40 miles per hour (65 km/h) across open country. They would suddenly burst out of the corn as the farm labourers reduced the crop to an

---

[1] Seamus Heaney, *The Names of the Hare* (1982)

island in the stubble. That's maybe why they were also 'the sudden-start, the shake-the-heart'.

They're normally solitary and live on the surface, unlike rabbits, which are colonists and live in burrows. One spring I saw a drove of five males chasing each other around and around a harrowed field in Rutland. This behaviour is about dominance and will give better access to females. The 'mad March hare' behaviour of two animals standing up and boxing was long thought to be males fighting, but it's actually a male trying to achieve copulation and a female trying to avoid it. This battle can last ages, and if another male approaches he will be chased off. Leverets will be born soon, as early as 1 April, in a grassy depression called a form. They emerge with fur coats and with their eyes open, so they're quickly self-sustaining – again, unlike rabbits.

The rainbow-hare reminded me of Kit Williams' 1979 children's book *Masquerade*, which contained pictorial and written clues for a treasure hunt for a golden hare made by Williams and buried in England: 'To solve the hidden riddle, you must use your eyes, And find the hare in every picture that may point you to the prize.' The hunt was hugely popular and caused a nationwide stir, but it descended into farce when the treasure was found. The solution led towards a spot under the tip of the shadow cast by a monument during the spring equinox. The *Sunday Times* claimed that the winner had discovered the hare by covert means. That's entirely in line with hares: evasive, mysterious, magical beasts: 'the creature no one dares to name'. Apart from Seamus Heaney, who named it seventy-two times.

On day two, after passing through Ringwood we cross a couple of lakes in the Avon Valley and see the western edge of the New Forest. Here the unpopular King William II, out hunting in the forest, was killed by an arrow fired by one William Tyrell. The arrow was said to have glanced off an oak tree and entered his chest, piercing a lung. It seems curiously appropriate that the oak, the king of trees, should have been involved in killing a king. Fearing charges of regicide, Tyrell escaped across the Avon at a point still called Tyrell's Ford. We passed it yesterday. His horse's shoes were said to be nailed on backwards, to confuse pursuers. Was this an assassination or an accident? If the oak tree did show a mark, it is hard to believe that even the most expert marksman could bounce an arrow off a tree and deliberately hit a king.

We've just seen some wood anemones sprinkled with lesser celandines and bluebells amongst a stand of trees. I hope that these three flowers are going to be with us all spring. The wood anemones have six white petals with a rosette of yellow anthers in the middle. The lesser celandines have yellow star-shaped flowers that stand out against the green woodland floor. They're sometimes called the 'spring messenger'. Gilbert White, the Hampshire naturalist, saw them out as early as 21 February. And the bluebells are coming, too, with their little drooping head like a cloche hat, and later we'll see them in their thousands, creating an appearance of blue ground-smoke through the woods. In the few hedges round here we're seeing the blackthorn flowers. These have six white petals and later they will make a snow-storm of the roadsides. The thorns are long and sharp; perfect for keeping livestock on the right side of the hedges. As the year rolls on the fruit of the blackthorn will come, the sloes, and they'll be picked to make sloe gin.

William Cobbett, the social reformer, farmer and journalist, rode this way in the 1820s, studying the lot of the rural poor. He was opposed to the Corn Laws, which placed a tax on imported wheat and made landowners rich but brought starvation to the farm workers. Cobbett was giving evidence to the Parliamentary Agricultural Committee against the landlord interest and wanted to see conditions for himself. The result is a fascinating snapshot of the English countryside in the early nineteenth century. In the resulting book, *Rural Rides* (1830), he notes that here in the New Forest deer were on the one hand fed hay from the public purse but on the other hand their increasing numbers meant that they were eating trees, also planted at public expense. Yet a poor man could be transported to Australia for catching any of this profuse game, which was, after all, on common land. It was another way of the aristocracy taking bites out of the common good. 'What are those deer *for*? Who are to eat them? Are they for the Royal Family?' Poor Cobbett was imprisoned for his radical ideas but his courageous journalism helped to make England a fairer place. He more than anyone else was responsible for the protest movement that led to the Great Reform Act of 1832, which removed some of the more corrupt electoral practices. *Rural Rides* is immensely readable, despite an apparent obsession with Swedish turnips and a dislike of drystone walls.

Mind you, Cobbett must have been difficult to live with. He disapproved of religious tracts, parsons, politicians and Shakespeare, whose work he dismissed as 'bombast, puns and smuts'. He hated tea and 'those ever-damned potatoes' which he was forever preaching against. What redeems him is his constant concern for the lot of the labouring poor in the English countryside. His books give us a snapshot of the rural England of the depressed 1820s.

On the path we see tracks in the mud: roe deer, fox and a large waterfowl I can't identify. On the roads we have to press against the hedges as large, glossy 4x4 cars roll by. These issue from expensive-looking old farmhouses along the edges of the New Forest. The car windows are closed and the occupants do not make eye contact with the scruffy walkers. There are usually horses in the fields next to these houses, and they're wearing horse-blankets. Around here even the animals wear clothes. The rough New Forest ponies, virtually feral, wander the country roads in these parts. They have their own thick hairy winter coats and do not wear expensive blankets. Like us, they pause, gaze over the gates at their wealthy cousins and pass on.

We walk into the shade of the New Forest near Fordingbridge, looking for the Knightwood Oak, the largest and most famous oak in the forest. We get to the plantation, which is pre-enclosure woodland: original forest. We crunch down a gravel path, walking past saplings from the original tree. At a bend on the right there is a rare example of inosculation, where an oak and a beech have fused together as if grafted. The join is surprisingly high up. This will sometimes happen when two branches rub together, abrade the bark and allow the living cambium to touch.

The Knightwood Oak is huge, with a girth of 24 feet (7.3 metres). It is over 600 years old and still going strong. The tree was pollarded over four centuries ago, having its head cut off to promote new growth which would then shoot back in spring. The result is that the trunk is not as high as it could be and the enormously thick branches shoot straight up. Frankly, it's not as attractive as an unmolested tree. This pollarding would have been done for two reasons. One was to provide foliage to feed livestock, in which case the branches were cut every couple of years or so. The second reason was to provide straight oaken posts for fencing, for which the branches were cut every ten years or so.

It's unclear why this particular tree was originally pollarded, but the practice was forbidden in an Act of 1698. Pollarding was open to abuse by the keepers as the foliage and posts were of value, and King William III needed timber for his new Navy. Wooden ships need many long straight timbers, and oaks provided the very best wood of all. If grown close together the trees stretch up to the sky and the trunks grow long. Buckler's Hard, the eighteenth-century ship-building village, is only a few miles away. Three ships that took part in Trafalgar were built there, and would have contained much New Forest heart of oak: *Agamemnon*, Nelson's favourite ship; *Euryalus*, on which official news of his death was written; and *Swiftsure*, which took in tow *Redoubtable*, the French ship from which he had been fatally shot.

We're walking back to the Avon Valley through the New Forest. A recent Forestry Commission survey of attitudes to woodland found that only 56 per cent of us made visits to the woods in the last two years for picnics or walking. That is the lowest number since sampling began twenty years ago. Most respondents blamed a lack of time, a lack of interest, or thought the woods were too far away. And yet most people are within six miles of Forestry Commission woodland, which is only about a quarter of an hour away by car. So why is there this decline in interest? Perhaps with the digital revolution gaining pace we are getting further from our roots in the land, and further from nature. Perhaps the woods are considered too boring when compared to screen-based entertainment. I'm optimistic, though. The new generation seems more aware of the need to reconnect.

In his book *Wildwood*, the woodsman-naturalist Roger
Deakin explained how he came to love the New Forest. Like
many of us it involved early exposure to the woods as a child
and a continuing interest as an influential adult. We are on the
hunt for England's only venomous snake, the adder, but Deakin
explains that the numbers of all snakes in the forest had
declined, including grass snakes and the smooth snake.
Humans persecute them like wasps. I've only twice seen an
adder in the wild, but we manage to find a collection of all the
native snakes, lizards and frogs at the Forestry Commission's
reptile centre near Lyndhurst. We walk in after closing time,
but a departing warden kindly lets us look around.

The clearings are deserted in the evening sunshine and the
snakes are soaking up the last remnants of heat on the stones.
A male adder lies basking in front of me. He's silvery in colour
and beautifully marked with heavy black zigzags down his back
and a broad V on his head. He would have emerged from
hibernation recently, a month before the females. He likes to
eat small rodents such as mice and voles. He waits for his prey,
strikes, then injects his venom. He'll then follow the scent of
the dying victim until he finds it paralysed, and then eats it
whole. He'll shed his skin in early April and then actively seek
a mate. If he finds one and another male approaches, the first
male will defend the female aggressively. That's when the
'adder dance' takes place between the competing males: they'll
raise their front half from the ground, attack, then entwine
with their competitor in a wrestling match. On finding a
receptive female our male will engage in a courtship display
which involves flickering his tongue over her whole body. If
she likes this their whole bodies quiver together and copulation
takes place. They then lie together for a couple of hours,
smoking.

The baby adders are born in late summer. Unlike other snakes the young are born live, not in eggs, and will be earth-worm-sized versions of their parents. They will hibernate in September or October, disappearing into the abandoned burrows of small mammals for the winter.

Adders occasionally kill small dogs that irritate them. Humans rarely die of adder bites: twelve in the last 100 years and the last case was in 1975. We probably have more chance of dying from the sting of a wasp. The poor adders have more to fear from humans because of the destruction of their habitat of hedgerows, heathland and rough grasslands.

Nearby is a large grass snake. It is dark brown and piled up like a link of sausages. These secretive snakes live near fresh water and feed on small frogs and toads. They are much larger than adders, sometimes growing over 6 feet (182 centimetres) in length, but are not venomous.

We continue amongst the trees of the New Forest. Spring is here, buds are bursting and the intense limey-green of fresh leaves makes it feel as if we're walking underwater on a seabed of leaves.

I've always loved walking in woodland: it feels good for the soul. But there is recent evidence that the natural environment might act as a tonic for the whole of the body because it's slightly poisonous. In an article in *New Scientist*,[1] toxicologist Mike Moore explains that when walking beside the ocean or in

[1] *New Scientist*, 15 June 2015.

woodland we breathe in an airborne soup of chemicals produced by plants, fungi and bacteria. In particular there are compounds called phytochemicals which contain antioxidants which act against pathogens, and volatile oils which give us the scent of plants. Moore argues that our ancestors evolved in a natural environment where they were exposed to low doses of these chemicals through inhalation and diet. These induce mild stress which in turn triggers repair mechanisms and enhances tolerance to bigger doses. This is called hormesis. The antioxidants found in the Mediterranean diet work in a similar way, by inhibiting a system that controls cell function and growth. When this goes wrong it can lead to diabetes, inflammation, some cancers and neuro-degeneration.

There is plenty of evidence that our bodies evolved around four million years ago to live as hunter-gatherers in a tree-dotted grassland savannah in Africa. So how on earth can we expect a cotton-wool kid in the city to feel even remotely human? The toxins in city air are made up of synthetic chemicals and mildew. Is it any wonder that children are developing unheard-of levels of asthma, obesity and depression if they aren't allowed to run around in the countryside?

My childhood friends lived in a rural village and played in fields and deserted railway cuttings, streams and amongst trees. We ingested a lot of dirt and ran until we were unable to speak. At school we played sports until tired enough to be controllable in the classroom. At home we ate unprocessed food and didn't drink sugary pop. A report from Natural England and the RSPB shows that children have lost the right to roam and warns that the mental health of twenty-first-century children is at risk because they're missing out on the exposure to the countryside enjoyed by past generations.

We've just noticed cows lying down before it rains. This

seems to keep a nice dry patch of grass beneath them. Who says cows are stupid? We try to see if they're facing north. They aren't. There was great excitement in 2008 when researchers at the University of Duisburg-Essen noticed that on Google Earth most cows were facing north, even in the Southern Hemisphere. Deer herds seemed to do the same thing. Eventually someone came up with the hypothesis that both species would have evolved in dense trackless forests or feature-less plains where the ability to sense magnetic lines would give a directional ability and thus an evolutionary advantage.

We're not far from Cuffnells, the country house Alice Liddell moved into when she married. It was she who provided the inspiration for Lewis Carroll's *Alice in Wonderland*, which opens with Alice sitting on a grassy bank surrounded by daisies while her sister reads a book with 'no pictures or conversation in it'. It's springtime, as it is at the beginning of so many childhood books. She sees the White Rabbit scurry past muttering 'Oh dear. Oh dear! I shall be too late!' and she follows him down a rabbit hole, falling down what seems to be a very deep well.

It's odd to think of Alice as an old woman, but she died at 82 years of age and is buried nearby in Lyndhurst. The book plays with the notion of time and physical dimensions and if you peer back at Alice's life, curious events begin to emerge. Two of her sons died in the First World War. She married Reginald Hargreaves, a fabulously wealthy magistrate, land-owner and cricketer, and the ceremony was held in

Westminster Abbey. She was a brown-haired child, and not a bit like the idealised blonde girl portrayed in John Tenniel's illustrations. Lewis Carroll, whose real name was Charles Dodgson, may have had ulterior motives in taking the Liddell children out for a rowing-boat trip on 4 July 1862, but they might have had nothing to do with an unhealthy interest in young girls.

The story of the book's genesis is almost better known than the book itself. Charles Dodgson, a brilliant young mathematician with a shy manner, befriends the Liddell family at Christ Church College, Oxford. Mr Liddell is the Dean, or head of the faculty. Dodgson becomes close to the family and starts taking the children on rowing trips up the Thames, beginning with the son Henry, then the young girls Lorina, Edith and Alice. They go in company with another adult. On the day in question there is boating, then a riverbank picnic when Alice asks for a story. Dodgson obliges, and she begs him to write it up for her. Eventually he does so and presents her with a handwritten and illustrated manuscript entitled *Alice's Adventures Under Ground*. The publishers Macmillan like it and it goes on to publication with a new title.

We now live in a prurient age in an atmosphere of suspicion and quick accusation. Dodgson, aka Carroll, has been accused of being a child-groomer and a paedophile. Evidence has been adduced in the form of the many photographs taken by him of young girls. Then there is the cooling of relations with the Liddells, and missing pages of his diary. However, a biography by Jenny Woolf concludes that the problem may have been that the eldest daughter Lorina was getting too fond of Carroll, not Carroll too fond of Alice. Either way, the picnic begat a lasting classic. I'm left wondering this: what was the book that Alice's sister was reading?

Just up the road, next to Chapel Lane, is an oak tree that Alice sat beneath while reading to her own children, and I plant another one in her memory.

It's dawned on me that spring provides the beginning of so many childhood books. *Alice in Wonderland*, of course, but also *Wind in the Willows*, *The Little Grey Men*, *The Hobbit* and so on. Adult books, too, *A Room with a View*, where the season represents a new beginning, *Lady Chatterley's Lover* by D.H. Lawrence: 'In the company of this common man the world was beautiful and direct. For the first time she felt the influence of Spring.' It's a season of beginnings.

We've walked out of the edge of the New Forest and now we're back in open country. There's more evidence that we may unconsciously cleave to an ancient environment. When humans are given unlimited resources they appear to re-make their surroundings into artificial savannah. In the eighteenth century, landscape designers such as Lancelot 'Capability' Brown and Humphrey Repton created the English Landscape Garden style for their immensely wealthy customers. One of Capability Brown's houses is near where we are now: Broadlands, at Romsey, which was Viscount Palmerston's house. With large bodies of open water and meadowland turf scattered with trees these vast parks were a fair simulacrum of the African savannah that our ancestors trotted around in. An afternoon spent in an art gallery will put you in front of quite a few landscapes of open grassland interspersed with trees. Something about this kind of landscape appeals to humans.

Living in a state of nature meant that our ancestors' lives were probably as Thomas Hobbes observed: nasty, brutish and short. But should we maybe find out what their bodies evolved to cope with, and then tune our surroundings to our own Stone Age body design?

The Hazda, a modern hunter-gatherer tribe, allowed themselves to be fitted with pedometers and it was found that the men walked around ten miles a day (16 kilometres) and the women around six miles (9 kilometres). This is in line with what the English tramps of the 1920s reckoned they could manage per day, on a poor diet. Gina and I found that after about eight miles our legs started objecting; ten miles was our daily average over the three months.

Once you start thinking about Hobbes' state of nature, all kinds of new areas open up. Biologist Paul Salopek, who is spending seven years walking the route that early humans took out of Africa to the tip of South America, points out that there is a neurological angle to walking speed and distance: 'You can make a pretty good evolutionary argument that we were designed to absorb information at about 5 kilometres per hour (3 mph).' This is presumably why motorways are wide and featureless, as at 120 kilometres per hour (76 mph) they would be terrifying if they had the bumps and trees of the countryside. Designing a more 'natural' environment, while leaving out disease and inconvenient predators, could be a lot of fun.

Tonight we're staying at The Three Lions at Fordingbridge, a restaurant with rooms, a sort of English auberge, and it's just great. This regime of walking ten miles or so through English countryside and then eating well and sleeping well is already feeling good. On my climbing trips I always found the walk-in to the mountain was as much fun as the mountaineering.

We're leaning on a wooden gate watching a herd of organic dairy cows being released into their new pasture. They leap and gallop with joy, kicking their heels and bellowing. It's quite a sight, well worth paying the extra few pence to have milk from a happy and fulfilled animal. The farmer's grinning, too. They do this for twenty minutes then settle down to grazing the sweet spring grass.

In Denmark there is a special day in mid-April when all the organic dairy cows are let out, and 'dancing cow day' has become a national spectacle. In England, though, more and more cows are being kept indoors for longer, or even all year round. This is known as 'zero grazing', and is increasingly used for high-yield herds, but scientific studies are showing that milk from pasture-fed cows is more nutritious and full of healthy omega 3 fatty acids. A peer-reviewed Dutch study concludes that if mothers and their infants up to two years old eat organic dairy foods the infants suffer a 36 per cent lower incidence of eczema.

We continue northwards up the River Avon. The name is a tautology: Avon means 'river' in the British Celtic language, so it's 'River River'. To distinguish it from the five other Avons in England it is known as the Salisbury Avon or the Hampshire Avon. In the spring sunshine we can see some of the many fish species through the beautifully clear chalk-stream. An angler I spoke to earlier saw some early barbel and what might have been a shoal of river carp hanging around in a large hole. Here there are Atlantic salmon, brook and sea lampreys, barbel,

bream, bullhead, chub, dace, perch and pike. Not to mention
seatrout. In fact this river has more species in it than any
other river in England, and that's because of the clear, clean
water.

When local canoeists were prevented from paddling on the
Avon by irate anglers, they discovered an ancient Act from
1664, during the reign of Charles II: '*The Act for making the
River Avon navigable from Christchurch to the city of Old Sarum.*'
The Act was not repealed, so there is still legal right of navigation. We are on our way towards Old Sarum, or rather its
modern successor, Salisbury, so we stop our fish-spotting and
walk on.

As we climb out of the River Avon valley north of the New
Forest, we see the devastation of the English countryside at its
worst, a sight that would make the countryman of 100 years
ago weep: the destruction of the hedgerows.

Great prairie-like fields open up before us, squared-off with
easy access for huge tractors and for minimal labour costs.
The result is a bland, featureless desert which blends into
Salisbury Plain beyond. What few hedges remain have been
turned into lines of machine-cut stalks with huge gaps.
Where a telegraph pole stands the chain-flail has lifted away
for a moment and you can see how the vegetation has tried
to grow up alongside the pole. Roger Deakin, in a chapter on
his own hedge-laying craft, writes this: 'I know of nothing
uglier or more saddening than a machine-flailed hedge. It
speaks of the disdain of nature and craft that still dominates

our agriculture.' It's scandalous. How on earth did we do this
to our countryside?

Hedges probably began when man first chopped out clearings in the original wildwood that covered much of post-Ice
Age Britain. This would have been a tangled mass of birch,
pine, aspen, elm and oak providing a huge, complex habitat for
insects, birds and mammals. To contain his livestock and mark
his boundaries Man would weave together small trees and
brushwood to create an impenetrable fence.

There is a popular belief that hedges are a recent addition
to the landscape, having been planted under the Enclosure
Acts of the early nineteenth century. Something like 200,000
miles of hawthorn hedge were indeed planted between 1750
and 1850 (the name 'haw' derives from 'hage', the Old
English for 'hedge'), but half of our hedges are older than
that, and many are hundreds or even thousands of years old.
We can date them by counting the number of woody species
per thirty yards: about one per century. In Devon, over a
quarter of hedges are over 800 years old, and many are
underlain by banks built in the Bronze Age, 4,000 years ago.
But hedging technology probably began long before that, in
the Neolithic Age, 6,000 years ago. There were advanced
woodcraft skills around then, such as the manufacture of
woven screens used in buildings and wattle and daub
construction. That means they knew about coppicing: cutting
trees short to use the flexible long shoots that grow back.
Some of our hedges might even date all the way back to the
original wildwood boundaries. It would be interesting to
know which ones.

In 55 BC Julius Caesar described the army-stopping hedges
planted by the Nervii, the most belligerent Belgic tribe in what
is now Flanders. The Nervii invented hedge-wars, still beloved

by the English suburban classes. 'They cut into the base of slender trees and bent them over so that many branches came out along the length; they then inserted brambles and briars so that these hedges formed a defence like a wall, which could not be penetrated nor even seen through.' This is a fair description of the hedge-layer's craft even today, and what could stop Julius Caesar can usually stop even the most persistent sheep.

In England, 30 regional variations of hedge evolved depending on the type of livestock being contained: beef-rearing counties such as Northamptonshire and Leicestershire use tough, bullock-proof binders to weave the hedge together, but sheep-rearing counties such as Derbyshire can manage with a lighter hedge, or drystone walls.

There are so many advantages to hedges. They're a natural wildlife corridor and provide breeding sites for birds and many other predators of pests. They help prevent soil erosion by controlling water run-off. They can provide crop yield increases by creating micro-climates, and where there are livestock they contain animals, shelter them from wind and rain, and provide herbs and plants essential to their well-being. They are also just so lovely to walk along.

Despite all this, the grubbing-out of hedges I witnessed as a boy in the 1960s accelerated, with nearly one-third of managed hedges disappearing between 1984 and 1993.

What led to the demise of the English hedge? The simple answers are over-population and the desire for profits. Around the time of the First World War new technology made intensive farming possible and the increasing population made demands for more food from the land.

In his fascinating book *Meadowland: the private life of an English field*, which describes a year in the life of one of his meadows, the farmer and writer John Lewis-Stempel explains how farming has changed completely. In the 1930s Britain's farmers grew enough food for 16 million people and now they have to squeeze enough out of the land for 40 million. And the population of these islands is 70 million and rising. It doesn't add up; something has to give. And it has.

Almost all grassland is now intensively grown, with a limited range of fast-growing grasses fed with fertiliser and sprayed with herbicides. As a result, Lewis-Stempel says, 97 per cent of old-style meadows have gone, and so have the traditional meadow grasses. Also, the practice of cutting the grass twice or three times in a season to make silage means that the first cut destroys the seed on the flowers before they have time to develop. It also disturbs or kills the ground-nesting birds and animals that used to live in the old meadows.

Now consider the hedges surrounding the meadows. Removing these allows larger fields, which make sowing and harvesting cheaper and easier, increasing yield and profits. Just increasing a field length from 360 feet (110 metres) to half a mile (800 metres) reduces the turning time for machinery by 80 per cent. Also, boundary hedges become redundant as farms are amalgamated, and fencing becomes a cheaper alternative to an expensive hand-laid hedge. But hedges are a crucial part of our English landscape and if we allow farmers to tear them up we lose something vital to our spiritual health. Surely they should be protected, just as our national parks are protected?

There is some good news, though. Throughout our spring walk we see signs of new hedges being planted, and the public seem more aware of their benefits thanks to TV and the internet. New technology might help, too, with smaller driverless tractors using satellite navigation coming soon, and the possibility of individual trees being connected to the 'internet of things'. In Melbourne, Australia, each tree in the city has been mapped and assigned an electronic identity and they are already receiving emails of appreciation from their human fellow citizens. I would love my oaks to be able to nature-report on drought, pests and their general sense of well-being.

Along the hedge-bottoms hedgehogs are stirring this spring. Their winter-long sleep is ending, and soon their short snouts will emerge and sniff the air. They emit all kinds of noises: grunts, squeaks and snuffles. They are hungry and will be looking for slugs, snails, beetles and worms. Their most dangerous natural enemy in England is the badger, and their last defence is to roll up in a ball and present their sharp 6,000 quills to the enemy. Sadly, this defence doesn't work against cars, and we regularly see squashed hedgehogs on the roadside. Hedgehogs are one of only three English mammals that hibernate: the others are bats and dormice. Amongst the insects, butterflies and queen bumblebees also hibernate.

When the temperatures drop in November and December and food becomes more scarce the hedgehog will look for a suitable nesting site in hedges, tree roots, piles of brushwood or – most perilously– in the bonfires built to celebrate Guy Fawkes night on 5 November. That's why bonfires should be built at the last possible minute. The nest itself, called a *hibernaculum*, is composed of dry leaves and grass and is up to 20 inches (50 centimetres) thick. The hedgehog will have prepared for her long sleep by fattening up hugely: she will weigh twice as much before hibernation as after it.

What happens during hibernation is extraordinary. This is a complicated energy-saving strategy, and is perilous as the animal is defenceless. The hedgehog becomes immobile, the body temperature drops from 35 degrees Celsius to 10 degrees Celsius, and the heart rate slows from around 190 beats per minute to 20. She will breathe once every few minutes.

If the winter is hard and the air temperature remains below freezing for days, there is a danger that ice crystals may start forming in the bloodstream. So if it gets too cold the metabolism has to switch on again and the animal will be roused to activity. As our climate warms up hedgehogs are hibernating less and less.

If only humans could learn to hibernate then astronauts could make long voyages to the stars without having to carry great quantities of food. Hibernation could help us tolerate major surgical operations, too. Contrary to popular belief, polar bears do not hibernate: their pulse slows but the body temperature does not decrease. This may be because the female has to give birth to cubs and nurse them during the long Arctic winter.

'Hedgehog courtship is an understandably cautious process, for the male in particular,' writes Hugh Warwick in *A Prickly Affair*,[1] 'this is a species where no really does mean no.' The babies are called hoglets and they are born with a membrane over their quills, which soon dries and can be cleaned off by the mother.

---

[1] Hugh Warwick, *A Prickly Affair*, Penguin (2010)

The old Romani, or Gypsy, way to cook hedgehog is to clean it (gut it) and then encase it in clay. This is then placed in the embers of a fire and, when ready, the hedgehog-brick is smashed open and the quills readily come away. The disappearance of hedges has coincided with the disappearance of the hedgehog. Numbers are down by more than 90 per cent. 'All the big conservation groups rely on charismatic mega fauna to sell a love of the natural world, which is a bit like reading *Heat* magazine to learn about love,' Hugh Warwick writes. 'Hedgehogs are the animal equivalent of the girl next door – the hedgehog allows us to have a connection with something truly wild in a suburban context.'

Beatrix Potter's *Tale of Mrs Tiggy-Winkle* is next to me now as I write, and I'm leafing through the illustrations. Hers is the hedgehog that children can learn to love: industrious and helpful to humans. There's something slightly disturbing about a wild animal dressed as a washerwoman, but that's the way children seem to like their fiction '. . . all through her gown and her cap there were *hair-pins* sticking wrong way out; so that Lucie didn't like to sit too near her.'[1]

If you really want to help hedgehogs, you could leave out saucers of minced meat, dog food or cat food, but not milk, which upsets their digestive system. Nor fish. Leave some corners of your garden wild in which they can shelter or hunt for their invertebrate prey, and punch holes in the bottom of your garden fences so that they can roam all night. Hedgehogs can cover the area of a golf course in one night, and modern garden fences prevent this. But the return of the English hedge would be the best news for this little animal.

---

[1] Beatrix Potter, *The Tale of Mrs Tiggy-Winkle*, Warne & Co. (1905)

The giant prairie fields around Salisbury are presenting us
with a problem. On my Ordnance Survey Explorer map I can
see a marked footpath crossing a number of fields. On lifting
my eyes I see a vast brown corduroy plain, with a huge tractor
belting up and down in a cloud of dust, rolling, by the looks of
it. The ancient footpath with its hedges has been totally erased,
and many footpath markers along here have been deliberately
removed. Now, do we stand on our rights and venture out
across the desert on a compass bearing, possibly to be flattened
by an immense machine? Or do we pick our way around the
edge, to be yelled at by an infuriated farmer? This problem has
arisen a few times, and we usually go round the edges.

I had a short career as a hobby farmer, running a rare
breeds farm in the Peak District, so I know just how
dangerous these rollers can be. I was once working up and
down a steeply sloping grass field, towing a big ballast roller
weighing about half a ton, with a small Ferguson tractor. The
idea was to roll flat the poaching caused by horses' hooves
over the winter, and it was a job I used to do every spring. At
the bottom of the field lay my neighbour's garden behind a
drystone wall. Behind the wall I was fairly sure he was doing
some weeding. On the down slopes we would whizz along at
speed, and on the up slopes the old grey Fergie would go
Chug, Chug, Chug, very slowly. On the last upslope run the
tractor suddenly lunged forwards and went chugchuggachug-
gachuggachugga, so I looked behind and saw to my horror that
the large yellow roller had become disconnected. It paused,
then started to roll downhill towards my neighbour's wall.

It would be doing about 40 mph when it went through the

wall, then through the house. What to do? I turned the Fergie
and pursued the thundering implement. We got in front of it
and I managed to hit both brakes at once just in front of the
right-hand corner. The wheels locked, the roller smote us hard,
turned violently, and started to chase us sideways across the
field. Eventually the whole entourage came to a halt.

This is why I walk around the side of fields when tractors
are around. I just wish that farmers would stop ploughing up
footpaths (by the way, the best poem I know about a tractor is
Ted Hughes' 'Tractor'. Go on, look it up).

We are putting in a long day of fourteen miles today, passing a
newly thatched cottage decorated with a pair of mad March
straw hares on the ridge. We walk past Grim's Ditch, a prehis-
toric earthwork, and I wonder what the people who dug it
thought of the spring. Was it a time of renewal after the hard
winter? Were most babies born then? Certainly most animals
around here are rearing their young in the spring, so why not
humans in the wild?

We're tired as we plod into the south edge of Salisbury. I'm
impressed by the way the countryside suddenly becomes town,
instead of first arriving at a straggle of houses, as in other, less
well-planned countries. Town planners are often reviled by
householders, but they hold a thin line between the green belt
and the more rapacious developers. One reason for this country
being such a glorious green garden is the good work of our
planners. It's one of the things that's working.

I've known Salisbury for years, coming time and time again

to the cathedral, but I realise that you never really know a town until you walk through it from end to end. The gardens were alive with birds and loud with bees, so different to the depressing monocultures of the prairielands to the south. There you will get several hundred acres of rape spectacularly coming into flower for a few weeks, then nothing. Honey from this plant also crystallises so quickly it is hard to extract it from the comb. City honey is better than that from the countryside for the reason that there are many more species of flowering plants coming into bloom at different times. Honey from the town can taste of elderflowers and limes in the spring, roses in the summer, and in the autumn it gets darker and spicier. Also, urban gardens are not drenched with pesticides.

Salisbury is dominated by the 404-foot cathedral spire. You can see it from miles away, and it looms over the whole town. It is the setting of *The Spire* by William Golding, the Nobel Prize-winning author. He is an author who is becoming neglected because his books are complex and stand apart from the kind of mainstream literature celebrated in the media. But Golding was rated by *The Times* as third on their list of the fifty greatest British writers since 1945, after Larkin and Orwell.

It was he who suggested the name Gaia, the Greek goddess of the Earth, for James Lovelock's hypothesis that the Earth is a single, self-regulating organism, including humans and other animals. He and Lovelock were walking companions and shared ideas. Golding is best known for *Lord of the Flies*, the account of a plane-load of British schoolchildren who are cast away on an island by a crash, and who swiftly revert to savagery. It may not be his best book, but it was his bestseller. It began a theme in his books of how humans band together to bully and murder vulnerable individuals. It happens in *Lord of the Flies*, *The Spire*, *Free Fall* and *Rites of Passage*.

We wander into the cathedral. I stand at the crossways, right where much of the action of the book takes place. *The Spire* is a dark, original book, full of pagan imagery and the medieval power of spring. It concerns Jocelin, the dean of a cathedral loosely based on Salisbury in the fourteenth century. He wants to build a spire on top of the existing tower to exalt God and himself, using money and preferment from his aunt, a mistress of the king. He sees the mason's model of the cathedral as a man lying on his back, and so the phallic symbolism of the spire is inescapable. It stands for Jocelin's hubristic will, the force that drives the pagan builders of the spire high up into the giddy air on subsiding foundations. This is too complex a book to attempt to summarise, but we're here to find spring, and in particular pagan spring. None of the builders of the cathedral are Christians, and they worship a fertility figure who may be Pan. They abscond during a crucial stage of the build to attend a spring ritual. This is historically accurate, as many churches were built on pagan sites to obliterate them, but their builders worshipped in the old way. You will find images of the green man carved by them in many Christian churches, and the sacred yew trees in their churchyards often pre-date the church.

I had dinner with Golding in the late eighties, a few years before his death. He had long white hair and beard and looked a bit like Jocelin. I knew that he disliked discussing his books, so avoided the subject. However, he did like small boats. 'It had the clumsy beauty of a double-bass.' It turned out that both he and my father had been navy lieutenants during the Second World War, and both had been on tank landing craft during the invasion of the Dutch island of Walcheren. Golding was on one of the LCTs converted to fire over 1,000 rockets at the defences, and he spoke graphically about how the deck of his ship glowed red-hot with the exhaust of the missiles, and how viciously the Nazi troops retaliated. 'A Christmas tree of exploding ammunition.'

Some think that Golding got his pessimistic view of humanity from close contact with children when he was a schoolteacher, but I suspect it had more to do with witnessing the horror of the Nazi regime. He saw the Nazi in himself: 'I am of that sort by nature,' he said.

As Jocelin lies dying he sees his spire through a window, and he also sees an apple tree in full spring blossom – a symbol of renewal. He formulates his last thought: '*It's like the apple tree.*' At last he achieves self-knowledge just at the moment of letting go of self. This ambiguous, paradoxical statement is maybe about the joy of life and death, dissolution into Nature, the oneness of all existence. Who knows? Golding was a writer of genius who wrote for the angels.

There is no apple blossom here yet. We have to walk westwards to Bath to pick up our next big footpath, the Cotswold Way, and so we have to make up a route following the valley of the River Wylye. Walking out of Salisbury we pass along a western road named Churchfields, dotted with churches. William Cobbett, on one of his Rural Rides, remarked that there were thirty churches in thirty miles in the mile-wide Avon Valley, and speculated that the population was larger in the far-off times when they were built. There were three more in the carpet-weaving town of Wilton, one of them an enormous church in Romanesque style, with a Byzantine look about it and a whopping great campanile tower. It feels like being in a piazza in Venice. There was much money and religion in this area at one time. Sheep, wool and carpets paid for these stones to be placed on top of one another. Salisbury Cathedral alone consumed 1,000 oaks. It all feels rather showy.

A few miles onwards we have a very different experience. I manage to get us lost and so we end up in the hamlet of Little Langford, where we find the tiny, exquisite church of St Nicholas. Above the Norman doorway is a twelfth-century tympanum, carved with a hunting scene. There is a huntsman, three dogs and a boar in woodland. It is dated to 1120, when this scene could have been witnessed a few hundred yards away from the doorway. That is exactly one hundred years before the start of the construction of the cathedral at Salisbury. Intriguingly, there is also a figure holding a staff that has burst into life with foliage sprouting from it. A tree-ful of birds observe the action. This probably is a likeness of Saint Aldhelm, who as the first bishop of Sherborne was preaching when his staff came into leaf. I guess that this was some kind of Christian–Pagan amalgamation. The Green Man was usually depicted as having foliage forcing its way out of his mouth, eyes and nose.

I step inside, to find the cool quiet interior much as it would have been in the twelfth century. There is an Elizabethan tomb in the south chancel, with an effigy of a ruff-wearing nobleman lying on it, waiting out the centuries that have passed in this place. The domestic scale of this place of worship feels more intimate than the huge churches we had been seeing.

Salisbury Cathedral's spire is a great shout of *'Halleluiah!'* at the cosmos, but even I, an unbeliever, feel the presence of God more strongly right here in the tiny church of St Stephen at Little Langford.

We can now see the site of Old Sarum, the original settlement of Salisbury, just to the north of the modern city. This was a Neolithic settlement for hunters and farmers, the very people who would be clearing the wildwood for livestock and hedging their boundaries. It is close to the great stone circles at Stonehenge and Avebury, and it would have been a city of high regard in those times, as confirmed by the burial barrows nearby. In the Iron Age it was built up into a hill fort and resisted the Romans in their time. A thousand years later it had its own cathedral and castle, but it became a waterless and dissolute place and was abandoned when the new cathedral was built down in the valley, where water was more easily had for the increasing population. Centuries later it became the most notorious of the Rotten Boroughs, still returning two members of Parliament despite having no actual inhabitants, only eleven voters who were landowners living elsewhere. The Pitt political family had it in their pocket. Tom Paine, in the *Rights of Man* (1791), pointed out that 'The town of Old Sarum, which contains not three houses, sends two members; and the town of Manchester, which contains upwards of sixty thousand souls, is not admitted to send any. Is there any principle in these things?' There was a principle, of course, the ancient English principle of the rich hanging on to power and privilege at all costs.

When he rode past on his way to Salisbury William Cobbett met a labourer coming home from work who told him '*they* make it bad for poor people'. He replied, 'it is not *they*, it is that ACCURSED HILL [Old Sarum] that has robbed you of the supper that you ought to find smoking on the table when you get home . . . I gave him the price of a pot of beer, and on I went, leaving the poor dejected assemblage of skin and bone to wonder at my words.'

'Who owns all this countryside?' I wondered idly as we plodded north, and I decided to look it up. The answer amazed me, but it wouldn't have amazed William Cobbett. *Country Life* magazine, not known for its left-wing tendencies, had a report on the most comprehensive land ownership survey since 1872. It found that just 36,000 individuals, only 0.5 per cent of the population, own over 50 per cent of rural land. Just ten individuals own one million acres between them, in a total of 60 million. And just one individual, Gerald Grosvenor, holds land worth £10 billion.

Never has so much been owned by so few instead of so many. Churchill would have been proud of them.

Kevin Cahill, the author of the report, *Who Owns Britain*,[1] has researched land ownership for ten years and concluded that 'a small minority still own a huge amount of Britain's land and what surprises many people is that over the last 100 years not a lot has changed. For the rich the pursuit of land is as important as it's ever been. They receive subsidies and most of their assets are held in trust, avoiding inheritance tax. The biggest change in land ownership in the past 100 years is that people who live in cities now finance the countryside whereas it used to be the other way around.'

---

[1] Kevin Cahill, *Who Owns Britain*, Canongate (2002)

Subsidies? I didn't realise that landowners receive money from the taxpayer for owning land. According to Cahill, 'in the UK the average "farmer" receives between £18,260 and £23,000 every year from the taxpayer for an average farm of 220-plus acres, whether or not he or she grows or herds anything'.[1] So they get around £83 in subsidies per acre, whereas urban dwellers pay taxes of around £18,000 per acre. Cahill's book reveals that land ownership is deliberately opaque in this country. The Land Registry does not record who actually owns the land, it records the freehold titles of domestic dwellings. Parliament attempted to correct this in 1873 with the *Return of Owners of Land*, the so-called New Domesday Book, but this was suppressed.

Ignoring whether this is fair or not, there is a far larger issue here, involving the price of land and thus the cost of houses. English homes are not only the smallest by floor space in Europe, they are also the most expensive, with the land they're built on costing a large amount of the total value. Because ownership is very hard to establish, no one knows how much land is available for development and because so few own so much, the price of land can be kept artificially high.

The irony is that half the UK population who pay direct taxes are effectively paying the 0.5 per cent who own the land farming subsidies which enable them to hang on to building land, further distorting an already rigged market. The result is that building sites cost two or three times what they should. As Cahill says, 'this is Britain's great property swindle'. It would be funny if it wasn't so ridiculous: the biggest con going on in this country is the cost of the houses we live in.

---

[1] www.newstatesman.com/life-and-society/2011/03/million-acres-land-ownership

I feel rather ambivalent about this because I would prefer the English countryside not to be built on, but it hardly seems fair to the hundreds of thousands of people pouring into this country not to give them an affordable house to live in. Even as one who was comfortably relaxing into a *Telegraph*-reading house-owning middle age, it just doesn't seem fair.

What has this to do with the English spring? Well, rather a lot, actually. An acre of farmland worth £5,000 that gets planning permission suddenly becomes an acre of development land worth between £500,000 and £1m. That's for a patch half the size of a football field. So our English spring is always at the risk of beady-eyed developers. Thank God for the planners, who seem to be our only defence against them.

There is a further issue here, one pointed out by *Country Life* magazine. There is a change coming which will shape the future of rural Britain. Land ownership is slowly moving from family estates, who actually live on the property, to corporate ownership run from centralised headquarters. 'Corporate ownership is management dominated, and, as such, deeply influenced by people with careers to mind, not permanent places in a local community to consider.'[1] And who owns the corporations? One of the unexpected results of globalisation and the concentration of the world's wealth in a few hands is that English property is being sold to the sort of people who have a house in the Caribbean, one in the Alps and one in Dubai. Now over 60 per cent of London properties worth over £2.5 million are owned by foreigners. The same is going to happen to up to 50 per cent of our English countryside. And how much do you think the new oligarch owner will care for the upkeep of wildflower meadows or footpaths?

---

[1] www.countrylife.co.uk/articles/who-really-owns-britain-20219

We're walking upriver along a footpath and we can see a pair
of red kites circling over a garden containing an open coop of
poultry. The lady of the house is standing there feeding her
hens, so I call to her from over the hedge. 'Lost any chickens
lately?' She looks at us as if we are tramps, robbers or worse.
'What's it to you?' she snaps. There is no point explaining
yourself when faced with stupidity of this magnitude, so we
leave her to her flock, and the hawks to their chicken take-
away.

This is Thomas Hardy country, his imagined Wessex, the
setting for his brand of 'Wessex novels' which he regarded as
money-makers to support his true vocation as a poet. It
consists of all of the counties of south-west England that we'll
be walking through: Dorset, Hampshire, Wiltshire and
Somerset. Plus Devon, which we won't, being behind us to the
south-west. As a young reader I became besotted with Tess of
the D'Urbervilles, a tragic maiden who (spoiler alert) flees to
Stonehenge after murdering her nemesis Alec (serves him
right), lies on the ancient altar stone (symbolism of sacrifice
here) and comes to a tragic end in a hangman's noose (a bit
unfair, surely?).

In his poetry Hardy has a good feel for nature, and I like his
description of a spring that's slow in coming, like ours: 'a backwards spring'.

> The trees are afraid to put forth buds,
> And there is timidity in the grass;
> The plots lie gray where gouged by spuds,
> And whether next week will pass

Free of sly sour winds is the fret of each bush
Of barberry waiting to bloom.
Yet the snowdrop's face betrays no gloom,
And the primrose pants in its heedless push,
Though the myrtle asks if it's worth the fight
This year with frost and rime
To venture one more time
On delicate leaves and buttons of white
From the selfsame bough as at last year's prime,
And never to ruminate on or remember
What happened to it in mid-December.[1]

Hardy's own spring as a poet also came late; he wrote most of his poetry after the age of 55. Reading them now, Hardy's earlier novels might sometimes seem depressing and melodramatic, but his imagined construct of Wessex has proved enduring and has spawned the kind of literary tourist trade that we will see later on our walk in Bath (Austen), Stratford (Shakespeare) and Haworth (Brontës). And why not? Anything that encourages people to read has got to be a good thing, but there are other, perhaps better, writers out there. I would like to make a case for Swindon (Richard Jefferies), Northamptonshire (Denys Watkins-Pitchford, John Clare) and the East Anglian coast (W.G. Sebald).

We continue up the Wylye Valley along a delightfully deserted country road, planting oaks every mile as we go. We could be in the 1930s. There are white domesticated geese grazing in the water meadows below us. This flock has just been let out onto the spring grass and they are clearly enjoying the fresh green 'bite'. These birds eat grass, like their

---

[1] Thomas Hardy, 'A Backwards Spring', April 1917

wild cousins the Greylag, but as they aren't ruminants and don't have teeth they need grit to macerate the grass in the gizzard. Birds have lost the ability to grow enamel and thus teeth. I can see there are piles of builder's sand and poultry grit around the fields to help the process. Geese cannot digest cellulose so they aren't as efficient as sheep or cows. As we pass they are quick to spot our movement and honk their disapproval. They sound like rusty car doors opening. I remember that in 390 BC the Romans were saved from a night attack by the Gauls by a flock of geese on the Capitoline Hill, and in the 1950s the Vietnamese Air Force used geese to guard their Grumman Bearcat aircraft (not the Grumman Goose, which was a seaplane). Don't laugh, they can give you a nasty peck.

Oh, to be in England
Now that April's there,
And whoever wakes in England
Sees, some morning, unaware,
That the lowest boughs and the brushwood sheaf
Round the elm-tree bole are in tiny leaf,
While the chaffinch sings on the orchard bough
In England – now!
And after April, when May follows,
And the whitethroat builds, and all the swallows!
Hark, where my blossom'd pear-tree in the hedge
Leans to the field and scatters on the clover
Blossoms and dewdrops – at the bent spray's edge –

That's the wise thrush; he sings each song twice over,
Lest you should think he never could recapture
The first fine careless rapture!
And though the fields look rough with hoary dew,
All will be gay when noontide wakes anew
The buttercups, the little children's dower
– Far brighter than this gaudy melon-flower!

Robert Browning was in northern Italy when he wrote those lines in 1845.

As we sit outside the pub eating our lunch in the sunshine I look back at the great obstacle of Salisbury Plain. We've decided that it's too hard to walk across in one day and we can't find suitable accommodation in the middle, so we're skirting round it. The plain is the largest remaining area of calcareous grassland in north-west Europe, and it is defined by its geology: a thin skin of poor soil covering a great chalk dome.

Despite the sparse living it has become something of a wild-life haven. It consists of around 300 square miles of chalky upland; half of it reserved for military training and half occupied by nature reserves. This blessed absence of people means that this spring we have rare plants growing there such as the burnt-tip orchid, the squinancy-wort and bastard toad-flax, not to mention the more abundant devil's bit scabious, mouse-eared hawkweed, hairy rock-cress and the wild parsnip.

All of this delicious plant life means that it's heaven for butterflies and bees, too. We have the Adonis blue butterfly, the male with his pale blue wings edged with a pencil outline, and the Duke of Burgundy, with little peacock-eyes on his wings. There are rare mining-bees and tawny bumblebees, all threatened elsewhere by loss of habitat caused by intensive farming.

It is depressing to realise what we're doing to our natural surroundings. According to geologists, we have been in the Holocene ('entirely recent') age since the last Ice Age about 12,000 years ago, but many environmentalists insist that we are now in a new age, the Anthropocene ('man age'). That's because we have exterminated so many other species that future geologists (if any) will see a sudden flatline of animals in the strata, together with a faint glow of radioactivity since atomic bomb testing in the 1950s. Some argue the Anthropocene should begin in the 1800s with the revolution in industrial manufacture that began in the north of England. Either way, they say, our human population is increasing like rats in a granary and if we don't control our population ourselves it will be controlled for us in the way parasites are controlled: by the death or sickness of the host. The host, in this case, being the Earth.

The *New Scientist* ran a more dispassionate series of articles on the subject and seemed to conclude that the problem was not so much sheer numbers of humans but the level of consumption. A middle-class couple in Los Angeles can use up as many resources as an entire village in Pakistan. So it is we in the first world, the wealthy, who are the problem. But as the world develops, how do you limit consumption? As P.J. O'Rourke said, 'There are 1.3 billion people in China and they all want a Buick.' And coming soon, 1.3 billion people in Africa who will all want a Mercedes.

David Attenborough, the BBC TV naturalist, who's seen at first hand the effects of human over-population on the animal kingdom, supports Population Matters, a charity advocating a reduction in our numbers. So do Jonathan Porritt and the Earth scientist James Lovelock, who wrote: 'those who fail to see that population growth and climate change are two sides of the same coin are either ignorant or hiding from the truth. These two huge environmental problems are inseparable and to discuss one while ignoring the other is irrational.'

The environmental polemicist George Monbiot dismisses these concerns with a put-down: 'It's no coincidence that most of those who are obsessed with population growth are post-reproductive wealthy white men: it's about the only environmental issue for which they can't be blamed.' He claims that it's the rich that are the problem and then he writes in the same *Guardian* article[1] 'The obsessives could argue that the people breeding rapidly today might one day become richer.'

But that is surely the point: the world cannot bear the weight of 10 billion wealthy humans. And who are we to tell anyone that they can't aspire to be better-off? Surely it would be kinder to us and our planet to have fewer, more comfortable people?

The world's population bomb is very relevant to the English spring. Net migration has risen to a record 330,000 a year during the reign of the present Home Secretary, a politician committed to stemming the flow. Theresa May announced at a recent party conference that as a result 'we need to build 210,000 new homes every year to deal with rising demand. We need to find 900,000 new school places by 2024. And there are thousands of people who have been forced out of the labour market, still unable to find a job.' This is risky talk for a politician. Most agree that limited, selective immigration benefits our country if we choose individuals who are highly motivated and highly trained. Our National Health Service depends on many such people, but where do we draw the line? And is it really fair to drain the best brains from Africa or India?

---

[1] *Guardian*, page 19, 29 September 2009

All these extra people inevitably have a bad effect on our countryside; 210,000 extra homes a year translates to around 875 built every working day, or about one home every two minutes. This will eat up acres of land which can never be replaced. Add in the extra schools and infrastructure needed to support the population explosion and it is surely clear to all that our countryside is under extreme pressure.

At this point accusations of racism are usually heard, but it's irrelevant where these extra people are coming from, or whether they're white, brown or green. If we value our countryside and its beauty we have to stop skating around this issue, an issue that no politician dares to approach, and make a clear statement: we have quite enough people in this country now, thank you. Do we really have a God-given right to inflict limitless numbers of children on the world?

We're walking on the verge of a fast road through a plantation of trees, and it's a scene of carnage. Every twenty paces or so we come across the corpse of another pheasant. They seem to be flying out of the wood low and slow as these birds do and are then being hit by cars. They then die on the verge. These are game birds, bred for shooting, and the RSPB says that around 50 million pheasants are released for shooting in Britain every year. It's an expensive hobby: 'Up gets a guinea, bang goes sixpence, down comes half a crown,' was the Victorian phrase, referring in turn to the cost of rearing each bird, the price of the shotgun cartridge and the value of the dead meat. Today those prices are around £30 for rearing,

30 pence for a cartridge and £1 worth of dead game. A day's shooting might cost you around £1,000. And you might not enjoy the meat: it's dark, dry and tough.

Conservationists are divided on the pheasant issue. The more left-wing dislike the moneyed classes who enjoy killing slow, disorientated birds with guns, but gamekeepers would say that other wildlife benefit from rearing game; wild birds can also hide in the snowberry bushes we see planted here to provide winter food and shelter for the pheasants, and they will also benefit from the thinning of the wood we're walking alongside. The fact is that pheasants would probably die out in this country if they weren't bred for shooting.

As a boy I used to poach for pheasants but my mother could never face eating them after plucking and cleaning. Around the same time, Roald Dahl's book about a child poacher was published: *Danny: the Champion of the World*. His dad was a poacher, too, and Danny invented a new way of bagging pheasants: scattering raisins laced with sleeping potion. The drugged birds rain out of the trees and Danny and his dad make a record haul of 120 birds. More fun ensues when the sleepy birds start waking up the next day. The most we ever bagged was two.

Spring was clearly important to the Neolithic builders of Stonehenge, as it is to any other animal trying to get through a hard winter. No one alive today really seems to know exactly what the monument was for: in this case we know less than our ancestors. There are plenty of theories. It is clear, though, that the site is aligned with the winter and summer solstices. For an intelligent animal keen to know when spring is coming, the winter solstice is significant as that's when the days stop getting shorter. We call it 21 December, and it's when the sun appears at noon at its lowest altitude above the horizon. The winter may well become colder after the solstice due to the lag in temperature rise, but at least the sun is coming back with steadily longer days. The summer solstice is when the long days of spring stop becoming longer: 20/21 June.

The spring equinox ('equal night' in Latin) falls on 20/21 March and is when the days and nights are equal in length: 12 hours each. The autumn equinox falls on the 22/23 September in the Northern Hemisphere and, as in spring, it's when all points on Earth theoretically experience the same length of day and night. So the builders of Stonehenge were probably observational scientists, using a hefty piece of equipment to make simple predictions about when the seasons were likely to change.

It's surprising to learn that this, England's most important monument, was bought for £6,600 at an auction in Salisbury just 100 years ago. A barrister, Cecil Chubb, bought it as 'a present' for his wife Mary. However, she was displeased as he had been sent to the auction to buy some curtains. Instead he returned with a load of old stones costing £680,000 in today's money. 'I bought it on a whim,' he said. Three years later Chubb gave it to the nation, and got a title in return: Sir Cecil Chubb, First Baronet of Stonehenge. It is not recorded if Mary got new curtains.

We are still puzzling our way up out of the Wylye Valley and manage to get onto the White Horse Trail. This footpath takes in all of the eight horse figures cut into the chalk hillsides of Wiltshire. We are walking round a corner when we suddenly see the Westbury White Horse miles up ahead, across yet another prairie field. This giant image, 180 feet (55 metres) high and 170 feet (52 metres) long is cut into the western escarpment of Salisbury Plain, on the edge of Bretton Downs and just below an Iron Age fort. It can be seen from up to sixteen miles away. There is no evidence for the horse's existence before the eighteenth century, and an engraving from the 1760s shows him facing in the opposite direction. However, the similar Uffington White Horse in Oxfordshire has been dated to the late Bronze Age, and it is quite possible that there was a figure here in the Iron Age that was overlaid with later versions.

I am reminded of Eric Ravilious' fine watercolour of the horse from exactly this angle. He gives him a sculptural muscularity missing from the real thing, and a racing steam train behind gives him movement. He could be galloping alongside. There's a sense of loss about it, though, somehow, the threat of a lost England. When it was painted, in 1939, the Second World War had begun and the Westbury White Horse was about to be covered up to prevent enemy navigators using him as a landmark.

The Cerne Abbas Giant is a similarly-sized hill figure in Dorset. He is spectacularly endowed, and postcards of him were said to be the only indecent postcards allowed to be sent through the English post office. He has become associated with fertility, and in springtime locals would erect a maypole on the figure, around which childless couples would dance to promote fecundity. Intercourse on the phallus itself would be certain to result in a child. A bit chilly, though.

I climb down to the White Horse from the Iron Age camp and stroke him on the head. His eye, six feet across, stares unblinkingly across the plain, across an eternal England.

After the Westbury White Horse we continue on the trail towards Trowbridge. On the way we pass the village of North Bradbury, where in the sixteenth century squatters' cottages were thrown up on common land. These were for cloth workers weaving at home for the Trowbridge clothiers. The squatters' cottages have an unusual legal history; if they could be built in a day and have a fire lit and smoke coming out of the chimney by sunset they were legally allowed to stay. The construction would therefore centre around a stone hearth and chimney, surrounded by hastily erected wattle and daub walls. These were a grid of woven sticks and mud. The chimney would be made of stone because of the heat of the fire. Some surrounding land was allowed to be enclosed with the cottage, and this was determined by how far the new owner could throw an axe or shovel from the four corners of the dwelling.

Living conditions in these hovels were frightful and disease was rife, with no sanitation and little opportunity to wash. There were usually only two rooms, a kitchen and bedroom for a family of perhaps ten children. William Cobbett, in his *Rural Rides*, reported, 'The labourers seem miserably poor. Their dwellings are little better than pig-beds, and their looks indicate that their food is not nearly equal to that of a pig . . . In my whole life I never saw human wretchedness equal to this.'

There was very often a privy next to the pigsty behind the

house, just as in rural China, where the single ideogram *pinyin* means both privy and pigsty. The pig ate the human excrement: recycling is nothing new. My old farmhouse in Derbyshire has exactly the same arrangement, a double-holed privy with an en-suite pigsty. Apparently the farm workers came back from the fields for a quick breakfast and had to perform their elimination swiftly, and in company. And in Tingri, Tibet, if you glance down the hole in the planks you'll meet the eye of a cheerful dog waiting below.

Later, in the early 1800s, tin baths became available, cheaply made of sheet iron dipped in molten tin to resist rust. There was a handle each end for carrying. Bath time would be once a week, and performed publicly in front of the fire, which would provide the warm water heated in whatever vessels they could find. The water would be drawn from an insanitary well outside. The order of bathing would be: father first, as main wage earner, then mother, then the children in descending order of age. The filthy water would be poured outside. Hence the injunction 'Don't throw the baby out with the bath water.'

We're not so very far from those days. My Scottish grandmother lived in a similar cottage to this during the summer, and tin baths were only just being removed from houses when I was a child in the sixties. They made very effective boats for navigating our local river.

It occurs to us as we walk past the site of these cottages that spring would have been a wonderful time of year. 'February fill-grave' was past, the cottage could be spring-cleaned and life was looking up.

CHAPTER TWO

Dawn chorus – cockerels – little egret – murmurations of starlings –
Edward Thomas – 'Adlestrop' – honey bees – traffic – Kennet and
Avon Canal – pillboxes – the Tithe barn – Chaucer – an Arctic
explorer – a Cold War bunker – Charlie the Farmer – The Map
that changed the World *– Jane Austen – Cotswold Way – skylarks*
– a stray dog – Richard Jefferies

It's five o'clock in the morning, it's dark but there's a hint
of dawn in the eastern sky. There are a few tentative
cheeps from the surrounding trees as I walk quietly down
to the bank of the River Biss, south of Trowbridge, in
Wiltshire. It's a week into our spring walk and I've come to
hear the dawn chorus with some fellow bird lovers. I've left
Gina fast asleep, as she's an evening sort of girl.

We assemble, fidgeting in the embarrassed manner of the
English, and wait for someone to tell us what we're going to
hear. Our expert David Culverhouse arrives and we're off
across Biss Meadows. And what a wonderful dawn chorus we
hear! First, the tiny wren with his mighty voice: *'Pip! Pip!*
Pip!' It's astounding how much volume this tiny ball of fluff
generates, and surprising, too, to learn that it is our most
common breeding bird. Then the blackbird, with the mellow
song that always conjures up damp English summer mornings
on the lawn. The great tit, with his two-syllable song, and the
chaffinch, which became a favourite that we heard all the way

up through England. David has an app on his phone that plays any bird song we're unfamiliar with, and soon the birds start answering the phone: greenfinch: *'Wheeeeze!'*, a moorhen *'Prrrrrr!'*, then the robin, who has a rather mournful, descending call which belies his cheerful, Christmas-card appearance. We saw a magpie with his black-and-white dinner jacket and his machine-gun call – *'AckAckAckAck!'* – and a blue tit sounding like a furious bicycle pump.

David tells us that these birds are singing to establish their territory and attract a mate. Even woodpeckers that don't sing make a noise that has the same effect: their drumming on resonant pieces of timber. He says we're lucky to hear so many birds this morning as the numbers of most of these species are falling.

There's a pond here, and in the clear chalk-stream river there are minnows, freshwater shrimps, mayfly nymphs, olive nymphs, burrowing mayfly, snails and stickleback. There are kingfishers, too, and heron fishing for all this tasty food. Heron numbers went from 80,000 to 2,500 in the severe winter of 1962–3, but they did recover. It seems that as long as they maintain a breeding population, birds and other creatures will make a reappearance if conditions swing back to favour them. The important thing is to prevent them becoming extinct.

There are many more birds calling as the sun comes up: a distant cockerel from a farm, a lesser black-backed gull, a mallard and reed bunting from the river, a cooing collared dove, bullfinch, chiffchaff, blackcap and missel thrush. Even David, who has trousered his phone by now, is startled when a loud croaking starts sounding from his bottom. 'Red grouse?' he asks in disbelief. The nearest one is probably 200 miles away. We look away in embarrassment; it turns out his phone is emitting unrequested bird songs and it takes some time to suppress.

There's a cry of delight from the humans as a white bird wheels in and lands on a patch of water on the meadow: a rare little egret. And as a finale to finish the morning off: a red kite circles overhead to see what all the fuss is about.

Over breakfast in the neighbouring Tesco supermarket we consider what we've seen. We all agree we've been lucky as we only expected to hear a couple of blackbirds. There's been a catastrophic decline in songbirds in recent years; anyone over 50 will remember dawn choruses from their childhood that were deafening, and there used to be hundreds of birds in my father's garden on spring mornings.

We've lost 44 million breeding birds in forty years. That's getting on for the human population of England. Starlings used to swirl in great mumurations of thousands above our house in Rutland in the sixties. They're down now by 79 per cent, sparrows by 71 per cent, lapwings by 80 per cent and cuckoos by 67 per cent. I haven't heard one cuckoo yet this spring. If this had happened overnight there would be an outcry, but just like the steady intensification of agriculture and creeping climate change, the decline in birds has been slow. People just don't notice a gradual decrease. Three-quarters of bees around here in the West Country have been wiped out in the last fifty years, but hardly anyone notices. There's been a huge increase in humans, but why? What are we all for?

What's so encouraging about the dawn chorus this morning is that Biss Meadows is a public country park, owned by Wiltshire's enlightened council, where conservation is a priority. The Meadows also provide a valuable floodplain to protect housing during flooding. It seems that it takes only a little thought and care for conservation measures to work surprisingly well, as we have seen this morning. Because of conservation efforts, things are better for red kite, corn buntings, tree sparrows, bittern, crane and stone curlews. It's another measure that's working.

Volunteers and friends of this park work in parties to make the place even more nature-friendly, and the Tesco supermarket and other companies in Trowbridge support this beautiful park for good business reasons. I take my hat off to them. Thank you.

We're crossing the hundred-year-old tyretracks of a bicycle ridden by Edward Thomas in his *In Pursuit of Spring*. In 1913, when he was just on the cusp of being prose writer and poet, Thomas took a journey from London to Somerset, on the way staying with friends near here, at Dillybrook Farm.

Thomas was a fine naturalist and was by then well respected as a nature writer of books such as *The Heart of England* and *The Icknield Way*. He was Richard Jefferies' biographer, too. Ted Hughes, another of our nature poets, has called him 'the father of all of us'. He was also an acute depressive. Winter was overrunning in 1913, he was feeling miserable, and so he decided to go and look for spring: 'I had a wish of a mildly imperative nature that Spring would be arriving in the Quantocks at the same time as myself . . . Spring would come fast, not slowly, up that way.' He set off on 21 March.

It is a strangely claustrophobic book: it seems that he feels trapped, not only in London, but also by his marriage and by his profession. As he gets into the countryside the writing becomes more and more poetic and the feeling of being trapped evaporates. For example, he introduces The Other Man, someone else who is cycling the same route, but whom he never names. I suspect he is Thomas's alter ego. He sees the man buying a caged chaffinch in a pet shop. It is placed in a paper bag. The man then surreptitiously releases it a few streets away, near Morden station. The symbolism is clear, but did it happen?

The book was written at a time when the threat of European war aroused feelings of insecurity in England, which in turn led to a longing for the countryside. You can see the same tendency in the books of Denys Watkins-Pitchford ('BB'), written in the 1940s, and the paintings of Eric Ravilious. When the nation's existence is threatened, part of you wants to creep back and curl up into nature. Edward Thomas's journey's end is Coleridge's Quantock Hills: 'the holy of holies of English poetry', where Romanticism began. This is a metaphysical journey of a poet's awakening. The writing is not just prose describing an exterior countryside; there is also a description of an interior landscape: 'the road was like a stream on which I floated in the shadows of trees and steep hillsides'. It's like the literary stream of consciousness that was about to become fashionable with Proust, Eliot and Joyce. 'The sun had both dried the turf and warmed it. The million gorse petals seemed to be flames sown by the sun.'

So far, so idyllic. But Thomas's peace is constantly interrupted by motor cars roaring by, covering him with dust. 'A motor car dashed under the "Lion" arch for shelter', 'hustled up the Exeter road by motor cars', 'A motor car raced by me.' You can just see Toad of Toad Hall at the wheel, shaking his fist at the writer on a bike. Modern traffic is the one thing that makes our own walking trip impossibly dangerous along country roads, yet in Thomas's time there was a tiny fraction of the number now in England. 'A motor car overtook me in the village, scattering a group of boys. "Look out!" cried one, and as the thing passed by, turned to the next boy with, "There's a fine motor; worth more than you are; cost a lot of money." Is this not the awakening of England? At least, it is the truth.'[1] Thomas was right in his sardonic way, England awoke to the desire for motor cars and now the roads are blocked with them.

A page later there is a half-formed hint of his later poem of English springtime, 'Adlestrop'. He writes: 'All the thrushes of England sang at that hour . . . ' and later, 'by a chain of larks' songs that must have reached all over England . . . ' He seems to be formulating the poem slowly in his head. The next year it came out like this:

> Yes. I remember Adlestrop –
> The name, because one afternoon
> Of heat the express-train drew up there
> Unwontedly. It was late June.
>
> The steam hissed. Someone cleared his throat.
> No one left and no one came
> On the bare platform. What I saw
> Was Adlestrop – only the name
>
> And willows, willow-herb, and grass,
> And meadowsweet, and haycocks dry,
> No whit less still and lonely fair
> Than the high cloudlets in the sky.

---

[1] Edward Thomas, *In Pursuit of Spring* (1914)

And for that minute a blackbird sang
Close by, and round him, mistier,
Farther and farther, all the birds
Of Oxfordshire and Gloucestershire.

I love this poem for all its misty evocation of a long-gone England.

As a small child I used to go with my mother to neighbouring Stamford by steam train, and all that mystery and excitement of being a traveller, the observer, is in this poem. The opening implies a conversation, but with whom? There is a glorious inconsequentiality about it all, as there is with our own spring walk. Nothing happened. 'No one left and no one came.' But everything happens: poignancy, a lost England, a spreading circular ripple of birdsong. Years later I went to Adlestrop, and it's all gone. The Beeching cuts axed the station, which was demolished. The steam engines are gone. There are fewer birds in Oxfordshire and Gloucestershire now, but I realised that England is not lost – England is eternal, and the sense of loss comes from within.

Later in 1913, depressed again and close to suicide, Thomas was given some advice by his American poet friend, Robert Frost. He pointed out that much of the prose in *In Pursuit of Spring* was close to poetry and that Thomas should bite the bullet and take up the art form. He knew what was wrong with his friend; it was what was familiar to anyone who has had to work under an unsympathetic manager: 'He was suffering from a life of insubordination to his inferiors' (he worked as a book reviewer and literary critic). In fact, there is some evidence that Thomas was already going down this path, and perhaps Frost was claiming undue influence. He even gave the advice – to stop indecision and get writing – in his own well-loved poem: 'The Road Not Taken': 'Two roads diverged in a wood; and I – I took the one less traveled by, And that has made all the difference.'

Edward Thomas was stung by this accusation of indecision, and the two friends fell out for a while. It may even have prompted his fatal decision to join the army: Thomas was killed at Arras in 1917. It was certain that he loved England. When asked why he had joined the Artists Rifles he stooped, took a pinch of the English earth and crumbled it between finger and thumb. 'Literally, for this.'

A passing dog walker has just asked why we started our spring walk on 20 March. Doesn't spring start on the 21 March? It's a good question, and the answer is that the actual date varies between 20 and 21 March. It also depends which spring you mean.

If you're an astronomer, the March equinox (equal-length days and nights) happens when the sun crosses the celestial equator on its way north. Astronomers (and navigators) imagine a great circle on the equally imaginary celestial sphere, which is a huge projection of the real Earth. Imagine a ping-pong ball (the Earth) hovering inside a giant balloon. Drawn on the outside of the balloon is the celestial equator, a projection of the real equator. As we know, the Earth's axis is tilted at 23.4 degrees, so the celestial equator is tilted, too.

The March equinox happens at the same time throughout the world but is converted into local time. In 2015, it happened at 22.45 GMT on 20 March. In Australia, in the

Southern Hemisphere, this equinox marks the beginning of autumn.

The solstice in 2015, when the sun is highest in the sky, was at 16.38 GMT on 21 June. That's the end of the astronomical spring. So we aimed to get to the Scottish border on the last full day of spring: the 20 June.

If you are a meteorologist, spring begins on 1 March and carries on until 31 May. Weather scientists do this so that the year is divided into equal quarters, which makes it easier to compare seasonal variations from year to year.

Robert Macfarlane is at the vanguard of a new breed of English nature writers. God knows nature needs supporters right now. In *The Old Ways* he states that Edward Thomas is the most important person in the book, who 'ghosted my journeys and urged me on'. Thomas, says Macfarlane, experienced 'the tension between roaming and homing'.

I first became aware of Macfarlane's writing on coming across his description of my Everest expedition's finding of George Mallory in *Mountains of the Mind*. He describes Mallory's Romantic obsession with the mountain (in the Wordsworthian sense), but I would add that there were darker forces that lay behind Mallory's desire: the drive of man to take hold of and subdue nature.[1] This was made explicit by Sir Francis Younghusband, president of the Royal Geographical Society. He was determined to get an expedition out to the

---

[1] See Graham Hoyland, *Last Hours on Everest*, HarperCollins (2013)

mountain. His 1920 presidential address hints at why he wanted Englishmen to climb Mount Everest:

'The accomplishment of such a feat will elevate the human spirit and will give man, especially us geographers, a feeling that we really are getting the upper hand on the earth, and that we are acquiring a true mastery of our surroundings . . . if man stands on earth's highest summit, he will have an increased pride and confidence in himself in the ascendancy over matter. This is the incalculable good which the ascent of Mount Everest will confer.'[1]

This 'incalculable good' has now brought Nature to her knees. But Nature is our parent, not a slave, and Younghusband's ambition will make orphans of us all. Whereas Chinese, Japanese and Tibetan cultures were content to accept high mountains as part of our oneness with the world, the aggressive new Victorians on the block wanted to stand on top of them, and like Ed Hillary, urinate.

In his third book, *The Wild Places*, Macfarlane describes his journeys into the few remaining wildernesses in Britain and Ireland. His experiences are interspersed with reflections on the people he meets, other writers, and man's inhumanity to Nature. It is pleasantly reminiscent of W.G. Sebald's books, with their discursive prose and quirky black-and-white photographs. In the earlier chapters, describing his roaming upon mountains and islands, he seems rather depressed by what we're doing to our planet, but by the end he has realised that wildness can still be found in the closer and more intimate parts of nature. In *Landscapes*, Macfarlane's next book, he expounds his love of the language of our natural surroundings, and I wonder whether, like Edward Thomas, his next move might be towards poetry.

---

[1] Royal Geographical Society, 1920 presidential address

We're passing a hand-painted sign for honey in the Wiltshire village of Knook and spot a man hammering a beehive together in a shed behind the house. I stroll in and hail him, and he emerges, still holding the hammer. The whole conversation is conducted with him holding it as if arrested in mid-swing. This is Den Procter, and I start by buying a jar of his Wiltshire honey – always a good opening gambit when trying to extract information. 'So how did the bees do this winter?' Not so good, it seems. They're afflicted with the varroa mite. He's been trying dusting the bees with powdered sugar – it sticks to the mite's footpads and is supposed to make them drop out of the hive. Doesn't do any good, though. Bees are in trouble here in the West Country, he says. The first thing he does in spring is to open up the hives and see if the bees have survived.

'So what's the one thing we could do to help bees?' Den becomes quite animated. Wildflowers. There are no wildflowers nowadays, and it takes two million flower visits to make one jar of honey. And they feed insects. Remember how your dad's windscreen was covered with bugs in the summer in the seventies? Don't get that any more. Same reason: farmers have sprayed pesticides to kill off the wildflowers and ploughed up every bit of meadow. No meadow flowers. Better off in the city.

We admire the artwork on the label of the honey-pot. I query the best-by date: end of 2018. 'Does honey go off, then?' No, no, no. They found perfectly edible honey in Tutankhamen's tomb. It was 5,000 years old. 'The label should say end of 7018 then?' Den looks at me as if I'm nuts and clearly thinks I've had my money's worth. We go back to our walking and he goes back to his hammering.

Den's right, of course. Bees are in serious trouble in England and all over the world, and that means trouble for us. They are the canary in the coalmine of food production: they indicate a serious problem. North America has lost half its bees in the last seventy years, and yet honey bees, wild and domesticated, account for 80 per cent of the world's pollination. A third of what we eat would disappear from our plates should the bee disappear. Beans, tomatoes, apples and strawberries all rely on the bee.

Not being ones to sit on their hands, our American cousins are doing something about it. The Obama White House recently announced that they are beginning a programme of support for bees and monarch butterflies which will improve millions of federal acres and cost millions of dollars. Most of that will go into providing habitat, but there is disappointment that they are not banning toxic pesticides and in particular neonicotinoids: 'neonics'. Several scientific studies have shown that these chemicals are reducing the numbers of queens produced and increasing the numbers of 'disappeared bees'; ones that never return to the hive. And yet in North America maize seeds are sprayed with these pesticides before planting.

A recent French study[1] has confirmed that individual bees are indeed harmed by neonics even though colonies temporarily produce more bees to compensate. The European Union voted to ban neonics, although it is interesting to note that the UK voted against the motion. What is worse, our government allows neonics in England. Following an application by the

---

[1] *Reconciling laboratory and field assessments of neonicotinoid toxicity to honeybees.* Mickaël Henry et al., 2015

National Farmers' Union, two of these pesticides can be used in four counties on oilseed rape crops.[1] We have large vested interests in chemical companies and industrial farming in this country, whose paid representatives claim that it is the loss of flower-rich habitat that is the problem. They're right, in a way. As we have seen, by 1984 there had already been a 97 per cent reduction of lowland meadow in the UK since the 1930s and now there are only 37,000 acres (15,000 hectares) left.[2]

This was because of changing agricultural practice: ploughing up meadows. And who is ploughing up the flower-rich habitat? The industrial farmers. It's the same old story: intensive farming, pesticides and desire for profits rather than wildlife.

We're stumbling alongside the road at 5.30pm on the grass verge as there is no footpath. It's raining and we have horrible walking conditions alongside a commuter rat-run between two towns. The cars are stationary and nose-to-tail for around a mile, waiting their turn to get onto an A road. Their drivers are returning from work, most of them looking overweight, tired and irritable. They don't make eye contact with the dishevelled walkers. Is there a tinge of guilt in their expression, or is it my imagination? They are the insiders and we the outsiders. When, later, we drive along the same road we have just walked along, the landscape seems from another country, dislocated and strange.

[1] www.bbc.co.uk/news/science-environment-34846629

[2] jncc.defra.gov.uk/PDF/UKBAP_PriorityHabitatDesc-Rev2010.pdf

I notice bluebells and forget-me-nots along this stretch, poking out amongst the debris of fast-food cartons and drinks cans. There are a couple of bees attempting to feed on them. My acorn looks lost where I plant it in the remnants of a hedge: it'll never thrive here. The sterile field is ploughed right up to the edge and looks soaked in chemicals. It's deeply depressing.

I nearly get myself killed somewhere along this section. When we walk on country roads without a verge I tend to walk outside Gina, swinging my map to give oncoming drivers something to see. If the road is curving to the right we are hidden by the hedges, but my hope is to jump into the field if approached too close. Everyone drives extremely fast on country roads, perhaps having seen too many TV car shows. I'm as guilty as anyone (and a car-lover myself, having sold a favourite to pay for this trip). A silver VW suddenly appears in front of me and I'm nearly hit by it. The driver seemed to be doing something with her phone. Shaken, we decide that we really have to stay off the roads where we can and try to make our way across country in future.

Heavy rain makes us abandon the walk for a few days at this point. It seems to be a cold spring this year and everything is grey and late. We decide to let the spring catch up with us.

We're now walking towards Bath along the Kennet and Avon Canal in bright sunshine on the 8 April. High pressure is to give us a gloriously dry, warm and sunny month. This is much more enjoyable; no cars, only the occasional narrowboat with a friendly skipper. The towpath is well paved – not too hard and not too soft. Canals don't tend to slope upwards so there are no hills to contend with. Life is good.

The idea to connect London with Bristol by waterway was first mooted in Elizabethan times. It was realised that the Rivers Avon and Thames were only three miles apart, so little digging would be necessary. Vested interests in the form of gentry and farmers opposed the idea as they were concerned about their income from turnpike roads and competition from cheaper produce from Wales. Because of this opposition the canal wasn't opened until 1810, but it had a brief prosperity until 1841, when the Great Western railway opened. The canal's fortunes declined and parts began to silt up until 1962, when work started to revive it.

This is another success story for conservation. Thanks to the Kennet and Avon Canal Trust we now have a beautiful resource for pleasure-boat owners and a habitat for over 100 species of bird: there are kingfishers, reed bunting and grey heron here. We saw lots of dragonflies and damselflies and the fishermen we passed were catching bream, carp and gudgeon, perch, pike, roach and rudd. Not to mention tench.

Humans are coming out, too, in the spring sunshine, laying out picnics on blankets beside the locks. We pass a concrete pillbox. After the evacuation of the British Expeditionary Force from Dunkirk during the Second World War this canal was designated one of the country's last-ditch defences: GHQ Stop Line Blue. Hastily built concrete boxes like this one were cast by local contractors, using scrap steel for reinforcement. They're about the size of a large garden shed and were manned only once in a false alarm by the Home Guard: Dad's Army. Presumably the Nazis would have invaded on specially built narrowboats decorated with swastikas, towed by goose-stepping horses. Surely letting the water out would have scuppered them. Paul, a digger-driving friend of mine who was dredging our local canal, fished out a long chain and a huge plug. Thinking nothing of it he went home for lunch. When he came back the canal was empty, and he was in big trouble.

My acorns are easy to plant along the canal. There is usually a deep hedge between towpath and countryside, so I try to replace any old trees that have died or fallen.

When we arrive at Bradford on Avon we walk into the great Tithe barn at Barton Farm. I wanted to see the magnificent oak roof of this Grade I listed building. The barn was built in the early fourteenth century, possibly about 1340, around the time of Geoffrey Chaucer's birth. The roof consists of fourteen great pairs of bent oaks along the 168-foot (51-metre) length, raised like giant chicken wishbones. Fastened to these are three levels of horizontal purlins supporting the rafters, which in turn support 100 tons of stone slates. It's one of the biggest and most glorious barns in the country, and belonged to the nuns of Shaftesbury Abbey, the richest nunnery in England. It was sold by the lord of the manor, Sir Charles Hobhouse, in 1915 and now is cared for by English Heritage.

Geoffrey Chaucer writes of spring at the very beginning of *The Canterbury Tales*:

> When April with his showers sweet with fruit
> The drought of March has pierced unto the root
> And bathed each vein with liquor that has power

To generate therein and sire the flower . . .
. . . Then do folk long to go on pilgrimage,
And palmers to go seeking out strange strands,
To distant shrines well known in sundry lands.
And specially from every shire's end
Of England they to Canterbury wend,
The holy blessed martyr there to seek
Who helped them when they lay so ill and weak.

The martyr was Sir Thomas a Becket, the Archbishop of
Canterbury, who was murdered on his cathedral steps by four
knights in 1170.

Here at Bradford on Avon we stay at a hotel that has its
own vineyard. There are 600 Reichensteiner vines in one acre
of walled garden. The wine is a pleasant medium dry white. As
England warms up over the next century or so, no doubt we'll
see more vineyards.

We've walked to our friend David Hempleman Adams' house
near Box. He's a big powerful man and has completed ski trips
to both Poles pulling sledges. He gives us some advice about
our long walk: don't think of the big picture, concentrate on
small targets. Give yourself treats when you get to your goals.
He says: 'You two might be starters, but are you finishers?' We
look at each other and hope so. For energy he used to eat a
whole pack of butter, a pound at a time, like a Mars bar. On
the way to the South Pole he read Margaret Thatcher's autobiography, carefully tearing out each page as he read it and

using it as lavatory paper. This saved having to carry the full weight of the book all the way to the Pole. As a result there is a trail of defaced Thatcheresque pronouncements all across the Antarctic wastes, a thought that will surely gladden the heart of any Labour supporter and will puzzle future archaeologists.

This morning we're all walking over to see his neighbour, Charlie the Farmer, another friend from a climbing trip. I want to talk to a Wiltshire farmer after walking through so much of the county. We cross the old Roman road to Bath, then walk up an avenue to his manor house at Monkton Farleigh. I notice there is quite a bit of hedge replanting on his land.

This must be the longest garden path in the country, about half a mile long. It gives the most stupendous view. We meet locals walking their dogs and stop to talk. Apparently there are mines under here, originally dug to provide stone for the city of Bath. They were taken over for use during the Second World War as ammunition depots. Then during the Cold War in the late 1950s the UK central government war headquarters were built somewhere under here, 120 feet down. It was to ensure that the government could still run the country after a nuclear attack. The bunker is still there. Its scale is huge: it's over half a mile long (1 kilometre) with 60 miles (96 kilometres) of roads. There was an underground lake of fresh water, power plants, food and fuel, and 4,000 government staff could survive for three months completely cut off from the rest of the country. They would have arrived by rail, and there was a secret branch of the London to Bristol railway tunnelling underground from Box tunnel. The prime minister of the day, Harold Macmillan, plus his cabinet, would have arrived by helicopter. There was even a BBC studio from which he could address his still-smouldering country.

Charlie the Farmer is in his kitchen and cooks us bacon and

eggs while we discuss farming. This is Sir Charles Hobhouse, the new incarnation of his ancestor who owned the Tithe barn. When I talk about hedges he groans. It turns out that if you replant hedges people push through them and make holes. Not ramblers, he said, they're all right, although some are a bit militant. It's mountain-bikers riding through his hedges. Intensive agriculture? The farmers' problem is the market. If supermarkets don't pay enough for food then the farmers have no choice but to use modern methods to intensify agriculture. Farmers around here are pouring milk down the drain rather than accept the few pence per litre that the supermarkets pay. The supermarkets are selling milk cheaper than water. You can't beat the market.

I get into a bit more detail.

'Do you think intensive agriculture is bad for England?'

'Well, that's a long subject but in short, no, I don't. A good sustainable balance is needed. There's nothing wrong with intensive agriculture as long as it follows good practice. In many areas intensive agriculture doesn't work, so this doesn't mean intensively farming the whole country. I also believe you can run intensive agriculture next to conservation and wildlife projects and areas to good effect. Telling the farming industry to ignore technology isn't a fair option. Most of us care about our precious asset and don't want to ruin it with greed, but we still have to make a living and keep pace with the world.'

'But doesn't the loss of 75 per cent of honey bees in the West Country concern you?'

'Yes, it does, and I do want more bees. We grow oilseed rape and peas and beans, which help. There is a movement now to grow 2–4-metre strips of pollen and nectar-rich grassland around arable fields. I've done this before and will certainly be doing it again. Bees are on the agenda in Western European farming at the moment. I'll be planting this sort of mix soon and by next summer should have some up and flourishing.'

I play with Charlie's young son for a while and wonder what kind of England he'll grow up in. I leave Monkton Farleigh with the feeling that these are bigger issues than can be dealt with by an individual farmer or landowner. These are matters for governments and the will of the people.

We're just walking into Limpley Stoke, along the Kennet and Avon Canal. There's an 1813 pumphouse down on the River Avon at Claverton that uses renewable waterpower in the river to pump water up to the canal here. It replaces water lost every time a boat passes through a lock, and it's old technology, green before its time. Another canal joins it here, long disused – the Somerset Coal Canal – and there are narrowboats moored up all around. We're stopping here to eat our picnic lunch on the grass lawn, admire the surroundings and think about the man who drew the map that changed the world.

On this spring walk I've noticed that the underlying rocks change the plants that we see. The chalk of Salisbury Plain was supporting a very different grassland habitat to these oolitic limestone river valleys with their thickly wooded slopes. And it was right here that the science of geology began with the man who surveyed the route of the Somerset Coal Canal: William 'Strata' Smith.

In the 1760s coal had been discovered nearby at Radstock, and mines sunk to take advantage of it. There was a ready market in the booming spa city of Bath, just nine miles away. The roads were terrible, though, and it was actually cheaper to get the coal from South Wales along the Monmouthshire Canal. So a canal was proposed to take the coal to a junction with the Kennet and Avon Canal; where we are now. William Smith, a surveyor, was contracted to plan the route.

The story that follows can be found in *The Map that Changed the World*,[1] by Simon Winchester. It is almost too painful to recount; because he was from humble origins, the son of a blacksmith, and had few powerful connections, his ideas and work were stolen and he ended up in a debtors' prison, but there is a happy ending. So what did he discover?

For centuries miners had realised that as they dug down through the rocks they encountered discrete beds of rock strata with different fossils in them. They learned when to expect the coal seams and were able to predict in which direction to dig. Smith learned all this in his early work surveying in the mines, so he can't have been too surprised when he observed the same sequence of strata appearing along the diggings of the new canal. It was like slicing through a layer cake. He noticed that the layers dipped towards the east. His great idea was to search the whole country to see if these strata were predictable elsewhere. After years of work he found that they were, and that the fossils always appeared in the same order. This is when he came up with his principle of 'faunal succession'. This was the idea that sedimentary rock strata contain fossilised plants and animals which appear in the order that they were laid down, and which can be predicted over large horizontal distances. It would lead to Darwin's ideas on evolution and everything that followed.

William Smith was also something of an epic plumber; when the hot springs failed at the Roman baths in the city of Bath in 1810 he was called in, dug down and found that the hot water had switched to a new channel. He not only restored the flow but made the baths fill quicker. I bet he turned up when he said he would and didn't overcharge, either.

---

[1] Simon Winchester, *The Map that Changed the World*, HarperCollins (2001)

You might think that scientists would honour such a man, but his maps of the geology of Britain were stolen, plagiarised and published more cheaply by the Geological Society of London, a group of well-connected amateurs. He fell into debt and ended up in prison. However, eventually he was recognised by a former employer, Sir John Johnstone, who ensured that his contribution was recorded. A new president of the Geological Society then bestowed on him a medal and the title 'The Father of English Geology'.

I'm sitting in the spring sunshine thinking about William Smith and looking at the millions of years of foliage and insects laid down in the rocks just across the valley. These are from the Mesozoic Era, maybe 250 million years ago.

There's been a hatch of mayflies just now and they're dancing over the canal surface. They are a primitive insect, and probably would have been around here in the Mesozoic. They have an immature stage when they live in fresh water, when they are called nymphs, then they emerge from the surface in a winged form to mate. The fish love these flies, and many of the anglers' artificial flies are made to look like them. The mayfly only lives for a day, and in one species the female only lives for five minutes. As a result they don't bother too much about eating, so they have vestigial mouthparts and empty digestive systems. The acorns in my pocket could live a thousand years. The timescales around here are mind-bending. William Smith's genius was to take a common observation about strata and think big about it.

We are now walking into Bath along the canal towpath, having crossed into Somerset over the beautiful Dundas Aqueduct that carries the canal across the River Avon. The towpath runs out on our side and I attempt to hitch a ride across the viaduct on a passing narrowboat. The crew try to stop, I try to leap on board and nearly fall into the water as the boat continues without me, its speed unabated. Gina wisely retraces her steps and regains the other side by walking the proper way under the bridge. See what she has to put up with?

Jane Austen moved here in May 1801, at this time of year, and it surely must have been exciting to come here from her father's provincial parish in Hampshire. Bath was still a fashionable spa town then, with a whirl of social engagements and balls. Perhaps it was too exciting, as Austen managed no published writing while she was living in Bath. In fact, she was not particularly happy here, and then her father died unexpectedly in 1805, leaving the family in a precarious financial position. Literary tourism takes no notice of such niceties, though, and there's a healthy Jane Austen industry with tearooms, glossy magazines and costumed actors.

The novels *Northanger Abbey* and *Persuasion* are largely set in Bath. In her writing, the town's topography, social rank and irony all go hand in hand:

'Prettier musings of high-wrought love and eternal constancy, could never have passed along the streets of Bath than Anne was sporting with from Camden Place to Westgate Buildings. It was almost enough to spread purification and perfume all the way.'[1]

Certainly the spirit of Regency Bath is alive in Austen's

---

[1] Jane Austen, *Persuasion* (1817)

novels, with refined sentiments and carefully coded messages. It's still alive here now. We're aware that the English accent has changed from the pleasant West Country burr of Dorset and Hampshire, spoken by people like Den, into something more like the Home Counties. Here, too, they speak what Gina calls 'Southern politeness'. A Yorkshire lass, she sometimes has trouble disentangling the message from the words, which very often state the opposite of what is meant. I have the same trouble.

The next day we march through the crowds of Bath tourists, feeling slightly out of place in our hiking boots and rucksacks. I have a vision of us as early Victorian explorers passing through an African village on the way to the source of the Nile. We sit on the lower lawn in front of the Royal Crescent and eat our picnic lunch in the springtime sun. This is probably the most stupendous piece of Georgian architecture in England. Although strictly speaking it's just 30 terraced houses in a row, with an Ionic-columned facade built of honey-coloured limestone in a great sweeping curve. It reminds me of the cliffs of Malham Cove in Yorkshire; after all, they're made of the same stuff. The Royal Crescent is just a cliff built by the beautiful, numinous fabricator: Man. I surreptitiously plant an acorn in the park hedge and hope that one day it will be part of the view.

We're setting out on the Cotswold Way, climbing up out of Bath along Dean Hill. I've been looking forward to getting onto this path for years. I used to drive down the M5 looking across at the Cotswold escarpment, dreaming of the day I could be free to walk its whole length. And here is that day. Furthermore, our route-finding should be easier for the next 102 miles as this is a well-marked national trail. Surely some Romans came this way, following the old British paths as well as their own roads? They could have walked all the way to Hadrian's Wall.

Our walk is starting well, as we've just passed a noticeboard telling us that the farmer is a conservationist and that the fields we are walking through are managed without artificial fertilisers or pesticides, to encourage wildflowers, insects and other wildlife. The farmer is a poet, too: 'Enjoy your walk and embrace the views, which nature here provides, For there's something special in these hills, And heavenly peace abides.' We're not used to this, having just come from the chemical prairies of Wiltshire.

We meet a group of scouts coming the other way. They're delighted as they're just completing the Cotswold Way from north to south. They are now avid for the fleshpots of Bath: ice cream and Coca-Cola. We walk off the conservationist-farmer's land, pass the racecourse and get up onto the plateau beyond.

Skylarks are singing here, so high we can't see them. I love this bird; it speaks of walking at dawn across great expanses of springy turf, with a free blue sky beyond. We're to hear skylarks all the rest of the spring whenever we're in open grassland without trees. The males fly straight up as high as 1,000 feet (300 metres), sing for several minutes, then drop to the ground slowly, still singing. Presumably if they lived in a woodland habitat they would sing while perched on tall trees, but as they have chosen these great spaces they have to gain their own height. Sometimes you just can't spot them against a cloudless sky, but the song seems all around us. Tennyson, in his elegy for his friend Arthur Hallam, *In Memoriam*, says: 'And drown'd in yonder living blue, The lark becomes a sightless song.'

The skylark's song has attracted writers and composers, although the physical bird is small, brown and nondescript, as are many ground-nesting birds. The twittering song is unusually long and complex, with up to 700 distinct syllables, and even has micro-dialects for different parts of the country. It was described by Meredith in his poem 'The Lark Ascending': 'He drops the silver chain of sound, Of many links without a break, In chirrup, whistle, slur and shake'. This poem inspired Vaughan Williams' 'pastoral romance for orchestra' of the same name, which has been voted Britain's favourite piece of classical music. The first few bars suggest the rising bird.

The song has distinct phases during the ascent, level flight and descent stages of the flight. The song serves as a territorial signal. If a neighbouring male changes his boundary and encroaches, then it provokes a reaction. A study has been done in which recordings of neighbours were broadcast from correct and incorrect boundaries, and it turns out that the song during the level phase of flight 'encodes for the individuality of the bird': in other words, the skylark can recognise his neighbour from the high-up, level part of his flight. This helps with territorial marking.

William Henry Hudson loved the skylark, too, and his description is a classic piece of writing that shades into nature mysticism at the end: 'The continuous singing of a skylark at a vast height above the green, billowy-sun-and-shadow-swept earth is an etherealised sound which fills the blue space, fills it and falls, and is part of that visible nature above us, as if the blue sky, the floating clouds, the wind and sunshine, has something for the hearing as well as for the sight.'[1]

Hudson shares this mystical quality with other nature writers. It is almost as if his experience transcends the five senses and becomes one weird, shimmering experience like another form of consciousness. Edward Thomas says of Hudson: 'The skylark is to him both bird and spirit, and one proof of the intense reality of his love is his ease in passing, as he does in several places, out of this world into a mythic, visionary or very ancient world.'[2]

These birds, though, are in trouble too: down 50 per cent in the last 25 years. It's the same old story: intensive farming, insecticides, herbicides. Skylarks are ground-nesting birds, vulnerable to trampling, rats and other predators, and haven't a hope without winter stubble fields and field margins to hide in. Autumn-sown crops are no use to the skylark, and most farmers want to plough every square metre for profit.

So why not let these declining species die out? After all, Nature is, as Tennyson said in the same poem, 'red in tooth and claw'. Darwin's theory of the survival of the fittest surely suggests that if we, the humans, are the species in the ascendant we should let market forces operate in nature and let other species die out. The problem with this view is that all creatures on Earth are part of a complex ecosystem on which we humans also rely. If we pull out one layer the whole edifice will collapse and we will have nothing left to eat. We're already seeing the consequences of this with the honey bee. The loss of the skylark would be a deeply regrettable thing.

'In the spring a livelier iris changes on the burnished dove,

---

[1] William Henry Hudson, *Birds and Man* (1901)

[2] Edward Thomas, *In Pursuit of Spring* (1914)

In the spring a young man's fancy lightly turns to thoughts of love.'

So wrote poor Alfred Tennyson, although in his case his fancy was turning to a young man: his friend Arthur Hallam. It is the tale of a miserable, unrequited love which resulted in something beautiful.

We bump into the vicar of Langridge working in the village hall. He likes the idea of us planting acorns and he tells us that his church is 1,000 years old. He feels a real continuity of tradition in his job. He tells us that every spring Charlcombe Lane is closed to let frogs cross the road. The villagers get buckets and help them on their journey to the local lake.

We're walking past an ancient field system which is showing the strip lynchets well in the evening sun. These big steps were supposed to be formed on a hillside when repeated ploughing accidentally led to a series of large ledges forming. This sort of agricultural terracing can be seen in Nepal, by the use of animal ploughing, but I have no doubt it was deliberate on the part of the ancient English farmer, too. A terrace is a far more stable platform to grow crops on and provides better footing for animals and man in such a landscape. It also controls rain run-off and erosion.

Spring was the season when the first ploughing took place. We are seeing many examples of ancient ridge and furrow in flat fields now returned to grass. These huge ripples in the fields are often seen from a train. What I didn't know is that they're a result of our old measurements of furlong and pole.

A furlong (660 feet or 200 metres) comes from the Old English, *furh* and *lang* for furrow and long. This was the length of the furrow in an acre of ploughed land. It was hard to turn a team of oxen so the furrow was made as long as possible. The ploughing was in a clockwise direction and so tended to heap the sillion, the thick shiny slice of soil up in the middle, forming the furrow, which would end up as rectangular strips of ploughed earth about 66 feet (20 metres) wide. The team would begin turning towards the end of the furrow, first left, then sharp right to come back down the other side, which made the furrows a long sinuous S shape. This led to some modern field boundaries also being curved, which a glance at a map will confirm.

The pole was a 16 foot 6 inches (5 metres) long stick used by the ploughman to encourage (all right, beat) the oxen. It would be a handy object to have around for measuring a field, and four of them gave the width of an acre. There is a surveyors' legend that the pole was legally defined as the combined length of the left feet of the first sixteen men to come out of church on a Sunday morning, but this sounds a tall story. What sounds more likely is that there was an old North German measurement of 16 Rhineland feet, the *ruthen*, which is much the same as a pole, and so it probably came over during the Saxon invasions in the ninth century, along with lots of Saxon left feet.

We have to cross the M4 motorway, and after the quiet fields the opposing streams of thundering traffic are shocking in

their intensity. There is a junction here, at Beacon Hill
Plantation, on the road between Bath and Old Sodbury, and we
are slightly surprised to see vehicles pulled up and a number of
men walking in the well-used woods. They have hungry eyes
and seem surprised to see us. There are condoms scattered
here and there.

Walking along the roundabout verges here we are seeing a
lot of Danish scurvy grass, the motorway plant of spring, with
a little white flower. It originated as a coastal plant, tolerating
salt-spray zones, and it will grow where our indigenous
grasses won't: where the roads have been heavily salted during
freezing conditions. Most vegetation dies off with salt-burn,
but not the scurvy grass. In the last fifty years it's moved into
more areas faster than any other plant in England. It is from
the cabbage family, rich in vitamin C, hence the name. Soon it
will be supplemented by dandelions, the yellow flower of huge
value to spring insects, and another coloniser of verges.
Children love blowing dandelion clocks.

We've just been joined on our walk by a dog. She's a young
yellow Labrador bitch, the national dog of the Cotswolds, and
she's clearly on the run. As we crossed the Bath Road at
Tormarton we saw her racing in circles around two walkers
who seemed to be throwing sticks at her rather than for her.
When we met the two men they seemed upset. She had joined
them miles back. She wouldn't go home. She was mad. They
were now worried that she would run across the road in front
of the speeding traffic and get herself killed. They seemed very
relieved when we promised to take her for a walk back in the
other direction.

I find a bit of binder twine and capture her. We are both
dog-lovers, and dogs know this. It may be our smell, actions,
voice, or maybe they use some kind of doggy psychic power,

but they do seem to know. She's a pedigree well-bred dog with an expensive collar. She's not mad, just very young and ill-trained. She's filthy, and she's having the time of her life.

So at last we now have a dog to walk. I've noticed that the few other people we meet walking through England are in the company of dogs. And as I like talking to people, talking to their dog first is a guaranteed ice-breaker.

We're crossing a huge field of sheep in Dodington Park and I'm feeling slightly worried that the dog might go for them. I released her a bit earlier, but instead of chasing sheep she's bouncing headlong through the ponds beside the River Frome, chasing ducks and barking with joy. The explorer W.E. Cormack, when crossing the island of Newfoundland, described her ancestors, the St John's water dogs. They were 'admirably trained as retrievers in fowling . . . the smooth or short-haired dog is preferred because in frosty weather the long-haired kind become encumbered with ice on coming out of the water.'[1]

The fishermen used them out in the Labrador Sea to retrieve fishing nets, so they became known as Labrador retrievers, even though they were from Newfoundland. And the Newfoundland breed is actually from Labrador. What else would you expect from the curious world of dog-breeding?

Our new dog is snuffling around in circles now, on the hunt for something fascinating. W.G. Sebald said his own writing style was like that of a dog sniffing around a field: 'If you look at a dog following the advice of his nose, he traverses a patch of land in a completely unplottable manner. And he invariably finds what he is looking for.'[2]

Born in Germany in 1944, Sebald emigrated to England and

---

[1] Cormack, W.E., *Account of a Journey Across the Island of Newfoundland*, Constable (1824)

[2] *New York Times* Book Review, 31 October 1993

became a university lecturer but wrote his books in German. He is a world-class writer and was being tipped for the Nobel Prize in Literature just before his early death. 'I grew up with the feeling that something was being kept from me' begins his essay *A Natural History of Destruction*.[1] That something was the fire-bombing and total destruction of the German cities with the strange absence, he felt, of any kind of response in German literature. The lecture takes us on a discursive journey through the holocaust, which seems to arrive at the conclusion that the Third Reich had brought the devastation upon itself by inventing the bombing horrors of Guernica, Warsaw, Belgrade, Rotterdam and Stalingrad.

I had to try *Rings of Saturn*. The book is part travelogue, novel, memoir and mythic text, and Sebald has invented a new kind of writing here. Ostensibly it is a walking tour of the East Anglian coast rather like our own spring walk, but the nameless narrator seems to be carrying the weight of Man's history upon his shoulders. Each chapter starts with an observation which then unreels into a series of connected but ever-expanding thoughts in a kind of literary Big Bang. A description of the narrow iron railway bridge across the River Blyth leads to a train that ran on the line that was originally ordered for the Emperor of China. The order was cancelled. That leads to Chinese dragons, the Forbidden City, the Taiping Rebellion and the mass suicide of the Taiping, the British opium trade that rotted the heart of China and the consequent destruction of the magic gardens of Yuan Ming Yuan by the British and French, ending with the death of the appalling Dowager Empress. In another chapter he starts with the traitor Roger Casement, then moves on to Joseph Conrad and

[1] W.G. Sebald, *A Natural History of Destruction*, Carl Hanser Verlag (1999)

on to his *Heart of Darkness*, which depicts the horror of the colonisation of the Belgian Congo. The book is interspersed with oblique black-and-white photographs.

Sebald died at 59 in a curious car accident that robbed us of a great writer who could have written more. He seemed a man overwhelmed by the twentieth century: 'History consists of nothing but misfortune and the troubles that afflict us, so that in all our days on Earth we never know one single moment that is genuinely free of fear.'[1] But his books are not depressing, they are filled with his wonderful, luminous human mind. After reading *The Rings of Saturn* I had to go back to the beginning and read it all over again.

We are passing Dodington Hall, home of James Dyson, the inventor of the bagless vacuum cleaner, and I knock at the door in the hope that our Labrador is his. There's no answer, but I expect he's upstairs doing some hoovering. We carry on, and I'm starting to think we'll be stuck with her for the rest of the walk to Scotland. What do we do if she kills a sheep? Are we responsible? Will she expect to sleep between us in the tent? We walk into the village of Coombes End and I spot a car slowly circling the village green, driven by an extremely ancient gentleman. He stops and rolls down the window. For some extraordinary reason his hairless head is covered with sticking-plasters. He ignores us and addresses the dog. She leaps into the car and, soaking and covered in mud, sits in the

[1] W.G. Sebald, *The Rings of Saturn*, Eichborn (1995)

front passenger seat. Without another word, they drive off very slowly into the distance.

We're getting up into the woods along the Cotswold escarpment and now I'm missing the dog. My boyhood was spent roaming the countryside in the company of the family's scruffy mongrel and he was up for anything: pulling my cart like a husky in winter, climbing the Scottish hills in summer, rolling in dead, rotting things whenever he could. My childhood reading was about other boys who had feral dogs: *Bevis* and William Brown. While William Brown has a wide following due to BBC Radio 4, the stories are simple fare. They also owe rather a lot to the stories of Saki. However, *Bevis: The Story of a Boy* (1882) is now virtually unknown, maybe because the protagonist is a more complex character. His author was one of our greatest nature writers.

Richard Jefferies is scandalously neglected, even though Edward Thomas wrote his biography and his admirers include John Fowles and Robert Macfarlane. But, now, unaccountably, he's unheard of. Don't just take it from me, here's Matthew Oates of the National Trust: 'Now, as our severance from Nature widens, so Jefferies's messages increase in importance. The prospect of Sir David Attenborough, one of his successors, lying forgotten a century from now beggars belief, yet that is precisely what has happened to Jefferies, the most deeply spiritual of our Nature writers and the first and truest nature conservationist. His message is simple: in Nature we truly belong.'

Jefferies' boyhood on Coate Farm in Wiltshire informed his writing throughout his short and troubled life. He struggled with TB and poverty and died at 38. He first had success with essays on the countryside in the *Pall Mall Gazette*, then wrote books of countryside observation – his novels came later. *Wood Magic: A Fable* introduces us to the child Bevis, who can talk to animals, birds and even inanimate nature. In the next book he is older and has lost this power but can exert more control on his surroundings. *Bevis: The Story of a Boy* laments a fast-disappearing countryside and interweaves that loss with the loss of a boyhood filled with boyish pursuits: shooting, camping, fishing and sailing. It struck a chord amongst the Victorian middle classes: a glimpse of a paradise lost on the departure to public school, and the awareness that the Industrial Revolution now had nature on the run.

As a child I loved the descriptions of building a gun and the mapping of a great lake. Arthur Ransome's *Swallows and Amazons* series owes something to *Bevis*; in both there are unsupervised children sailing home-rigged boats and making maps of waterways like proto-Empire builders. However, the Ransome children are insipid in comparison to Bevis and his friend Mark, who kill, skin and eat their food. He also beats his spaniel, Pan. He is more of a wood-spirit than a boy.

Jefferies' *After London* takes on the themes of Bevis and develops them into a post-apocalyptic adult novel about a future London drowned in a poisonous swamp. He could almost be describing a sea-level rise caused by post-2100 global warming. His characters live in a new medieval society in a revived wildwood and there is feeling of post-industrial longing for a simpler world. William Morris borrowed Jefferies' utopian themes for his own *News from Nowhere*, and indeed the Arts and Crafts movement was a reaction to

Victorian industrialisation, just as the ecological movement is maybe now reacting to the digital revolution.

Jefferies writes eloquently of spring birdsong: 'It is sweet on awaking in the early morn to listen to the small bird singing on the tree . . . The bird upon the tree utters the meaning of the wind – a voice of the grass and wild flower, words of the green leaf; they speak through that slender tone. Sweetness of dew and rifts of sunshine, the dark hawthorn touched with breadths of open bud, the odour of the air, the colour of the daffodil . . . all that is delicious and beloved of spring-time are expressed in his song.'[1]

In a short side-trip I go on a pilgrimage to Coate Farm, where Jefferies was born, near Swindon. A few hundred yards away is Coate Water, the original of *Bevis*'s New Sea and the inland sea of *After London*. There is a museum here, run in the farmhouse by Jefferies' admirers, and I am taken to see the Council Oak, which is a real tree that is still growing on the banks of the New Sea. I plant an acorn in the hedge. In the unexpectedly grand farmhouse, which ruined his father but gave so much to the literary world, you can meet Richard Jefferies in spirit.

His last book is the most haunting. *The Story of My Heart* is an account of a man's awakening to nature. He knows there is more to the universe than meets the scientific eye: 'From standing face to face so long with the real earth, the real sun, and the real sea, I am firmly convinced that there is an immense range of thought quite unknown to us yet.'

He knows he is dying of tuberculosis but he accepts death like an animal lying in a snare:

---

[1] Richard Jefferies, *Field and Hedgerow; Being the Last Essays of Richard Jefferies*, Longmans, Green & Co. (1889)

'It is eternity now. I am in the midst of it. It is about me in the sunshine; I am in it, as the butterfly floats in the light-laden air. Nothing has to come; it is now. Now is eternity; now is the immortal life.'[1]

---

[1] Richard Jefferies, *The Story of My Heart: An Autobiography*, Longmans, Green & Co. (1883)

CHAPTER THREE

Going the Cotswold Way – Julius Caesar: 'This whole island is one horrible forest' – the Wildwood – a red squirrel could cross England without touching the ground – The Man Who Planted Trees – magpies – Yetis – a Land Rover – sacred groves – Cider with Rosie – a car accident – pagans – racing cheeses – fairies

We're wading along the wooded edge in a sea of bluebells. The Cotswold Hills roll up from the Thames Valley in the east and terminate in an abrupt escarpment above the Severn Valley: the Edge. We have far-reaching views of the Severn estuary, the Malvern Hills and beyond them the Black Mountains of the Welsh border.

The geologist William Smith would have told you that the Cotswolds are composed of Jurassic limestone, which was quarried to make these delicious golden-brown stone villages below us. J.B. Priestley was fascinated by this colour and wrote that 'the truth is that it has no colour that can be described. Even when the sun is obscured and the light is cold, these walls are still faintly warm and luminous, as if they knew the trick of keeping the lost sunlight of centuries glimmering about them.'[1] To me they look like the crust on Stilton cheese, and I wish I could just walk up to one of these houses, cut a slab off and eat it.

---

[1] J.B. Priestley, *English Journey*, Victor Gollancz (1934)

The bedrock gives rise to a grassland habitat on the hills and these dense woods on the edge. The Cotswold Way, the national trail along the escarpment, was the idea of a couple of visionary and determined people backed up by hard-working followers, like most things worth doing in our country. Ever since Charlie the Farmer's remark about militant ramblers I've had a different view of the bearded, fleece-wearing types that stride past us. I realise that a great deal of the grunt work of conservation is done by people like this, in their own time. So I take my hat off again.

We're in Claypit Wood near Hawkesbury Upton and we're seeing the first big display of bluebells today, 13 April. There's wild garlic, too, which we are going to see in the old woods all the way up to Scotland. There are also primroses, wood anemones and cuckoo-pint. No actual cuckoos yet, though, which surprises me.

There are some lovely houses along here, and earlier we passed Horton Court, which has a twelfth-century Norman Hall built by one Hubert de Rye, whose ancestor saved William the Conqueror's life during the revolt in Valognes in 1047. Passing these places makes me realise what a successful land-grab the Norman Conquest was and how very well William's henchmen knights did out of it. Like the oak-planting knight, they ensured their families' prosperity for centuries.

Before Horton Court on this time-travelling path along the Cotswolds we walk through the vast eleven-acre fort at Old Sodbury, enlarged by Roman conquerors a thousand years before the Normans and excavated by Iron Age Britons centuries before that. The local farmer kindly keeps the inside of the camp well mown so walkers can pass through it. As you stroll through you can imagine the people that lived here and enjoy the view which hasn't changed much in 2,000 years: the great silver serpent of the Severn river winding across flatlands towards the sea, with endless black hills beyond.

'This whole island is one horrible forest,' Julius Caesar was supposed to have said of Britain. In our English mythology there was a great wildwood in Roman times, covering the whole land from shore to shore, enveloped in a silence broken only by the singing of countless birds. A squirrel could have travelled from shore to shore without touching the ground. It would have been a red squirrel, of course. Richard Jefferies' *After London* is a return to this Arcadian state, and much of our literature from Robin Hood, *Sir Gawain and the Green Knight* and Shakespeare's *Midsummer Night's Dream* is concerned with a vast, impenetrable wood.

The problem is, it's not true. Oliver Rackham, in *The Last Forest*, says this: 'There are, for a start, two versions of forest history: one cannot be true, but the other may be. Forests are one of the most prolific fields of pseudo-history – a consistent, logical, accepted corpus of statements, copied from writer to writer down the centuries. We still read, for example, that forests necessarily have to do with trees, that medieval England was very wooded; that the king's hunting was protected by savage laws and extreme punishments . . . The story reads well and makes excellent sense, but it has no connection with the real world; it cannot be sustained from the records of any actual forest or wood.'[1]

---

[1] Oliver Rackham, *The Last Forest*, J.M. Dent & Sons Ltd (1989)

Rackham makes a point here about the historical definition of forest: an area, typically owned by the sovereign and partly wooded, kept for hunting and having its own laws, rather like the New Forest. It did not necessarily consist of trees.

Rackham knew a great deal about trees. He was an academic whose doctoral thesis explored the limits of photosynthesis and plant growth. His results dealt with the rate of carbon dioxide uptake into water and the action of the enzyme that catalyses carbon dioxide into sugar. These suddenly look very relevant today, with concerns about the amount of CO_2 in the atmosphere and its effects on plant growth. His lifetime study of ancient woodland management led him into conflict with the Forestry Commission, whom he criticised for planting conifers, and countryside managers who were planting non-native species.

His writing style is similarly academic and admonitory. He tells us in *Woodlands* (2006): 'Some Facts of Life. Coppicing and pollarding. Older readers will have been taught that trees die when felled and woods disappear because people cut them down. The reality is more complex.' He goes on to explain that most native trees in England do die if completely cut down and the roots grubbed out, but they do well when coppiced and pollarded, and that was the way some ancient woodlands were managed by man.

After the last glacial period 12,000 years ago (we usually call this the Ice Age), Britain was left as barren tundra emerging from under the retreating ice-walls of the glaciers, which had reached as far as a line between the Bristol Channel and Brentwood in Essex. It looked much as Spitsbergen does today. Pioneer trees such as Scots pine, willow, birch and rowan slowly established themselves. The climate steadily became warmer and these trees were supplanted by deciduous species creeping northwards every spring: juniper and yew, the now nearly-extinct small-leaved lime, elm, holly, then our familiar oaks, hawthorn, ash, maple, hornbeam, hazel, cherry and crab apple.

A peak was reached around 8,000 years ago, when this original wildwood covered around 90 per cent of the land. By the time Julius Caesar arrived, though, more than half of it had already been cut down. A more reliably attested remark by Caesar suggests that the original coniferous forest had all but gone by the time the Romans arrived in 55 BC: 'There . . . is timber of every description, except beech and fir.' By the time the Domesday Book was written 15 per cent was left. By 1900 it was down to only 5 per cent. After the First World War there was so little timber remaining that the Forestry Commission was created, planting fast-growing, non-native conifers like Sitka and Douglas Fir and clearing what little native woodland was left. Native woodland plants and animals suffered severely under the new shade-making conifers. By 1990 only 2 per cent of ancient woodland was left.

However, things are now looking up. Thanks to people like Rackham and organisations such as the Woodland Trust the bulk of new planting in England since the 1990s has been of native species, and on our walk through the country I can testify to that. It's another thing that's working. There's still more to be done, for example 85 per cent of the little remaining ancient woodland has no legal protection. There's too much over-grazing by livestock and deer. Sheep are a particular menace to my young oaks. I'm keeping my eye on them.

As we walk through England we keep seeing patches of land with regular rows of white plastic tubes sticking in them. They look like war cemeteries, the dead as regimented as they were in life, but instead of marking death they are marking hope: each one contains a slender sapling, protected from sheep. People seem to be becoming more tree-conscious.

Yongshun Ma was a Chinese lumberjack in Heilongjiang Province who cut down over 36,000 trees in the course of his career, but planted more than 40,000 to pay off his debt to nature. And in the novella *The Man Who Planted Trees*, Jean Giono describes how, while on a walking tour in a desolate valley in Provence he runs out of water but is rescued by a shepherd. It turns out that this man is single-handedly planting a whole forest of oaks to restore the ruined valley. When the narrator returns years later from war, shell-shocked and needing recuperation, he finds that the valley has become a paradise of trees and springs. The French authorities assume it is a natural reforestation and the valley is eventually populated by 10,000 grateful citizens. This story was taken to be true by most readers, but Giono eventually admitted that it was fiction. It was the story he was most proud of, he said.

We've just seen a pair of magpies foraging near Foxholes Wood, and we recite 'One for sorrow, two for joy'. This old rhyme suggests that this bird has occult powers of prediction: 'Three for a wedding, four for a death . . . '

The collective noun for magpies is a 'tidings'. These birds have been seen grieving for their dead, laying wreaths of grass. Our ancestors were acute observers of wildlife and probably realised that magpies are in fact amongst the most intelligent of creatures. The cognitive parts of their avian brain are proportionally the same as those of the great apes, and a 2004 study suggested they have the same intelligence as gorillas, chimpanzees and orang-utans.

'Five for silver, six for gold . . . '

Contrary to folk-wisdom, magpies are not attracted by shiny objects, but they can recognise themselves in a mirror. Experiments have been conducted where a coloured mark is made on the neck of a magpie subject and the bird is observed looking into the mirrors around the cage and attempting to scratch off the mark. This does suggest that they have self-awareness, an example of convergent evolution with humans.

I once saw a parliament of magpies. I opened the bedroom curtains early one Somerset morning to find the entire garden covered with the birds: there must have been over a hundred of them. They were silent, and it was a chilling sight, rather like Alfred Hitchcock's film *The Birds*. No one knows what this rare behaviour is for. Old countrymen might well assume the magpies were meeting with the Devil.

> Seven for a secret, never to be told.
> Eight for heaven,
> Nine for hell,
> And ten for the devil's own sel'…!

Another sign of spring in Dursley Woods: wood anemones. These are the white flowers with six petals and a yellow centre that we saw first in the New Forest. They have delicate pink on the underside. They carpet the woods around here, and like bluebells they try to flower, pollinate and set seed quickly before the tree canopy closes overhead. However, their seed is rarely viable in Britain so they spread very slowly by means of underground roots. The resulting carpets of wood anemones are another sign of ancient woodland. They are a lovely partner to the bluebells. They have little bulbs beneath the surface where they store the energy to reproduce. They have a slightly musky smell, giving them their old country name: smell fox.

We're walking down into Wotton-under-Edge, where a friend is picking us up and will kindly give us a bed for a night. After tonight we've decided to evolve a base-camp system, where we stay in one place for a few nights, if possible, then walk further and further north from it, returning each evening by bus or train. Soon we'll take a cottage for a week, and when the weather warms up we'll camp. Steve is another mountaineering pal and he's excited as he's recently spotted Yeti tracks on Gangkhar Puensum, Bhutan's highest mountain. We gaze at his images of indisputably bipedal tracks in the snow. I wonder what these fabled creatures might do in spring. Would they retreat from humans up into the icy Himalayas? Or hide in leafy forests?

At North Nibley we're climbing steeply up to the Tyndale monument, built to honour William Tyndale, who translated the Bible into English and was burnt at the stake for his pains. He was challenging vested interests in the Church, a dangerous thing to do in these parts. There's another Cold War monitoring bunker up here somewhere, built in case Russia burnt the whole of England at the stake. Robert Burns had it right: 'Man's inhumanity to man makes countless thousands mourn.'

Down in the next village I check out the local garage. There's always something interesting behind the workshop in these places, and we spot an old Series I Land Rover. It looks as if it's been dug up from the bottom of a bog. There's no engine so I offer the garage £400, but I get a slow shake of the head. Prices have obviously gone up in the Cotswolds.

It's 14 April, we've made it past Dursley and we're standing at Uley Bury, another of the many Iron Age forts along the escarpment. There is a cross-shaped kestrel hovering above us, absolutely still. Then it slopes away across the big wind. I'm wondering how the builders survived up here in cold spring weather. It must have been a hard life and even fetching water would have been a struggle. It seems that a good lookout was paramount when selecting sites, not access to water. The Incas were the same. There's a Romano-British temple nearby at West Hill, and the village of Nympsfield gives us a clue to sacred groves somewhere around here. The name is a mixture of Celtic and Old English: *nimet* (Celtic for holy place) and *feld* (Old English for open space).

Roger Deakin, the writer-woodsman, is good on this subject. He explains in a whole chapter of *Wildwood* that the village names of Nymet or Nympton are related to the Celtic *nemeto*, Gaulish *nemeton*, and Old Welsh *nimet*, all meaning the same thing: sacred groves. Down in Devon the Romans had to concentrate military power at a fort called Nemetotacio, the 'Road Station of the Sacred Groves', to counter resistance from native people reluctant to give up their sacred trees. I wonder if the same resistance was met here. Deakin connects this religion to the one we met in Salisbury, the worship of the Green Man, and describes some of the Christian churches featuring this motif in their carvings. His face, sprouting with leaves from eyes, nostrils and mouth, seems almost agonised.

In *Sir Gawain and the Green Knight*, one of the Arthurian romances, there is a beheading game, where the Green Knight has his head repeatedly struck off by Sir Gawain, only for it to

re-grow. It suddenly occurs to me that this might be a reference to tree pollarding, and wonder if the trees in sacred
groves were pollarded in a ceremonial, religious rite leading to
re-growth and re-birth in the spring? Pollards are famously
long-lived; up to a thousand years. Could this be a kind of cult
of eternally-renewing life?

We're at Painswick town – 'the Queen of the Cotswolds' –
staying with my Uncle Jim, who was the doctor around here
for years. One of his patients was Laurie Lee, author of *Cider
with Rosie*, one of the seminal texts for those who like to
believe the Cotswolds are Ideal England. In the book he tells
of his boyhood in nearby Slad around the time of the First
World War, just before the motor car changed these villages
forever. There are gaitered, booted and bonneted old folk in
this autobiography who address each other as thee and thou, a
rural idyll of harvests, endless sunny days in summer and
freezing Christmases in winter. I loved the book as a boy, with
its hint of fruity eroticism:

"'Go on,' said Rosie. I took a deep breath . . . Never to be
forgotten, that first long secret drink of golden fire, juice of
those valleys and of that time, wine of wild orchards, of russet
summer, of plump red apples, and Rosie's burning cheeks.
Never to be forgotten, or ever tasted again . . .'[1]

Of course, it wasn't all like that. Doctor Jim has disturbing
stories of the living conditions that he encountered amongst the

---

[1] Laurie Lee, *Cider with Rosie*, Hogarth Press (1959)

Gloucestershire rural poor in the sixties. Childhood illnesses were often fatal, and pregnancies sometimes disastrous.

Laurie Lee walked from the Cotswolds out into the world, and became a poet, novelist and writer of documentary films, amongst other things. His film *Journey into Spring* was an early example of the British natural history film. It was made by British Transport Films, a unit which paradoxically promoted the newly-nationalised British railways by extolling an unspoiled rural Britain.

Doctor Jim and I go on a pilgrimage to Slad church to see Laurie Lee's grave, with the Woolpack opposite. He had a seat in the pub with his name on it. There's a red admiral butterfly fluttering around the church and the warden says he's been trying to catch it and release it outside. It lands on Lee's stained glass, right on the words of his poem 'April Rise'. Laurie Lee might have laughed at that, the sheer corniness of it on this April morning:

> If ever I saw blessing in the air
> I see it now in this still early day
> Where lemon-green the vaporous morning drips
> Wet sunlight on the powder of my eye.[1]

Today we're walking from Stroud. We see the stream of emergency vehicles racing towards Painswick as we're driven to the day's starting point: an unmarked police car, then an

---

[1] Laurie Lee, 'April Rise'

ambulance, a fire engine, then a marked police car. We speculate what kind of accident could merit such a huge call-out. We only hear what happened as cousin Sally drops us off in Stroud. The mobile phone rings: her mother, Jim's wife, has flipped her car upside down in the middle of town. We don't know how to help but jump out of the car to let Sally race back home.

I'm rather fazed by this, and I manage to get us lost in some woods, walking south instead of north. I'm trying to navigate by map and compass and take a road that curves the wrong way. Gina, who is somewhat younger than me, is brilliant at navigating with her smartphone and soon has us back on track. But the day is lost and we decide we'd better head home to find out the worst. It turns out that Jane, who is a tough woman, has got away with just a black eye. She's been delivering meals to the elderly around Painswick for years but feels that now maybe it's time to stop.

On our return to the walk the next day I try to persuade the taxi-driver to take us all the way, but he's in a furious hurry, sweating profusely, shouting and hurling his mini-bus around the country lanes. It's a horrible experience. He drops us off miles away from the right place. It strikes me that most of the cars we see on our walk are being driven by people who are in a tearing hurry.

This walk has had a strange effect on my own car driving; I find I'm going slower and looking at the countryside more. This makes drivers behind me apoplectic with rage. When we're walking we sometimes just sit down in the verge and watch for ten minutes. All sorts of interesting things start to happen: we see a caterpillar crawling slowly up a stem. A shrew appears in amongst some roots. A bird will whirr in and sit on a branch and cock its head. Adjust a feather.

'A poor life this if, full of care, we have no time to stand and stare,' wrote William Henry Davies, the poet-tramp who was helped to publication by Edward Thomas. He also wrote *The Autobiography of a Super-Tramp*, the book that gave the English rock band their name.

Sometimes when I'm planting the acorns I kneel, bury my face in the grass and breathe in, just to feel it all. Passing car drivers might wonder whose bottom is thus raised to the sky. William Davies would have understood about the life in grass verges – he was what my father called a milestone inspector. He lived in a house at the end of his life, though, near here at Nailsworth.

While we're staying in Painswick Doctor Jim reveals to us something completely unexpected. He produces a green folder of cuttings and photographs simply marked '*Pan*'. I have it next to me as I write.

Painswick is a particularly beautiful town, built out of creamy stone from the local quarry. It grew wealthy on the wool trade, but is now wealthy by virtue of being in the Cotswolds. During the Civil War the church was occupied by the Parliamentarians, and Royalist bullet and cannon-shot marks are still to be seen on the tower. It is famous for its churchyard, which is filled with not one but 99 ancient yews and many fine tombs. This has been described as 'the grandest churchyard in England',[1] and buried right here is a mystery.

---

[1] Alec Clifton-Taylor, *English Parish Churches as Works of Art* (1974)

The town has a well-hidden pagan past. Every spring the people of the town held a 'Feast Sunday', when they processed from the churchyard to the woods near an ancient beacon. Here they would indulge in drunken merriment and Bacchanalian rites of the most debauched variety. Young men would race through the streets, lashing any young women they met with thongs which were supposed to confer fertility. This was witnessed by Robert Raikes, the founder of the Sunday School movement. This spectacle, he said, 'would have disgraced the most heathen nations. Drunkenness and every species of clamour, riot and disorder formerly filled the town on this occasion.' What he saw on that day led him to create the Sunday Schools.

In 1739 one Benjamin Hyett built a Palladian mansion here, to the north-west of the town. He also commissioned the building of a temple-like structure called Pan's Lodge, and in the rococo gardens he erected a man-sized statue of the Greek god Pan. A painting of Pan's Lodge names the town 'Panswyck', and shows the god playing his pipes to a group of ladies and gentlemen. Another house near the churchyard, 'Fiery Beacon', contains an image of Pan's head, again playing his pipes. More strangely, Hyett was allowed to attach a statue of the god to the south wall of Painswick church.

However, in 1950 the vicar, Reverend Jackson, disgusted by the revelry, ordered a group of churchgoers to enter the churchyard at night and tear down the statue of Pan, which had remained there for 200 years. They buried it in an unmarked grave in the churchyard, and the burial party were sworn to secrecy over its whereabouts. Today only one or two residents know the location of the grave.

All of this bears some examination. Hyett's activities could be dismissed as an outpouring of then-fashionable

neo-paganism from the local gentry, or he could have learned
something about the town's rituals which he wanted to mark.
Some place-names provide more hints. There is a nearby farmhouse named Bacchus, there is Jack's Green on the other side
of the valley – named after the May Day festival character
Jack-in-the-Green – and there is a village named Paganhill just
down the valley, famous for its maypole but now a suburb of
Stroud.

This could be a very ancient tradition. Painswick was a
Roman settlement, and a Roman altar existed at the site of the
present church's communion rails. The Roman colonists would
have brought certain rites which begged for blessing from the
gods in spring to safeguard their sheep and goats, which were
grazed in the surrounding woods. Wolves were a considerable
menace in England until around 1433. The relevant Roman
festival was the *Lupercalia*, or festival of the wolf-god, the Lycian
Pan, and it may even be pre-Roman in ultimate origin. It
honoured the wolf that suckled the twins Romulus and Remus,
the founders of Rome. Dogs were sacrificed, and the youths, or
Luperci, dressed in sacrificed goatskins and raced around, beating
young women with goatskin thongs to ensure fertility and to
ease the pain of childbirth. Curiously, the Painswick Sunday
Feast ritual was associated with a dish called puppy-dog pie;
Painswickians are to this day known as Bow Wows.

Another possible clue to Painswick's pagan roots is a legend
attached to the churchyard and its remarkable number of yew
trees. As we have seen, this species of tree is associated with
pagan sites. Tradition asserts that there were 99 yew trees and
that any attempt to grow 100 would end in disaster. Thus the
one-hundredth tree may be a symbol for something else. On
the outside wall of the church's north aisle is an ithyphallic
figure from the fifteenth century: a carved figure clutching an

erect penis. It faces due east and thus greets the morning sun. Does the phallus somehow represent the one-hundredth yew tree?

So far, so tenuous, but in Doctor Jim's file there is an envelope filled with photographs. One shows an empty plinth on the church wall marked 'Pan's plinth'. Others show the particular spot in the graveyard where the statue of Pan is buried. It is easily identifiable, as the shadow of the 42nd yew tree falls over it at the spring equinox. One photograph even shows the measurements in inches of the rectangular shape in the turf: 36 by 58 inches. If the Church of England is ever relaxed enough to allow an excavation, an important artefact could be recovered. I don't suggest that Pan is replaced on his plinth, though. He lives in the woods.

Butterflies are whirling around my head as I walk down the chalk slope. The thin soil is warm in the spring sunshine. We're now on Prestbury Hill, just south of Cleeve Common. This is a butterfly reserve on unimproved grassland: that means flower-rich grassland that hasn't been treated with fertiliser. There is a delicate balance going on here: there are just enough food-plants but not too many, just enough grazing to keep grasses from growing too tall, but not too much grazing in summer. Just enough saplings can provide cover and food for butterflies, but if they spread they can take over the whole area and spoil the grassland, so they have to be cut back. It's a wonder that the conservationists and farmers can juggle all these factors.

As a result, though, they have brown argus on rock-rose (with a curious Latin name: *Helianthemum nummularium*), small blues on kidney vetch (*Anthyllis vulneraria*) and chalk-hill blues on horseshoe vetch (*Hippocrepis comosa*). On our way here today we've seen peacocks and small tortoiseshells and a red admiral (which is a contraction of red admirable). The butterfly people here are proud of their dark green fritillary, which will be flying in July, their duke of Burgundy, which needs large-leaved cowslips, and the lace border that looks just like the edge of a handkerchief stuck to a plant-stem. There's also large Skipper. I've seen a few of these when sailing, usually shouting.

The bluebells are starting to haze. There are so many millions of them that they look like a ground-fog creeping along the understorey of these ancient woods. They get their flowering and leafing done early, before the canopy closes over them. The poet Gerard Manley Hopkins loved them. 'I do not think that I have ever seen anything more beautiful than the bluebell I have been looking at. I know the beauty of the Lord by it. Its inscape is mixed of strength and grace, like an ash tree.'[1]

Hopkins' inscape is the essential being of the flower: its unique God-given identity. Instress is what he calls the impulse that carries the concept of the object into the mind of the observer. The poet's job is to help the reader apprehend the inscape of an object by capturing its uniqueness and communicating it.

Poor Hopkins was another of our tortured writers, torn between homo-eroticism and the Catholic faith. He became a Jesuit priest. He had a huge influence on modern poetry by inventing sprung rhythm, a precursor to free verse. He'd

---

[1] Gerard Manley Hopkins, *Journal*, 18 May 1870

become fascinated by old forms of Anglo-Saxon verse such as *Beowulf* and invented his own form. 'The Windhover' is one of the most impressionistic, metaphysical things he wrote. On the surface it is about a kestrel. It is also about Christ's sacrifice:

> I caught this morning morning's minion, king-
>> dom of daylight's dauphin, dapple-dawn-drawn Falcon, in
>>> his riding
>> Of the rolling level underneath him steady air, and
>>> striding
> High there, how he rung upon the rein of a wimpling wing
> In his ecstasy! then off, off forth on swing,
>> As a skate's heel sweeps smooth on a bow-bend: the hurl
>>> and gliding
>> Rebuffed the big wind. My heart in hiding
> Stirred for a bird, – the achieve of, the mastery of the thing!
>
> Brute beauty and valour and act, oh, air, pride, plume, here
>> Buckle! AND the fire that breaks from thee then, a billion
> Times told lovelier, more dangerous, O my chevalier!
>
>> No wonder of it: shéer plód makes plough down sillion
> Shine, and blue-bleak embers, ah my dear,
>> Fall, gall themselves, and gash gold-vermilion.[1]

It is a pity that Hopkins couldn't feel free to follow his own nature. He did help to free poetry from the dum-de-dum of centuries, though. Like other nature writers he also frees words so that they start to bleed into other forms of existence.

---

[1] Gerard Manley Hopkins, 'The Windhover' (1877)

Other poets owe a debt to Hopkins; do I detect an echo at the beginning of *Under Milk Wood*?

> It is Spring, moonless night in the small town,
> starless and bible-black, the cobble streets silent and
> the hunched, courters'-and-rabbits' wood limping
> invisible down to the sloeblack, slow, black, crow-
> black, fishingboat-bobbing sea.[1]

Spring Bank Holiday this year is going to be on 25 May, the last Monday in May, as is determined by statute. It's an important date around here as it's the day of the world-famous cheese-running on Cooper's Hill. We're going to be renting a cottage on the Witcombe Estate near Birdlip, within sight of the course.

We ask a local lady about this extraordinary event. It's probably another pagan spring festival and connected to the idea of rolling things down a hill, which is always great fun and slightly dangerous. The hill forts along the Cotswold edge would surely have kept round boulders ready to roll down on intruders. Later, burning bundles of brushwood were rolled downhill to welcome the return of the new year after winter. There was an Iron Age hill fort on Cooper's Hill, and later a Roman villa at the foot of the escarpment. Roman snails are still found on the slopes.

In modern times the villagers of Brockworth have continued the tradition, which some think was done to preserve their

---

[1] Dylan Thomas, *Under Milk Wood* (1954)

rights to the common. Tradition layers on top of tradition. What happens is this: a 9lb Double Gloucester round of cheese is rolled from the top of Cooper's Hill and is pursued by running competitors: about twenty young men. The first to run down the one-in-one gradient hill and cross the finish line wins the cheese. The idea is to try to catch it, but the cheese is given a head-start. The reason for this is that a well-rolled cheese can reach 70 mph (112 km/h) and could potentially kill a competitor. The event has now become world-famous and winners have come from as far afield as Japan and America.

Double Gloucester is a hard cheese once made from the milk of Gloucester cattle, a traditional breed from these parts. The milk is particularly suited for cheese-making as it's high in butterfat and protein. The breed nearly became extinct but was revived in 1972 when just one herd remained. Stinking Bishop cheese is also made from Gloucester milk; the name comes from the perry used to wash the rind and is nothing to do with malodorous divines. The perry is made from the Stinking Bishop pear which was bred locally by a Mr Bishop who had an ugly temper. Irritated one morning by the lethargy of his kettle, he got out his gun and shot it.

The Double Gloucester is particularly suited for this kind of competition, which demands perfect roundness and the strength to survive high revolutions (around 1,000 rpm at the finishing line). A soft Brie just wouldn't do. A case protects the perimeter of the cheese, something like a wooden racing tyre. No one seems to know exactly why Single and Double Gloucesters are so named; the Single is whiter and crumbly, while the Double has a stronger, more savoury flavour. The reason for their naming is probably because whereas the Single is made from full-cream milk from the morning's milking and skimmed milk from the evening's milking, the Double gets full-cream milk from both milkings. The Double is allowed to age for longer than the Single – six months versus three weeks – and it's a slightly firmer cheese. The distinctly yellow tinge used to come from a flower that we've been seeing around here: Lady's Bedstraw (*Galium verum*). Why bedstraw? Because it was used to stuff mattresses as it repels fleas. It has the scent of new-mown hay.

The race is dangerous, like many of these traditional village sports, leading to sprains and broken limbs. It attracts huge crowds of around 15,000 people and in 2010 the event was cancelled because of health and safety fears. In May 2013, a police inspector warned the 86-year-old cheese maker Diana Smart of Churcham, who has supplied the Double Gloucester racing cheeses since 1988, that she could be held responsible for any injuries. Foam cheeses were briefly substituted, but since then sense has prevailed.

These English spring festivals are persistent, probably because everyone wants to get out after a dull winter and enjoy the good weather, possibly because we have some atavistic memory of celebrating the spring. When I was a youth in Rutland we used to take part in the Hallaton bottle-kicking, which happened every Easter Monday. It was a contest between the nearby Leicestershire villages of Hallaton and Medbourne, which always descended into a riot between hundreds of men in a sea of mud. It started with a parade through the villages, and a hare pie was laid on the site of an ancient pagan temple (this is possibly a memory of the pagan worship of the goddess Eostre, who gives us the name Easter). Then the pie was flung into the crowd. This 'hare pie scramble' always descended into a vicious fight. After the pie was eaten the real fun started: the bottle-kicking. The only rules were no knives, no eye-gouging and not too much stran-gling. A small wooden keg of beer (the bottle) was wrestled by the competing teams in a giant, seething rugby scrum across a muddy stream and through barbed-wire fences and hedges. The aim was to carry the keg into the rival village. Or away from it: the rules seem unclear. The best of three contests won. Afterwards everyone retired to the pub to recover from their injuries.

Back in Gloucestershire, in nearby Tetbury, there is woolsack racing at the end of May, where men and women race up Gumstool Hill carrying heavy sacks filled with fleeces. In Wiltshire, in the village of Urchfont, there is still a tradition of scarecrow-making at the beginning of May, and on the same weekend in Hastings there's a parade for Jack-in-the-Green, who is a Green Man figure. His effigy leads a crowd of 1,000 to the castle, where he is sacrificed to free the spirit of summer. Then there are the Lancashire Bacup Nutters, who dress up as Moorish pirates every Easter Sunday and perform dances. But possibly the oldest spring dance festival in the country is at Padstow, Cornwall. The 'Obby 'Oss ('hobby horse') is a Celtic tradition and once again celebrates the coming of spring. Crowds of local people banging drums and singing follow the two 'Osses, which are cloaked frames – one red and one blue. Underneath are the local young men who try to catch the local young women as they pass through the town. Being caught under the black cloaks is thought to bring good luck, fertility and accusations of sexual harassment.

We've just found a Roman snail, *Helix pomatia*. It's a huge brute; twice the size of our common snails at a couple of

inches across, and it has a lovely brown-banded creamy shell.
These were brought to England by legionaries sometime after
AD 46. The cooks would feed them on milk and peacocks'
brains to fatten them up, and they were no doubt served as a
special treat in the nearby Roman villa at Witcombe. Some
managed to escape from the larder and ran, or slithered, for
the hills. However, they didn't go far. Their migration range is
between 13 to 19 feet (4 to 6 metres), which might explain
why they've stayed so close to the villa. They hibernate and
will lay eggs in June, and the offspring may live as long as
twenty years. Cunning gardeners know that if you move a
common snail more than 65 feet (20 metres) it won't find its
way back to your lettuce. Just flinging it over the neighbour's
hedge won't work, unless you use a catapult. These beauties
are protected by law, though, so it's illegal to kill, injure or eat
them unless you are French, in which case you call them
escargot and eat them as a delicacy. It's worth pointing out
that our admirable Wildlife and Countryside Act 1981 was
introduced to comply with a European directive. It's not all
about wonky bananas, you know.

The spring car drivers are out. After walking through
silent Witcombe Wood and across the delightfully named
Birdlip Hill we've had to cross another torrent of motor cars
at the Air Balloon roundabout. This is one of the rare places
where a major trunk road climbs and crosses the Cotswold
edge. The A417 from Gloucester to Cirencester, built along
the old Roman Ermine Way, collides with the A436, and a
great tangle of traffic results. A heat-haze rises from the
glittering cars, and as we pick our way between the
stationary bonnets I am struck at how unhappy the drivers
look. Many of them are on the phone, or texting. Some of
these monsters muster over 500 horsepower, more than a

racing car, yet the drivers look disengaged from the business of looking where they're going. We have a friend, a cyclist, whose wife was crushed and killed by a lorry that came up from behind them as they rode along. And I once overtook a truck driver on the M4 who was reading a newspaper balanced on the steering wheel. At least it was *The Star*, so the stories were short.

We plunge back into the Scrubbs woods with relief and resolve to avoid roads as much as we can. There are great views from the promontory here. William Cobbett came this way after a tedious journey across the 'miserable country' around Cirencester:

'I looked down from the top of a high hill into the *vale of Gloucester!* Never was there, surely, such a contrast in the world! This hill *Burlip Hill*; it is much about a mile down it, and the descent so steep as to require the wheel of the chaise to be locked; and even with that precaution, I did not think it over and above safe to sit on the chaise; so, upon Sir Robert Wilson's principle of taking care of *Number One*, I got out and walked down . . . All here is fine; fine farms; fine pastures; all enclosed fields; all divided by hedges; orchards aplenty . . . Gloucester is a fine, clean, beautiful place; and, which is of a vast deal more importance, the labourers' dwellings, as I came along, looked good, and the labourers themselves pretty well as to dress and healthiness.'[1]

Cobbett was gazing over the farmland, but around one's feet the short turf still supports many lime-loving herbs. There are several species of orchids here, such as early purple orchid, bee orchid and musk orchid. There's a lovely tall blue flower here, too, with an odd name: Viper's Bugloss. All this abundance

---

[1] William Cobbett, *Rural Rides* (1830)

supports butterflies, moths and local snails. The din of the traffic recedes behind us, and I plant an oak to celebrate.

I'm now standing with one foot on the south bank of the River Thames and the other on the north bank. It's all Julian's idea. He's joined us for a few days of walking while we're staying at the farm cottage at Witcombe. I always introduce Julian Champkin as The Man Who Knows Everything, like Alexander von Humboldt or Edward Gibbon. Actually it would be hard to know everything these days as human knowledge is doubling every eighteen months and its half-life is shrinking: the time it takes to become obsolete or just plain wrong. Julian exhibited only one oddity on our days together. Every time I planted an acorn he was overcome by the need to urinate on it.

One thing Julian knows is that we're walking past the true source of the River Thames, at Seven Springs, just four miles south of Cheltenham. So we've stopped to look at this, another sort of spring. Thames Head is traditionally taken to be the source, even though the Winterbourne stream dries up seasonally there (the name means a water source that dries up in summer). The River Churn, however, flows all year round into the Thames and its source is right here, which is fourteen miles further from the mouth of the Thames. There's a plaque that reads '*Hic tuus o tamesine pater septemgeminus fons*', which Julian translates as 'Here, O Father Thames, is your sevenfold spring'. The combined flow from the seven springs emerges from this culvert under the Gloucester road. Then Julian pointed something out; if there are seven springs upstream from here then surely the longest of the seven springs on the other side of the road is the true source? At which point I reply: you can take some things too far. I plant four acorns here, just to be awkward.

The proto-Thames trickles away from us to become the Father Thames of so many writers, including Kate Bush:

> Oh! England, my Lionheart!
> Peter Pan steals the kids in Kensington Park.
> You read me Shakespeare on the rolling Thames –
> That old river poet that never, ever ends.
> Our thumping hearts hold the ravens in,
> And keep the tower from tumbling.

We are standing in a stream that connects ultimately with the sea, but are we standing in the same river as the one we see in London? The Greek philosopher Heraclitus seemed to think not: we cannot step twice into the same stream. Plato took it further: 'We both step and do not step in the same rivers. We are and are not.' Joseph Conrad, the great writer-sailor, took this notion of flux further still and connects it with some sort of oneness. His river flows on into the sea and dissolves into a great ocean at the beginning and end of his short novel, *Heart of Darkness*:

'The sea-reach of the Thames stretched before us like the beginning of an interminable waterway. In the offing the sea and the sky were welded together without a joint, and in the luminous space the tanned sails of the barges drifting up with the tide seemed to stand still in red clusters of canvas sharply peaked, with gleams of varnished sprits. A haze rested on the low shores that ran out to sea in vanishing flatness. The air was dark above Gravesend, and farther back still seemed

condensed into a mournful gloom, brooding motionless over
the biggest, and the greatest, town on earth . . .'

Marlow, a narrator character, tells his story, an excoriating
account of Belgium's brutal colonialism in the Congo, in which
the victims lost their lives and the victors lost their souls. At
the end Conrad, perhaps the best-ever prose writer in English,
tells us something important about the nature of the universe:

'Marlow ceased, and sat apart, indistinct and silent, in the
pose of a meditating Buddha. Nobody moved for a time. "We
have lost the first of the ebb," said the Director suddenly. I
raised my head. The offing was barred by a black bank of
clouds, and the tranquil waterway leading to the uttermost
ends of the earth flowed sombre under an overcast sky –
seemed to lead into the heart of an immense darkness.'[1]

The Cotswold Way has brought us through Lineover Wood,
and there's something here I want to see. This 120-acre
(50-hectare) wood is situated on a north-facing section of the
Cotswold escarpment and is now owned by the Woodland
Trust. The name means lime bank in Anglo-Saxon, and there
are some of the large-leaved limes here that are now rare in
Britain.

This woodland has been managed since ancient times, and
there's a lime stool here which is at least 1,000 years old. A
tree stool is the stump left after the original tree was felled.
Shoots grow from these stumps very fast; sometimes 2 inches

---

[1] Joseph Conrad, *Heart of Darkness*, *Blackwood's Magazine* (1899)

(5 centimetres) a day and they would have been harvested every few years for poles or logs. I'm thinking about the pre-Roman sacred grove cults again, and wonder if there were promises of eternal life based on trees like this apparently living forever.

There's a 600-year-old beech here, too, one of the largest in England, and we stand admiring it for a while. It's a vast tree, 23 feet (7 metres) in circumference. It looks like the Green Man, with his contorted features and green foliage thrusting out from crevices in the bark.

There are shrubs here, too, amongst the trees: hazel, hawthorn, blackthorn and holly. The Trust has planted a 15-acre area with oak, field maple and shrubs to make a new wood pasture habitat. This will be grazed by livestock whose dung will provide food and living for insects and fungus. The animals will keep the shrubs under control, and maybe in future the trees could be pollarded high so that the animals can't reach the fresh shoots, as with the Knightwood oak. You can see a clear browse line on trees in wood pasture, which is as high as the cattle can reach for the fresh foliage. Giraffes would do well around here.

As with the other conservation projects we have seen, encouraging one species brings others along, too. All the flowers on the understorey are attracting insect life, which in turn brings in spotted flycatcher, great spotted woodpeckers and treecreepers. Volunteers have put up nesting boxes which are now inhabited by tawny owls. They have put up well-written informative notices, too, with lots of activities for children. I feel lucky to live in a country with such well-intentioned people around. Thank you, Woodland Trust.

We walk out of the wood on another carpet of bluebells and dog's mercury. There's lily-of-the-valley, too, with its lovely white

flowers that are rather like hats that might have been worn by
Sir Arthur Conan Doyle's Cottingley Fairies. The Sherlock
Holmes author was a spiritualist as well as an amateur sleuth,
and he had been commissioned by *The Strand Magazine* to write
an article on fairies. It was December 1920, and England was
still in the grip of post-World War spiritualism. The death of
thousands of men in the trenches had resulted in a fascination
with the afterlife and a craze for psychic mediums amongst those
left behind. When Doyle heard that two young girls in
Cottingley, West Yorkshire, had photographs of real fairies with
wings, he was bowled over. The pictures duly appeared in *The
Strand Magazine*, together with Doyle's enthusiastic description.
They featured one of the girls gazing adoringly at what looked
like classic storybook fairies, complete with gossamer wings and
tiny musical instruments. Doyle felt the need to re-name one of
the girls Alice, a reference to Lewis Carroll's *Alice's Adventures in
Wonderland*. The edition sold out in a few days.

Others were less impressed. One critic pointed out that the
fairies had distinctly Parisienne hair-styles and another wrote:
'Knowing children, and knowing that Sir Arthur Conan Doyle has
legs, I decide that the Miss Carpenters have pulled one of them.'

Eventually, in the 1980s, Elsie and Frances admitted that
they had faked the photographs using cardboard cut-outs.
Doyle would never know. Perhaps he should have listened to
his own creation:

'It is my belief, Watson, founded upon my experience, that
the lowest and vilest alleys in London do not present a more
dreadful record of sin than does the smiling and beautiful
countryside.'[1]

---

[1] Arthur Conan Doyle, *The Adventure of the Copper Beeches, The Strand
Magazine* (June 1892)

I have just knelt in dog poo. My technique of planting acorns is to kneel down in the verge and dig a hole, planting the acorn on its side as recommended. The problem is, with the springtime grass now growing longer, it's hard to see what I'm doing.

The filth is all over my trousers and all over my boots. The dog must have been an enormous, obese brute. It stinks, and I must get it off. So I clamber into the field, remove my trousers and boots and hop around in the long grass, half-naked and uttering cries like 'Urrrgh!' and 'Urrrrrrgh!'

Another party of boy scouts chose that moment to march round the bend and confront this apparition. Trained, no doubt, to be on the lookout for middle-aged men with their trousers down, they ignore me and press on.

Dog-owners act in strange ways. The hedges in the countryside are festooned with blue plastic bags filled with dog excrement. It should, of course, be bagged and put in the bins provided by the council. It will never bio-degrade in the bag and it is a horrible eyesore. It shouldn't be left on the ground as canine faeces transmit diseases such as toxocariasis, which can cause blindness in children, and neosporosis, a nasty parasite of cattle. A common sight round here is an immaculately dressed owner gazing into the far distance, trying not to look connected to darling Poopkins on the other end of the lead who is hunched over, grinning and straining and producing another Cumberland sausage of revolting ordure.

I am adapting my oak-planting to local conditions: from now on I try to remain on my feet and wade into the hedge.

Spring is travelling faster through the country every year, Julian informs us, and now arrives eleven days earlier than it did during the Victorian era. At Kew Gardens crocuses have been coming up nearly two weeks early, and in 2014 small tortoiseshell butterflies arrived 26 days early. The speed of spring is calculated by measuring the time and the distance between related events, so bluebells might flower in Gloucestershire on 13 April, but 200 miles further north they may not flower until a week later, on 20 April. That would give a 'speed' of around 1.2 miles per hour (2 km/h).

Professor Tim Sparks, at Coventry University, has made a study of thousands of records going back over 124 years and has worked out that between 1891 and 1947 the season used to move up the country at around 1.2 miles per hour, travelling 28 miles per day. Now, though, spring manages 45 miles per day, at a dizzying 1.9 miles per hour. That's about the same speed as someone swimming a leisurely breaststroke, all day and all night.

The speed of the seven individual events that were measured differed, with trees catching up with the new, faster spring rather slower than insects. Ladybirds arrive at 6.5 miles per hour, swallows arrive at 2.4 miles per hour, and hawthorns come into leaf at 6.3 miles per hour, but they come into flower at 1.9 miles per hour (which suggests that different signals drive leafing and flowering in hawthorn). Orange tip butterflies arrive at 1.4 miles per hour, frogspawn travels at a speed of 1 mile per hour and oak trees come into leaf at 1.3 miles per hour. And apparently the spring doesn't travel in an exact south-to-north line; its passage is more like a diagonal line drawn up through England from Penzance to Berwick-on-Tweed, just like spring temperatures.

This change has a bearing on the success or failure of all English wildlife, but it is hard to know what to do about it. The climate has been changing in this country since the last Ice Age and will until the next Ice Age – if it comes. As we all know, we're experiencing global warming, which is leading to earlier springs. All we can do is to study what's happening, learn how we might help and try to reduce humanity's impact on spaceship Earth.

At Stanway we cross the stream that rises in Lidcombe Wood. For at least a thousand years it has driven watermills at the foot of the escarpment in an entirely renewable way. In 1291 the Abbey of Tewkesbury owned no less than three corn mills and one fulling mill here. Fulling was the process of beating woollen cloth to clean it from the sheep's oils and to make it thicker. In Roman times slaves worked ankle-deep in vats of stale human urine, pounding the cloth with clubs. The ammonia salts cleaned and whitened the cloth. The urine was so valuable it was taxed, so presumably slave-visits to the latrine were conditional. By the Middle Ages Fuller's Earth, a soft, clay-like mineral, was being used instead of urine. Watermills were introduced to do the pounding, no doubt much to the relief of local slaves.

Wool was the wealth of the Cotswolds for centuries, but only sites like these hold any clue to the long-gone woollen cloth trade. In the twelfth century it used to be said that in Europe the best wool was English, and in England the best wool was Cotswold. The reason was that this area was ideal for sheep, and the Abbeys ran huge flocks of Cotswold Lions, a large local breed with long fleeces. I had a couple of these and they were beautiful, but also remarkably greedy and stupid.

One day they escaped and ate my yew hedge. This is poisonous to livestock and led to their painful death, despite my best efforts with a stomach pump and charcoal. This is why yew trees are kept behind stone walls in churchyards.

Medieval merchants became rich and spent fortunes on wool churches as well as building fine houses for themselves. At that time 50 per cent of England's economy was due to wool. A number of laws were put in place to increase consumption, including burial of the dead in woollen shrouds, leading to the expression 'you can't pull the wool over my eyes': i.e., I'm not dead yet. However, persistent fiddling by the Tudor political classes, together with foreign competition, led to a steep decline in the wool trade.

By 1635 the uppermost mill had become a paper mill, still recorded on my map. The last mill is still going after all these centuries. When the cloth industry collapsed at the end of the seventeenth century this mill was converted to grind corn, which it still does. There is a massive 24-foot waterwheel made in cast-iron by one James Savory in nearby Tewkesbury in the mid-nineteenth century and the mill was in turn a wood-sawing mill, an electric power generator and it now grinds local wheat between a pair of French grindstones to make a fine local product: Stanway Flour.

Walking past Stanway House, a Jacobean manor house, I heard a rhythmical thumping which I couldn't figure out until later: it's a hydraulic ram, a water-powered device which uses the principle of water-hammer (like the banging in pipes). It uses the flow of a river to pump a small amount of water uphill. Like the waterwheels and the Claverton pumphouse, this is an old technology which was green before its time: almost free to run and completely sustainable. You can do something similar in the bath with a plug.

We're just topping-out on the summit of the Cotswold Way, Cleeve Hill. At 1,083 feet (330 metres) it's the highest point in Gloucestershire and the air feels thin. The other name for it is Cleeve Cloud, which I prefer. A bit farther on there's a superb viewpoint. We can see well into Wales, and we can even imagine we can see the Quantock Hills over 90 miles away (140 kilometres). To the north we can see Evesham Vale, where we leave the Cotswold Way and head towards Stratford. There's a golf course up here and it will have consumed around 111 acres (45 hectares) of natural heathland and turned it into lawn, fed with tons of fertiliser and pesticides and sprinkled at times with large amounts of water. The Campaign to Protect Rural England says golf courses damage the Green Belt and public access to the countryside. 'As well as taking vast amounts of land out of public access, golf courses are extremely water-intensive,' says CPRE. On the plus side, golf fans claim that the sport is a way of enjoying the countryside. There are at least three objections to this: firstly, golf courses are not really representative of the English countryside; secondly, their generally lowland locations take farmland out of production; and thirdly, they are only open to those few who can afford the fees. There are class and power dimensions to this debate, as is usual in England (but less so in Scotland): better-off people play golf. I'll give my golfing friend Kip Wake the last word. 'On our golf course I've seen hares, kingfishers, rabbits and hawks. That's better than a load of houses.'

CHAPTER FOUR

William Morris – Spring Thicket – News from Nowhere – *Bill Bryson* – *the Appalachian Trail* – *passenger pigeons* – *at last we hear a cuckoo* – *we've lost over half in twenty years* – *deforestation in their West African winter home* – *memorial benches* – *humanity: a plague on the Earth* – *which apocalypse: hot or cold?*

The spring tourists are out in Broadway, one of the Cotswolds' showcase villages. There are several huge coaches parked up in the broad high street, and many Japanese tourists enjoying the sunshine. I wonder if they find the Cotswolds as exotic and beautiful as we find their culture.

In one of the shops is a postcard of *Spring Thicket*, a design by Broadway's most famous resident, William Morris. We climb up to Broadway Tower, where Morris once lived and worked. *Spring Thicket* is one of his last wallpaper designs, with heavily stylised open-cup lilies in white together with swirling green leaves on a pale blue background. It was inspired by the spring foliage he saw in the woods around here. I went on a Morris pilgrimage once by narrowboat to Kelmscott, his manor house on the Thames. I asked the lock-keeper where the house was, and he gestured rather impatiently into the distance. 'I don't know why everybody wants to look at his house. All he did was make cars.' In fact cars were just about the last things William Morris would have made; he was a textile designer, a novelist, a poet and a socialist revolutionary. In fact, if he had made cars they would have been rather beautiful, but they weren't invented until the end of his lifetime. I expect he would have driven a Morris Traveller, a sort of half-timbered cottage of a car.

Morris was a hugely influential figure in Victorian England, and that influence continues in the work of C.S. Lewis and J.R.R. Tolkien. In fact, Tolkien was quoted as saying that he could not better the Morris books that he read in his youth, and that he borrowed the names Gandolf and the horse Silverfax from Morris's *Well at World's End* for his own *Lord of the Rings*, changing them slightly to Gandalf and Shadowfax.

Morris was born into a wealthy middle-class family in Essex, and he burned with a life-long guilt at being able to afford luxuries that he felt should be available to all: 'I do not want art for a few, any more than education for a few, or freedom for a few.' He was artistically talented and, much influenced by the writing of his contemporary, art critic John Ruskin, he started to produce beautifully-made textiles, furniture and interior designs in medieval style. He loathed the way that Victorian industrial capitalism turned out shoddy, ugly goods made by unhappy workers to furnish the homes of the proletariat. Instead, his mantra was 'Have nothing in your houses that you do not know to be useful, or believe to be beautiful.'

The paradox was that his designs were expensively hand-made and were thus only affordable by the better-off. His firm Morris & Co. became hugely popular with the aristocracy and upper-middle classes and moved into premises in London's Oxford Street. He was aware of the conflict and felt guilt at 'ministering to the swinish luxury of the rich'. He became a leading light in English Socialism and wrote a utopian novel, *News from Nowhere*, which owes something to Richard Jefferies'

After London, which had been published five years before. In his
novel Morris describes an ideal society based on Marxist principles in a pastoral landscape.

Morris can also be credited with eco-socialism, the principles of which he developed later in life within the Socialist
League. However, Morris might have been the original champagne socialist; he and his family were once rowed up the
Thames to Kelmscott Manor by a boatman with whom he
declined to share his champagne breakfast. Whatever you think
of Morris's ambiguous relationship with money, class, art and
wealthy patrons, the fact remains that he was a nature-lover
and *Spring Thicket* is a lasting design that is still sold today –
even as a smartphone case. What would he have made of
modern-day China, a pseudo-Communist state, churning out
cheap goods, including mobile phones? 'I have spoken of
machinery being used freely for releasing people from the more
mechanical and repulsive part of necessary labour; it is the
allowing of machines to be our masters and not our servants
that so injures the beauty of life nowadays.'

In the end, William Morris loved beauty, and cared deeply
that men and women should all equally share in beautiful lives.
He also loved the Cotswolds, as you can see anytime you look
deeply into the intricate design of *Spring Thicket*.

On the way up to Broadway Tower we see a drystone wall
being rebuilt, and it provides a good excuse to stand and
regain our breath. This is the kind of job farmers do in spring
after the lambing. The fresh limestone is almost white in

colour and chalk-soft, very different to the abrasive grey grit-stone walls we will see later in the Peak District. Julian has done a fair bit of walling and shows us how the big through-stones hold the two outer skins of wall together, without the use of mortar. All the techniques of traditional drystone walling are on display here. First, different sizes of stone are selected and laid out in rows. They look as if they've been recently quarried, rather than picked out of the field, as were the first walls built around here. The topsoil is then dug away along the line of the wall so that the large, flat foundation stones lie on harder subsoil. Then string is pegged out to give two straight edges, and a wooden batter frame set up to give the size and shape of the wall. This is an A-shaped, easel-like framework made the same size as a cross-section through the wall. Finally the waller starts laying the stones, beginning with two rows of stones that gradually diminish in size as the wall goes up. The through-stones, or tie-stones, don't project here in this wall as they do in Derbyshire – the latter give you a handy foot-step to climb over the wall, although farmers hate you doing this. The waller fills in the gap between the two facing walls with small hearting stones. At the top is laid a line of coping stones standing on their edges, which also help to tie the two faces of the wall together. The end result is a thing of beauty, and a suitable alternative to hedges in this area where these aren't possible to cultivate, due to poor growing conditions.

William Cobbett loathed stone walls. He was taking one of his rural rides out of Cirencester:

I came up hill into a country, apparently formerly a down or common, but now divided into large fields by stone walls. Anything so ugly I have never seen before. The

stone . . . lies very near the surface. The plough is continually bringing it up, and thus, in general, come the means
of making the walls that serve as fences. Anything quite
as cheerless as this I do not recollect to have seen . . .
these stones are quite abominable.[1]

Of course, Cobbett hadn't seen barbed wire, as it wasn't
invented until 1867. Walls cannot compare to hedges in
natural beauty, certainly, but where there is no option except
wire or a wall I would choose a wall every time.

We've had to rescue five lambs from the wrong side of walls
or fences; in fact, Julian has become quite adept at this. The
first alert is the sound of piteous bleating, then the sight of a
lamb running up and down alongside a fence, with a lone
mother looking anxiously at the small hole through which her
child has escaped. We always made sure that the correct lamb
was matched with its mother: having kept sheep myself I know
that well-meaning ramblers can misunderstand sheepy anxiety.

Broadway Tower stands high over the surrounding landscape, with its top nearly 1,100 feet above sea level. You can see
sixteen counties from up here, and we can see the next week of
our spring walk across the Vale of Evesham, towards
Birmingham. The great landscape designer Capability Brown
was at work here, too, having been commissioned to design this
ornamental folly for the Earl of Coventry. Although supposed
to be in Saxon style, the design is more like a Norman tower.
After a chequered history it was rented as a holiday retreat by
Arts and Crafts medievalists including William Morris and his
friend and fellow artist, Edward Burne-Jones. It was here that
William Morris started his campaign for the preservation of

---

[1] William Cobbett, *Rural Rides* (1830)

historic monuments and founded the Society for the Protection of Ancient Buildings in 1877. He was appalled at the way in which over-zealous Victorian restorations scraped away historic features of ancient churches, and he called his new society 'Anti-scrape'. In particular, Morris was bothered about the practice of restoring ancient buildings to an imagined state from the past, while at the same time destroying later modifications which he felt documented their history. This was 'forgery'. Instead, he believed, ancient buildings should be repaired, not restored. His principles are still followed today, and as usual with Morris, his aesthetic instincts seem right.

At the top of the hill the three of us collapse with relief on one of those wooden memorial benches that you see more and more alongside walks throughout England. They usually come with a brass plate announcing something such as 'This was the favourite view of Ernie (1921–1992) and Eileen (1922–1999) and they spent many happy hours here together'. It seems a sweet way to remember a beloved friend and to share something beautiful with strangers. Some of these bench-marks are mildly humorous, such as the one on Hampstead Heath which reads:

> 'Now in years astride my eighties,
> this Elysian seat I have vacated,
> but gentle neighbour sigh not yet,
> I've only moved to Somerset.'
>   (Ben W, 1912-)

I hope that Ben has now taken a higher Elysian seat in heaven. If all 70 million of us in the United Kingdom had a memorial bench we would have them stretching arm-rest to arm-rest in a line all the way through England – then four times around the world.

We continue along the Cotswold Way, heading towards its northern end at Chipping Campden. This has been a wonderful path, the best I can remember in England. It's easy to walk, dry underfoot and well-marked. The villages are lovely, the views stupendous, and there are pleasant places to stay. If you walk from south to north as we have, the light is behind you and you can see detail without being blinded by a low sun. The prevailing wind is also behind you, so there is no feeling of a chill blast in your face.

This is so easy compared to the Appalachian Trail, the longest footpath in the world, which stretches along the eastern coast of the United States for almost 2,200 miles, from Georgia to Maine. It consists of barely-marked trails in dense woods, with the ever-present threat of black bears and homicidal Americans en route. Earl V. Shaffer was the first to complete it non-stop in 1948. He had walked a section of it in the thirties with a friend who was killed in the Pacific theatre during the Second World War. Shaffer had also fought in the war and his long walk was part therapy and part tribute to his lost friend. His book, *Walking with Spring*, described his epic journey, which took 123 days from April to August, averaging seventeen miles a day (the trail was just over 2,000 miles at the time). Shaffer carried no tent and wore army boots and, like us, he walked northwards with the spring as the weather warmed. When he arrived at the end the trail authorities refused to believe he had completed it until he showed them photographs and endured their cross-examination.

In his immensely entertaining book *A Walk in the*

Woods[1] Bill Bryson describes how he and his friend Katz attempted to follow Shaffer's footsteps. They managed 870 miles, more than a third of the total distance. They suffered considerably, got fit, lost weight and kept off the booze. Bryson claims that every twenty minutes on the Appalachian Trail Katz and he walked further than the average American walks in a week: 1.4 miles, or 350 yards each day. This seems incredible. He explains that it's nearly impossible to walk anywhere in America, as any English pedestrian tourist visiting the country well knows. Bryson was even honked for walking through towns. His neighbour drives 800 yards to work, and another drives 100 yards to pick up her child from a friend's house. He thinks Americans are steadily losing the use of their legs. The British are not much better: when America sneezes, Britain catches a cold. I notice that when we stay in London we walk everywhere, far more than at home in the country where every single journey is by car. We certainly feel better walking ten miles a day on this spring walk, we feel fitter, eat and sleep better. Gina calls it 'happy tired'.

A more shocking revelation in Bryson's book is the changes in the North American landscape. Indiscriminate chopping down of trees and the extermination of the buffalo were followed by the loss of the passenger pigeon, a bird that was once the most numerous in the world. In Ontario in 1866 one flock a mile wide and 300 miles long took fourteen hours to pass overhead. Yet the species, that at its height may have numbered 9 billion, lost its woodland habitat east of the Rocky Mountains and was hunted for cheap slave-food until Martha, the last known specimen, died on 1 September 1914 in Cincinnati Zoo.

---

[1] Bill Bryson, *A Walk in the Woods*, Broadway Books (1998)

This appalling story brings two thoughts to mind. One is the astonishing fragility of such a species that can collapse from 9 billion to total extinction in less than one human lifetime. The second thought is that our own species now numbers a rather similar 7 billion. The latest UN study[1] has calculated the human population in 2100 is going to be around 11 billion, and that's an upwards revision of over 2 billion extra mouths to feed: more than the present population of China and the USA combined. Several recent studies suggest that with the help of present technology planet Earth can support around 2 billion humans at a European standard of living, so we're already three or four times over-booked. Sir David Attenborough, the BBC naturalist, certainly thinks so:

'I've seen wildlife under mounting human pressure all over the world and it's not just from human economy or technology – behind every threat is the frightening explosion in human numbers.'

He makes it quite clear where the fault lies: 'We are a plague on the Earth. It's coming home to roost over the next 50 years or so.'

It is not only naturalists that are concerned. 'The more people there are, the more food we need, the more space we occupy, the more resources and consumer goods we wish to have and the more development has to take place.' So says Prince Philip, Duke of Edinburgh, who has met more world leaders than most. But what are the politicians saying? Absolutely nothing, apart from the Green Party – with one MP. No politician dares risk discussing their constituents' inalienable right to inflict yet more children on the planet. No religious leader says anything except 'go forth and multiply'.

---

[1] www.un.org/apps/news/story.asp?NewsID=51526#.Vk4y7nbhDIU

The issue is dismissed as one for posh rich men who blame poor Africans for over-producing children, when it's the over-consumption of the West that's the problem.

Our vanity as a species cannot conceive of extinction, but human ingenuity is such that some kind of fate that befell the passenger pigeon might be waiting for us. It might be a genet-ically modified virus or some completely unexpected loss of habitat or food supply.

What would nature look like without humans? Two more American books give a clue: *One Second After*[1] is a novel that deals with the after-effects of an EMP nuclear-bomb attack on the United States by Iran and North Korea. The electro-magnetic pulse causes the nation's electric power grid to collapse, leading to a mass die-off of the population from 300 million to 30 million, largely because of loss of refrigeration and the rise of typhoid and cholera.

The World Without Us[2] is more of a thought-experiment book, speculating what would happen if the human population of the world suddenly vanished overnight. The author, Alan Weisman, had already written articles for *Discovery* magazine about the Korean de-militarised zone, a 160-mile (250-km) long strip of mountainous land between North and South Korea which had been left to nature since the cessation of hostilities between the two countries in 1953. It has now become an involuntary park, and is one of the most well-preserved areas of temperate habitat in the world, with Siberian tigers, Amur leopards and Asiatic black bear living amongst nearly 3,000 plant species. No humans enter the zone. *The World Without Us* extends the idea world-wide and shows us what would be left of our civilization after a

[1] William R. Forstchen, *One Second After* (2009)

[2] Alan Weisman. *The World Without Us*, St. Martin's Thomas Dunne Books (2009)

few hundred years: very little. For example, New York would rapidly disintegrate due to a silting-up of sewers and subways, leading to collapsing foundations. Rainwater damage to buildings would destroy them in a few centuries, and nature would sweep in from parkland to reclaim the crumbling ruins. After 500 years all that would be left of us would be a few cast-iron fire hydrants, stainless-steel washing-machine drums and some plastics. Before long the only evidence of humanity left for curious aliens would be radio-active elements, some ceramics, bronze statues and the Mount Rushmore sculptures to show them what the top bit of humans looked like. Tectonic subduction would erase all traces of us within a few million years as the present-day continents slide under new ones. And that would be that: no traces of humans in a blink of a geological eye.

I regard this kind of literature as survivalist fantasy, something like *After London*, but it has a curious attraction – especially if you or your descendants are survivors. The positive news is that nature can recover surprisingly swiftly from humanity's worst depredations, but only if a breeding population survives. It might be hard for the dodo or the passenger pigeon to return, but new, wonderful species would soon arise if only we let them. As the Roman poet Horace said: 'You can drive nature out with a pitchfork, but she will always come back.' The conclusion surely must be that we should strive to keep as many individual species alive as possible, in case we might like to see a panda or a dodo again.

The cold spring weather has an effect on our plans. I originally hoped to walk throughout the season for three months, letting it overtake us so that by the time we reached Scotland the spring should just be over, and summer on its way. It's been an unseasonably cold start to the year, so we'll have to have a lay-off to let the season catch up.

We tramp through the woods, chestnuts in full flower on either side, their candles now so heavy that the boughs sway more slowly than in winter. There are some huge specimen trees here, absolute beauties of different species I can't identify. Someone spent a lot of money here a couple of centuries ago. The house comes into view, three great gables standing over the ornamental garden that produced T.S. Eliot's first poem from the *Four Quartets*, 'Burnt Norton'. I move more cautiously, aware that this is a private house. I peer over the wall, and there it is.

In late summer 1934 the poet had been visiting a friend and near-lover, Emily Hale, and whilst walking past the house he wandered into the overgrown garden. The atmosphere of time-less decay had a disturbing effect on him. He had some kind of a mystical experience, and breaking a poetic silence of six years, Eliot wrote a poem about time.

> Time present and time past
> Are both perhaps present in time future,
> And time future contained in time past.[1]

Tom Eliot wasn't the only writer interested in the notion of time. Our nature-mystic Richard Jefferies wrote, 'Now is eternity; now is the immortal life.' And William Golding seems to be writing about something similar at the end of Jocelin's life, when he witnesses the apple tree blossom in *The Spire*.

---

[1] T.S. Eliot, *Burnt Norton*, Faber (1941)

Twice I have had a suspicion that time is not quite what it seems. Once was near the summit of a high mountain where, desperately hypoxic and at my limit of exhaustion, time seemed to be collapsing into a great 'Now', containing all past and future. I think I was dying. The second time was when following a drama script under bright lights in a radio studio. I was seeing the words on the page and hearing the actor's speech. I could see the script before and after the event-horizon of the spoken words, so I could see past, present and future, yet the words I could hear were cutting through the material of time in the Now. For a moment I had the strong sensation of moving through time as a ship's bows cut through a sea. It was a dislocating feeling. The text on the page you are reading in your present has a past at the top of the page and a future at the bottom. And yet it was written in my present and so, as Stephen King points out, writing is both time travel and thought-transference.

Einstein said this: 'People like us, who believe in physics, know that the distinction between past, present and future is only a stubbornly persistent illusion . . . the only reason for time is so that everything doesn't happen at once.'

Maybe everything has, is and will happen all at the same time, just as a book contains a text which we cannot read in an instant but have to laboriously read through word by word. Or maybe we are more like a snail crawling around a clock face, endlessly pursuing the minute hand but unaware that the clock face reads all times at once. Scientists seem unable to solve this riddle, but some of our nature writers seem to be able to approach it.

Eliot's poem shares images with the other poems in the *Four Quartets* which repeat like musical themes, such as the four seasons (spring appears in *Little Gidding*), or the sun shining for a precious moment, capturing a moment of eternity, or the repeating theme of this very rose garden.

Theologically the poem is about grace – maybe. It is about an England under severe threat – perhaps. But if Eliot had known about the 'burnt' in Burnt Norton he might have written a different poem. The house was owned by one Sir William Keyt MP, whose wife left him after he started an affair with a maid, Molly Johnson. The baronet attempted to run his butler through with a sword, suspecting him of being an informant, but the butler stuffed his bed with pillows to deceive the would-be murderer. The butler had also taken a fancy to the ubiquitous Molly. Keyt then built an extravagant mansion next door for his mistress. Molly, obviously a keen bird-watcher, was supposed to have said 'What is a Keyt [kite] without wings?' The besotted baronet embezzled money from his son and built two wings, only for Molly to run off with another man in 1741. Sir William, on one last drunken bender, then set fire to Norton and incinerated it and himself. Curiously, all that was left of the baronet was a few bones, his keys and a pocket watch. I suspect that he didn't die in the fire but did a Lord Lucan and decided it was time to take up a new life elsewhere. The heat of the fire scorched the side of the existing mansion, hence the name.

This story has been the basis of a novel written by the present inhabitant of Burnt Norton: Caroline, Countess of Harrowby, a glamorous and kindly lady. She shows me round the house and grounds a few weeks later. It turns out that the house was occupied by one Lady Lincoln at the time when Eliot wandered into the garden, so strictly speaking he was trespassing. He was a somewhat odd character; Virginia Woolf described him as 'a polished, cultivated, elaborate young American . . . But beneath the surface it is fairly evident that

he is very intellectual, intolerant, with strong views of his own
& a poetic creed.' This man of surface and also depth was
clearly struck by the atmosphere of this extraordinary place.

The main impression I come away with is of a feeling of
permanence. The absence of any traffic noise at all, together
with the age of the house and the quiet stands of trees, gives a
strong feeling of timelessness: exactly the feeling of the Eliot
poem. The same house has thus been the source of two literary
works by two different writers: one inspired by a whirl of
human passion, betrayal and despair, and one by a quiet
moment in a sun-filled garden.

We've just seen the first swallows, swooping and swerving
around the field. One flits past the side of my head, skidding
past by inches. They are the most agile flyers, taking insects
on the wing at tremendous speed. They've just come 6,000
miles from southern Africa on their annual migration. Here's
Ted Hughes:

> A Swallow
>> Has slipped through a fracture in the snow-sheet
>> Which is still our sky –
>
>> She flicks past, ahead of her name,
>> Twinkling away out over the lake.

The ancients thought that swallows hibernated over winter,
and Carl Linnaeus believed that they generated spontaneously

from mud at the bottom of lakes. Their migration was not even fully understood by the great naturalist Reverend Gilbert White, the author of *The Natural History and Antiquities of Selbourne* (1789). His book takes the form of a series of observations in letters to fellow naturalists. He searched for swallows and house martins hibernating in a 'benumbed state' in 'secret dormitories' in Selbourne. He was still looking for evidence of torpid swallows just weeks before his death. Presumably he couldn't accept that a bird weighing less than an ounce could fly thousands of miles to South Africa then return to exactly the same place it was hatched.

In every other respect, White was a superb nature writer and can be regarded as our first published naturalist and ornithologist. He understood the vital connections between living things in a way still not entirely understood by agri-businesses, but above all he was an observer. Here he is observing the nightjar catching insects on the wing:

'The powers of its wing were wonderful, exceeding, if possible, the various evolutions and quick turns of the swallow genus . . . I saw it distinctly, more than once, put out its short leg while on the wing, and, by a bend of the head, deliver somewhat into its mouth . . . I no longer wonder at the use of its middle toe, which is curiously furnished with a serrated claw.'

Richard Mabey, in his biography of Gilbert White, shows how expressively he wrote in a style to suit the birds he observed:

'What is striking is the way Gilbert often arranges his sentence structure to echo the physical style of a bird's flight. So "The white-throat uses odd jerks and gesticulations over the tops of hedges and bushes"; and "Woodpeckers fly *volatu undosu* (in an undulating flight), opening and closing their wings at every stroke, and so are always rising and falling in curves".[1]

It is due to the work of naturalists such as Gilbert White that England is probably the best-recorded wildlife site in the world. Because this country industrialised first, we did nearly everything else first, including, paradoxically, recording the very species that industrialisation was going to exterminate.

Julian's news about the speed of spring is augmented by a climate change report by Natural England, which is based on the observations of thousands of volunteers and the records of people like Gilbert White. The study assumed a 2 degrees Celsius increase in temperature by the year 2080. They studied over 3,000 English species and decided that there are going to be gains and losses over the next sixty-five years. I've been wondering about the non-appearance of the cuckoo, and that's one of the birds most at risk from climate change. On the bright side there will be winners as well as losers. And here's where it gets unfair.

Despite England emitting more greenhouse gas per capita than most countries since the Industrial Revolution, we are in a fortunate position. Most of our wildlife species are at the northern end of their range. As the country warms up, those animals, plants and insects will be able to extend their range northwards and higher in altitude (because temperatures tend to decrease as you go north and up). Those already up there

---

[1] Richard Mabey, *Gilbert White*, Profile Books (2006)

will have to squeeze up a bit or move out. So it might be grim up north right now, but soon it's going to be green.

I've already seen the little egret on my dawn chorus walk and soon it will be joined by the great egret, the spoonbill, emperor dragonflies, chough, corncrakes, nightjars, roseate terns and many other butterflies and other insects. Wasps, bees (hooray), ants and the Dartford warbler may do better. There may be twice as many winners as losers, but the losers will include many birds that live on uplands in the north: the curlew, hen harriers and ring ouzels.

The seas around us will be changing, too. Because they're shallow and enclosed the English Channel, Irish and North Seas have already warmed up four times as quickly as the worldwide average, and haddock and cod have moved around 200 miles (320 kilometres) to the north. In their place have come hake, red mullet and sea bass.

Is there anything we can do to help? Yes, a great deal. Motorway verges are already wonderful wildlife habitats, as the numbers of hawks circling will testify. These, together with railway embankments, can be improved to provide corri-dors for species extending their range. More wetlands can be established as these are wonderful resources for wildlife – as we will see later. Farmers like Charlie are starting to leave strips of pollen-rich grassland around the edges of arable fields. In our own gardens we can leave wild places and encourage flowers. Don't bother mowing the lawn: let wild-flowers thrive for the bees. Don't bother to strim the wilder corners of your garden, and please discourage cats from killing your new garden birds.

We're very lucky in this country that the early effects of climate change will be less harmful than in other places, such as low-lying islands or drought-stricken countries, and our knowledge of conservation is going to be vital. What will happen if the temperatures keep rising is another matter.

We're now in Chipping Campden, which became the centre for the Cotswolds Arts and Crafts movement at the beginning of the twentieth century, much influenced by the craft ethics of John Ruskin and William Morris. There are many beautiful houses here, but they're hardly affordable by Morris's socialist workers. Electric gates and raked gravel have replaced sagging wooden fences and dung-splattered farmyards. I conclude that the Cotswold villages have lost much of their *Cider with Rosie* charm by becoming wealthy and manicured, but the country-side this spring looks as wonderful as ever.

We've come to the end of the Cotswold Way, or the begin-ning – depending on which way you look at it. It has been a wonderful path and every bit as good as I had hoped.

In Bill Bryson's *The Road to Little Dribbling* (2015) he revisits some of the English places he travelled to in *Notes from a Small Island* (1995) and comments on the delightful fatuity of the English. As he points out himself, Bryson is one of our most welcome immigrants, and one who loves the things about England that I love. 'Nothing – and I mean, really, absolutely nothing – is more extraordinary than the English countryside,' he proclaims, 'and what a joy it is to walk in it. England and Wales have 130,000 miles of public footpaths, about 2.2 miles of path for every square mile of area. People in Britain don't realise how extraordinary that is.'

He's absolutely right. We're lucky in England and Wales to

have so many footpaths, unlike North America where it's so hard to walk anywhere legally. And there may be even more rights of way that we don't know about. Not far from where we are now is Crudwell, the site of a recent legal ruling on footpaths. After a recent Court of Appeal ruling that the paths are legal rights of way, nearly 1,000 footpaths and bridleways could be reinstated after 200 years of being left off the map. An ex-Ramblers Association secretary, John Andrews, won the case to reopen the bridleways after twenty years (a bridleway is a footpath in which it is also legal to ride or lead a horse, but not necessarily a bicycle).

The two Crudwell bridleways were marked out by land commissioner, Daniel Trinder, in the early 1800s during the Enclosures, when large areas of common land were being enclosed and divided up into privately owned plots. They were found on an early nineteenth-century map, but Wiltshire county council had refused to restore them.

Lord Dyson, Master of the Rolls, decided that despite the 'linguistic imperfections' of the 1801 Inclosure Consolidation Act, Trinder had had the power to 'set out and appoint' public bridleways and footpaths.

He said to the court: 'We have been told that there are believed to be between 500 and 1,000 cases in England and Wales where public footpaths and bridleways set out and appointed by commissioners are not currently recorded in the relevant definitive maps.'

So what happens now? Let's hope those unrecorded bridle-ways will be reinstated. But there's a greater threat to footpaths. Any historic paths not officially recorded as public rights of way by 2026 will be extinguished, meaning thousands of well-trodden paths, and other potentially useful routes, would be lost forever. Keen walkers might like to get out

there and make sure their local paths are walked once a year
and recorded.

The spring blossom is out in the Vale of Evesham. This exceptionally fertile valley is the centre of a healthy market garden
industry, and the famous orchards are giving a great display of
fruit-tree blossom this year. I remember that the Japanese word
for orchard is 'flowering snowstorm', and I see drifts of
blossom float by in the sky.

John Moore wrote 'It hurts afresh every time the blossom
comes and goes; it is so beautiful and brief.'[1]

He was considered 'the most talented writer about the
countryside of his generation'[2] and was a pioneer conservationist. He was also a Fleet Air Arm pilot during the Second
World War and a bestselling author. He has a refreshing take
on the English countryside, and he isn't a doom-monger. In
The Seasons of the Year he points out that England is simply a
garden, and its beauty is manmade and artificial. The natural
state of an England without us would be a mixture of light
scrub, low woodland, heaths and rushy marshes. That was the
English landscape up until 1760. Since then the countryside
has changed in accordance with the demands of the farmer.
The growing population needed corn, so the Cotswolds
switched from sheep pasture to arable. We needed milk, so
cornfields changed into pasture. We want sugar and so the

---

[1] John Moore, *The Seasons of the Year*, Collins (1954)
[2] So said Sir Compton Mackenzie

fens fill with thousands of acres of sugarbeet. Moore goes on to say that these changes profoundly affect our wildlife. Partridges wax and wane with the length of stubble: when men hand-cut the corn with scythes they left long shaggy stubble that gave cover for the partridges, and so they prospered. Then the binder came along, making a short stubble, and the birds rapidly declined. The combines came next, leaving a long stalk, and so the populations bounced back. The latest combine-harvesters cut low to use the straw and once more the partridges lack cover and their numbers have dwindled. Moore's point is that we must expect the countryside to change with the demands of the population and technological advances. I would add that if the population grows too large the demands on the countryside will lead to permanent damage. John Moore is a wonderful writer. Try him.

I love his advice on how to appreciate nature: 'The wise man, I think, whether he looks at a little moth or at a spring orchard, always feels he is looking at it both for the first and for the last time. His joy and wonder are always mixed with a sense of the briefness and the frailty.'[1]

We continue to walk past blossoming fruit trees. White plums and damsons are the first to appear, followed by pink apples and white pears. The wild plum trees originally came from the Middle East; Armenia or Mesopotamia, but the plum was rapidly domesticated by early humans and has turned up in

[1] John Moore, *The Seasons of the Year*

Neolithic sites. Pershore plums are particularly juicy, and their story really took off in 1827 when the landlord of the Butcher's Arms pub in Church Street discovered a seedling of a wild plum growing in the ancient Tiddesley Wood on the outskirts of Pershore. This became known as the Pershore Yellow Egg Plum, and by 1870 no less than 900 tons were being sent to market every year. This became such an event that the Great Western Railway named one of their steam trains the Pershore Plum.

It might seem odd that someone could find a viable commercial fruit hanging around in a wood, but plums are related to blackthorn which forms a big part of the hedges around here. They produce sloes every autumn which we collect to make sloe gin. Plums are related to damsons, but not to quinces, which belong to the apple and pear family.

Quinces are sharp-tasting but hardy and were cultivated before the apple, and in fact many ancient sources may be mis-translated as apple when the fruit was really a quince. Plutarch tells us that a Greek bride would bite into a quince to perfume her kiss before entering the bridal chamber, 'in order that the first greeting may not be disagreeable nor unpleasant'.[1] It occurs to me then that Eve's apple may in fact have been a quince, so perhaps she was preparing for her bridal encounter with Adam instead of bringing the woes of the world upon his race by biting into the apple of knowledge. Could those mis-ogynistic, bearded old Bible scholars have possibly got their facts wrong?

---

[1] Plutarch, *Roman Questions*, 3.65

It's spring in Shakespeare:

> O Spring, of hope and love and youth and gladness
> Wind-wingèd emblem! brightest, best and fairest!
> Whence comest thou, when, with dark Winter's sadness
> The tears that fade in sunny smiles thou sharest?
> Sister of joy! thou art the child who wearest
> Thy mother's dying smile, tender and sweet;
> Thy mother Autumn, for whose grave thou bearest
> Fresh flowers, and beams like flowers, with gentle feet,
> Disturbing not the leaves which are her winding sheet.[1]

We have to find a route north from here, aiming towards Stratford-upon-Avon. On the way we're passing through the Vale of Evesham and Shakespeare's Forest of Arden. As a kid reading Shakespeare at school I always wondered what the Forest of Arden would look like. In *As You Like It* the forest seemed something like an enchanted jungle. In it everything turns topsy-turvy: people start cross-dressing, women take control and men learn about love. In the forest of *A Midsummer Night's Dream* things get even weirder; fairies gain special powers and a man grows an ass's head. For Shakespeare, then, the forest was an enchanted place, but the modern Forest of Arden is now a place of country clubs and motels. We walk to Stratford-upon-Avon past a huge railway engine scrapyard at Long Marston, which is also home to the surprisingly named Shakespeare County Raceway drag strip. I'm fairly sure that Bill Shakespeare wasn't into fast cars, but we begin to get an inkling of the huge literary tourist trap that's waiting for us in Stratford.

---

[1] William Shakespeare, *The Two Gentlemen of Verona*, Act 1, Scene 3

We join the River Avon by the racecourse and walk in on
the Shakespeare's Avon Way footpath, past the Royal
Shakespeare Theatre, where a Shakespeare taxi whizzes by. We
pass the Shakespeare In Love bridal shop and then the
Shakespeare Ink body-piercing shop. There's a Shakespeare
Fish Bar, and for the dragsters there's a Shakespeare Garage
Doors business. You get the idea. As we walk out of Stratford-
upon-Avon along the canal we see the last gasp of Shakespeare
literary tourism at Mary Arden's Farm – his mother's family
home.

What if Shakespeare didn't write any of the plays that we
think he did? Does it really matter to Stratford? If the Loch
Ness Monster didn't exist there would still be a healthy trade
in signage around Inverness.

One intriguing fact that's just emerged is that Shakespeare
was quite possibly a pot-head. Fragments of 400-year-old clay
pipes from his garden were analysed by a technique called gas
chromatography mass spectrometry and found to contain
cannabis. Other pipes from next door seemed to contain
cocaine. So what was going on?

There was quite a lot of smoking going on in the late
1500s. Sir Walter Raleigh had just returned from Virginia,
bringing back North American *Nicotiana*: tobacco which
contains nicotine, and Sir Francis Drake may have brought
back coca leaves from Peru containing cocaine (*Erythroxylum*).
Some claim there's a hint in Shakespeare's Sonnet 76, where
his subject is lack of inspiration and he writes:

> Why is my verse so barren of new pride,
> So far from variation or quick change?
> Why with the time do I not glance aside
> To new-found methods, and to compounds strange?

Why write I still all one, ever the same,
And keep invention in a noted weed,
That every word doth almost tell my name,
Showing their birth, and where they did proceed?

The suggestion is that here he is rejecting cocaine (a 'compound strange') and leaving invention inside the cannabis weed (a 'noted weed'), instead of smoking it and having drug-inspired dreams. So was William Shakespeare off his face when he was writing *The Tempest*? It certainly reads like it. But so much is unknown about the Bard, except that he brings good business to Stratford.

Heading out of town the next day we join the Stratford-upon-Avon Canal, which is going to take us to Birmingham. It's great walking: no cars, no hills, easy oak-planting in the hedges.

At last, I'm listening to a cuckoo. We're on the towpath of the Stratford-upon-Avon Canal, near the tiny aqueduct at Yarningdale. The cuckoo is calling from a small wood, just to our east. There is a slight echo, which adds to the haunting nature of the song. Woodlands echo because of reflection from all the leaves: you'll notice there is no echo after the leaves fall. It's after midday on 23 April and it seems late to me this year.

The cuckoo is a much-loved bird in English culture as the herald of spring. Yet it's always been known as a cheat and a parasite, which led to insults in medieval English such as 'cuckold' and 'cuckoo in the nest'. Aristotle was the first to observe and record that the bird made no nest but deposited her egg in another bird's nest, and the Reverend Gilbert White called this habit a 'monstrous outrage on maternal affection'. The cuckoo's behaviour disturbed God-fearing naturalists such as White as it suggested its behaviour was mechanistically selfish instead of part of a divinely benevolent plan. This became such a bone of contention that the mere mention of the bird at the British Ornithologists' Club would lead to outbreaks of fighting amongst the members.

What the cuckoo does is quite extraordinary. The male advertises his presence to females with his well-known call. After selection and mating, the female sits silent and motion-less and observes her prey: the nests of meadow pipits, dunnocks and reed warblers. Once the host birds are away feeding (or sometimes distracted by the male cuckoo) she launches herself into the nest, smashes and eats one original egg and lays her own egg in just ten seconds. Her egg simu-lates the host eggs almost perfectly; the green speckled eggs of the reed warblers or the spotty brown eggs of meadow pipits. She flies off, never to see her offspring again.

The embryo in her egg is part-formed and beats the remaining chicks by hatching half a day ahead. The parasitic cuckoo chick then heaves any remaining eggs or chicks over the edge of the nest onto the ground, where they smash and die. There is no time for the chick to learn this behaviour so it is almost certainly pre-programmed.

The unwitting adoptive parents feed the monster chick, which grows several times bigger than the hosts. They are driven to a frenzy of feeding by a clever deception, noted by Dr Nick Davies of Cambridge University, who spent 23 years observing cuckoos on Wicken Fen. In his excellent book,

Cuckoo: Cheating by Nature[1] he explains how the chick does it: 'The cuckoo chick has this amazing begging call,' he says. 'It sounds like a whole brood of hungry chicks.'

It might seem easy to foster your offspring in this way, but it isn't. 'Foisting your parental duties on somebody else may seem to be a wonderful thing to do . . . but over evolutionary time, the hosts fight back so that the poor cuckoo has to work incredibly hard to be lazy, simply because it has to overcome all of these defences. What we witness is a fantastic arms race between parasite and host.' The reed warblers of Wicken Fen fight their parasite with a series of stratagems, such as learning to reject eggs that differ very slightly from their own. These behaviours are in turn overcome by the cuckoo.

This evolutionary arms race between host and parasite is only one of the aspects of Davies' fascinating book. It made me realise truths about the way we fit into nature, and what happens when a parasite overmasters a host. We humans made a giant step by the evolution of consciousness, which led to further giant steps – such as the invention of printing, which disseminated knowledge, and the Industrial Revolution, which ramped up cheap production – and we now stand at the beginning of our biggest step, the Digital Revolution, which I guess will take our consciousness out of physical bodies. Our host, the natural world, cannot evolve controlling stratagems fast enough and we are now in danger of killing our host: planet Earth and her precious cargo of species.

It might be some consolation to the dunnocks, reed warblers, pied wagtails and meadow pipits that the cuckoo is in decline: numbers are down by 65 per cent since the 1980s. There have been a number of studies done to find the reason

---

[1]   Nick Davies, *Cuckoo: Cheating by Nature*, Bloomsbury (2015)

why. As Nick Davies observes, the cuckoo is in a finely balanced arms race with the host species and times its arrival in England to match the breeding season of the host species here. One reason put forward is that as spring temperatures increase the host birds are laying their eggs earlier by five to six days, suggesting that the cuckoo is missing a narrow window of opportunity.

One study[1] looked at this timing in depth. It found no correspondence between cuckoo decline and any decline of host species, and found that instead the earlier breeding of reed warblers may actually benefit cuckoos. It concluded that reduced prey, mainly caterpillars, available during the breeding season and bad conditions along migration routes or on the overwintering grounds in sub-Saharan Africa might be behind the decline in cuckoos.

Another study,[2] using satellite-tagged cuckoos, confirmed this suspicion and revealed several surprises. First, the cuckoo migrates back to Africa much sooner than previously thought: as early as 3 June, with 50 per cent of the sample leaving by the end of June. Secondly, these 'English' cuckoos only spend 15 per cent of their time here. One individual spent 47 per cent of his time in Africa and 38 per cent of his time on migration. Refuelling sites are vital during migration, and the River Po in Italy is one favourite area. These individuals were found to skirt round the Sahara Desert rather than commit to one mammoth cross-desert flight, as was previously thought.

---

[1] Douglas, D.J.T., Newson, S.E., Leech, D.I., Noble, D.G. & Robinson, R.A. (2010), *How important are climate-induced changes in host availability for population processes in an obligate brood parasite, the European Cuckoo?* Oikos, Early View doi: 10.1111/j.1600-0706.2010.18388.x

[2] British Trust for Ornithology Cuckoo Tracking Project: www.bto.org/science/migration/tracking-studies/cuckoo-tracking/about

Many seemed to fail to find food in sub-Saharan Africa and returned north, a known survival stratagem. Deforestation in its African winter home and lack of food on the migration routes now seem to be the most likely reasons for the decline in the species.

There's another reason. According to the *Telegraph*,[1] every year 5 billion birds attempt to fly from Africa to Eurasia and 1 billion are deliberately killed by humans. Using birdsong recordings and other wily devices the trappers of Cyprus, Malta and elsewhere use guns and Chinese-made mist nets to ensnare the birds and kill them. The only difference we could make is to boycott Chinese-made goods until these illegal nets are stopped at source.

The cuckoo will remain popular amongst humans. The oldest English song we have, 'Sumer is icumin in', celebrates the bird in the Wessex dialect of Middle English and was probably written around 1270 by William of Winchcombe, a scribe at the priory at Leominster. It's a surprisingly complicated polyphonic song in which one performer starts, to be followed by a second singing from the beginning after what we would call a bar. It's the type of song known as a round, which may still be recognised in modern music such as the Beach Boys' 'God Only Knows', which is another complex song. Translated, the first verse goes:

> Summer is a-coming in,
> Loudly sing cuckoo
> Groweth seed and bloweth mead
> And springs the wood anew
> Sing cuckoo!

---

[1] www.telegraph.co.uk/news/earth/8102878/Songbirds-poached-and-eaten.html

The ewe is bleating after her lamb,
The cow is lowing after her calf;
The bullock is prancing,
The billy-goat farting,
Sing merrily, cuckoo!
Cuckoo, cuckoo,
You sing well, cuckoo,
Never stop now.
Sing, cuckoo, now; sing, cuckoo;
Sing, cuckoo; sing, cuckoo, now!

There are scholarly suspicions about this song and there may be more in it than meets the eye, like the bird it celebrates. It reads like a straightforward welcome to spring and early summer, but lacks certain words found in other renewal songs, and some of the words and farmyard noises may have double meanings. The cuckoo was certainly a symbol of adultery and duplicity. Shakespeare had this: 'The cuckoo then, on every tree, Mocks married men: for thus sings he, Cuckoo; Cuckoo, cuckoo: O, word of fear, Unpleasing to a married ear!'[1]

So the song may be ironic, but what the monkish writer really intended is probably lost forever.

If global warming is happening and springs are getting earlier, why is this spring we are walking through so cold? It seems that trying to predict climate change is like trying to predict

---

[1] William Shakespeare, *Love's Labour's Lost* (Spring at V, ii)

the outcome of a football match by watching one second of play. Is that ball going up or going down? Is that team all at their end or the opposition's end? The timespan that humans have been measuring is so short that any meaningful long-term change is hard to spot. The climate usually changes over eons, and Ice Ages have been arriving every 100,000 years or so lately. It is worth remembering that the English countryside itself was created by global warming: during the last Ice Age England was a bleak, treeless desert.

I've been following the climate change debate in the newspapers and online for years – and getting more and more perplexed. In my youth there was a fear that we were heading for another Ice Age, and I remember it being discussed around the family table. On 11 January 1970 the *Washington Post* reported that 'Colder Winters Herald of New Ice Age' and in 1972 a group of glacial-epoch experts at a conference agreed that 'the natural end of our warm epoch is undoubtedly near'. Then *Newsweek* magazine ran an article titled 'The Cooling World' on 28 April 1975. It promised famines, drought, tornadoes and starvation. In conclusion it claimed that 'the present decline has taken the planet about a sixth of the way toward the Ice Age'. Scientists suggested ways to warm up the world: scattering soot at the poles was my favourite. Generating lots of carbon dioxide wasn't suggested.

Now, of course, we're all terrified of galloping global warming. I have myself witnessed glacial melting in the Himalayas over the past thirty years and there's no doubt that something big is underway. The glaciers in the Tian Shan mountain range have lost a quarter of their mass over the last five decades, mostly because of melting due to increased summer temperatures. That's about five gigatons every year, and a gigaton of ice is an ice cube one kilometre square. Over nine expeditions to Mount Everest I vaguely noticed the snowline moving upwards every year and the glaciers receding. An American climbing friend, David Breashears, spent several years climbing around the mountain and taking photographs from exactly the same places as the first reconnaissance party in 1921, Guy Bullock and George Mallory. When he showed me the pairs of images the differences jumped out: the glaciers are obviously disappearing. Like the slow diminution of songbird populations in England this gradual change isn't noticed until you consciously make comparisons: it just creeps up on you.

It's clear that something is afoot in the countryside we're walking through, and it seems to be to do with climate change. But we're too close to the wood to see the trees.

What is fascinating is the war between the Global Warming fraternity – the Warmists (most scientists, the left-wing Greens and the *Guardian* newspaper) and the Deniers (people who would like to carry on happily consuming, the right-wing, and the *Daily Telegraph*). These two camps insult each other regularly (I like to read the *Guardian* and *Telegraph* on alternate days: it keeps me on the straight and narrow). Christopher Booker in the *Sunday Telegraph* on 2 August 2015 gleefully claimed that Arctic ice appeared to be increasing in extent, and further claimed that polar bear numbers seem to be increasing. In the *Guardian* George Monbiot rushed into print with 'How to prove Christopher Booker wrong in 26 seconds'. Booker retaliated with 'climate liars hard at work'. And so on. The finger-jabbing goes on between Warmists, too. The excitable Monbiot (whom I know well, having been his colleague at the BBC working on nature programmes) is accused of backsliding on nuclear-power issues. Another is spotted taking a Mercedes limousine to the BBC TV studios instead of cycling.

'Hypocrite!' And so it goes on, with much heat and little light.

All of this is reminiscent of Jonathan Swift's Gulliver's travels to Lilliput and the quarrels between the tiny, foot-high people there. There were two factions: those who broke their eggs at the big end (Big Endians) or the little end (Little Endians). By the time Gulliver arrives, 11,000 Big Endians have been put to death by royal edict, others have fled to the court of Blefuscu, the neighbouring island. Swift, the satirist, has a serious point, he is satirising the conflict in England between the Catholics (Big Endians) and Protestants (Little Endians). You might accuse Swift of trivialising important issues, but he didn't dare be explicit, and we've nearly arrived back at that point with the climate change debate. No one seems to dare to question the facts presented by either side for fear of being branded Denier or Warmist. But they all enjoy a good apocalypse. Both sides promise famines, drought, tornadoes and starvation.

Where does all this leave us with the English spring? Too hot or too cold? Or will we get both warming and an Ice Age? The *Guardian* seemed to be suggesting a double apocalypse in the headline 'Will global warming trigger a new ice age?' on 12 November 2003.

Climatologists now know much more than they did in the seventies, a great deal of research money is being spent, and all the evidence points towards anthropogenic (man-caused) global warming. But there are worrying signs of an enforced consensus amongst scientists. During the 'Climategate' scandal at the University of East Anglia, hacked emails between climate scientists appeared to discuss hiding inconvenient data. John Tierney of the *New York Times* wrote: 'These researchers, some of the most prominent climate experts in Britain and America, seem so focused on winning the public-relations war that they exaggerate their certitude, and ultimately undermine their own cause.'[1]

Enormously important decisions are being made by governments on the basis of this research, billions are being spent and people are being made to change their behaviour. Those of us who love nature and want to protect it would quite like some clear answers from the scientists. What can we do about it?

'Mama Earth is in a crazy mess, it's time for us to do our best, from deep sea straight up to Everest,'

so raps Sean Paul in 'Love Song to the Earth'.

He goes on:

'Six billion people all want plentiness, some people think this is harmless, but if we continue there'll only be emptiness.'

I couldn't have put it better myself.

---

[1] John Tierney, E-Mail Fracas Shows Peril of Trying to Spin Science. *New York Times*, 1 December 2009

CHAPTER FIVE

The Little Grey Men – killing animals – young poachers – aggressive duck behaviour – Birmingham – a scrapyard – Tolkien – Morris dancers – the Doctrine of Signatures – canals and barges – torture of bulls – did Romans drive on the left? – the Space Shuttle

'*T*he spring is sprung, the grass is riz, I wonder where the birdies is?*' The message is chalked on the pub blackboard. It's a good question: the countryside seems empty of birdlife today. The pub landlady doesn't know who wrote the rhyme: just that her father used to recite it.

The season of spring begins two wonderful books set in this part of England. Not far from here is *Little Grey Men* country, the setting for a series of books that has captivated many children and adults. The author, Denys Watkins-Pitchford, taught art at Rugby School, and is another of our neglected English nature writers. His elder brother died young and he himself was considered delicate so he was kept at home to be educated. As a result he roamed the fields and streams of Northamptonshire alone, learning about fishing and hunting. He was an artistic child and excelled at drawing the creatures he saw. After a spell studying art in Paris and the Royal College of Art he took up a teaching post at Rugby School in 1930. There he started writing articles for the *Shooting Times* under the pseudonym 'BB'. This refers to the heavy type of lead bird-shot he used for shooting geese. Too young and delicate for the First World War, he was too old for the Second. His recognised literary success was a children's book, *The Little Grey Men*,[1] which won the Carnegie Medal. He is rather like Richard Jefferies in some ways: both share the same close observation of nature and both are unsentimental about it. Being hunters made them both watchers of wildlife, but BB's work as an artist gives a visual acuity to his writing.

It is springtime at the beginning of *The Little Grey Men*. 'It was one of those days at the tail end of winter, when spring, in subtle way, announced its presence. The hedges were still purple and bristly, the fields still bleached and bitten, full of quarrelling starling flocks; but there was no doubt of it, the winter was virtually over and done with for another seven months. The great tide was on the turn, to creep so slowly at first and then to rise even higher to culminate in the glorious flood, the top of the tide, at midsummer.' The book is a celebration of the English country; the wonder, the beauty and the power.

This book had a profound effect on me as child, and I would recommend it to any parent who wants their child to discover a love for the countryside. The story is about the last gnomes in England, who live inside a hollow oak tree on the banks of the Folly Brook somewhere in Warwickshire. BB's own introduction says it best: 'They are honest-to-goodness gnomes, none of your baby, fairy-book tinsel stuff, and they live by hunting and fishing, like the animals and birds, which is only proper and right.' They're about the same height as buttercups, they wear beards and Dodder, the eldest, wears a bat-skin cape (with the ears left on) and a wooden leg made with an acorn

---

[1] Denys Watkins-Pitchford, *The Little Grey Men*, Eyre & Spottiswoode (1942)

cup. They are centuries old, and they were born before Man was civilised. Their world is the small, intimate world of the English countryside populated by otters, kingfishers and badgers, all of whom have the power of speech. Their England was threatened even then; BB was writing this in 1941, with the whole country expecting invasion. There is new tarmac leaking off the roads which poisons the Folly and the gnomes' lives are always threatened by Man. When the time is right (when the wild iris bud splits), they leave on an epic quest for their brother Cloudberry, who had left to look for the source of the Folly the previous year and had never returned. Always there is an awareness of what the wildlife is doing:

'Two male blackbirds who were running round each other in a love duel (their tails fanned and crests depressed) also saw the boat push off, and even they forgot their jealous anger and flew up to the oak tree to see how the gnomes fared.'[1]

They have adventures even more gripping for a child than the true-life adventures of Kon-Tiki and Mount Everest. The pivotal point in the novel is an encounter with the Pan, the god of all animals. Dodder invokes him at midnight on Midsummer's Eve to deal with Giant Grum, the gamekeeper in Crow Wood who has been killing the wild animals and birds of the wood.

There is something else in BB's fiction. When you're a child his books are positive and inspiring, but when you re-read them as an adult you realise that underneath his invocation of the countryside there's a valedictory note; a farewell to childhood and a farewell to a lost England.

---

[1] Denys Watkins-Pitchford, *The Little Grey Men*

BB, the artist, drew his own illustrations of animals and plants which perfectly convey his world. Although his watercolours are excellent and feature on many of his book covers, it's the scraperboard drawings that stand out. This technique uses hardboard washed with white china clay, over which is sprayed a layer of black India ink. It was a single-colour technique suited to economic book illustration. Using a sharp tool, the artist scrapes fine lines in the black surface through to the white underneath. The result is exquisitely detailed line drawings which BB used as headpieces and tailpieces to the chapters. So you can study real creatures such as field-mice or geese, or the fictional ones such as the gnomes Sneezewort or Baldmoney.

The names of these gnomes give an insight into the compendious knowledge of our countryman ancestors. Each BB character is given the name of a plant, presumably because they're just good names. Dodder is a parasitic plant which can actually 'smell' hosts such as clover and potatoes and grow towards them. Its tangled appearance gives it the folk names of wizard's net, devil's guts, devil's hair, devil's ringlet, gold-thread, hailweed, hairweed, hellbine, love vine, pull-down, strangleweed, angel hair and witch's hair. Most inhabitants of this country now struggle to tell the difference between oak and ash, yet here are thirteen names for the same insignificant plant. Perhaps it's like our pub-quiz knowledge of sport, cars, celebrities and shopping.

The plants that give the other characters' names also suggest a hinterland of human knowledge: sneezewort causes sneezing and is poisonous. It's also called sneezeweed, bastard pellitory, fair-maid-of-France, goose tongue, sneezewort yarrow, wild pellitory and white tansy. Baldmoney was dedicated to a god, Baldr, and Cloudberry was also known as salmonberry, bakeapple and knoutberry. It has a delicious fruit full of vitamin C which northern seafarers valued. The Norwegians are now trying to develop this commercially so that's one plant that may survive. It makes a delicious jam, a bit like blackberry.

The point is that every plant or animal in our habitat was intimately known for its food value, medicinal uses or behaviour. For example, our common weed called fat hen could once again be a vital part of our diet if we had nothing else to eat. It used to be eaten in England as a vegetable, and it's still fed to chickens (hence the name). The shoots and young leaves are like spinach and the seeds are full of protein. Quinoa is a close (and trendy) relative grown for its seeds. It would never occur to us now to collect a weed for eating, but it was widely consumed in Iron Age settlements and has been found in the stomachs of bog bodies, the ancient victims of killings who were dumped in peat bogs which have preserved them. Fat hen is still widely cultivated in northern India as a food crop.

We've lost most of this knowledge about our natural surroundings because it's no longer of any use to our daily lives. Like the complex rigging and knotting learned by the seamen of Nelson's navy, it's an obsolete technology which now seems irrelevant. The difference is that we're in danger of sinking the ship we live on, and we've forgotten most of what we knew about it.

There is a darker sequel to *The Little Grey Men*, entitled *Down the Bright Stream*.[1] It begins in spring again, and this

---

[1] Denys Watkins-Pitchford, *Down the Bright Stream*, Eyre & Spottiswoode (1948)

time they go on an expedition with their brother, Cloudberry,
who it turns out had flown on the back of a wild goose to
Spitsbergen the previous year. He was waiting for them in the
oak tree when they returned home at the end of the previous
book. However, their brother turns out to be shockingly,
murderously unreliable. Then the Folly is wrecked by Man,
who is diverting it into a reservoir. 'It was a shame that such a
bright spring morning should be so heavy with disaster. For
the Folly meant everything to the gnomes. It had been their
loved companion for generations, it had provided them with
fish, it had sung them to sleep, it had borne them safely back
from the perils of Poplar Island and sinister Crow Wood.'[1]
They are forced to leave England but manage in the end to
escape to a safer land.

It's springtime, too, at the beginning of BB's masterpiece for
adults, *Wild Lone: The Story of a Pytchley Fox*.[2] Set in fox-
hunting country, it's the story of one fox and his battle against
his great adversary, Man. Things we may have seen a hundred
times are described in a fresh way:

'It was the time of day when the wood-pigeons come in to
roost, and now they were wheeling in a rushing grey cloud
round and round the wood. Suddenly, and at the same moment,
they swept back their wings, and all landed in a clappering,
bustling cloud in the tops of the oak trees farther down the

---

[1] *Ibid.*

[2] Denys Watkins-Pitchford, *Wild Lone: The Story of a Pytchley Fox*. Eyre &
Spottiswoode (1938)

wood. It was quite a minute before every bird had settled down. Some had perched on thin, whippy branches and, being heavy birds, strove for a moment or two to retain their balance, bending this way and that and flapping their wings. When all were at rest, a strange hush fell, and in the exquisite silence a far song-thrush was singing.'[1]

BB had a great ability to put himself inside the mind of the creatures he wrote about. We stalk with the young fox as he grows from cub into adult male, we smell the first mother partridge that he scents and kills, and we're right with him in the midst of his fight with a badger who steals his food. Always, though, one implacable enemy pursues him throughout his life even when he's a newborn cub: Man. 'The place reeked with the hated scent that smelt of death and the end of all bright beautiful things – the wind, the night woods, warm blood and wild yearnings.'

Like that other schoolteacher William Golding, BB seems to dislike humanity. But he had a tragic life in some ways, and maybe this informs his writing. His son Robin died young and in 1974 his wife, Cecily, became ill after working in the garden while a farmer was spraying his fields at the other side of the hedge. She died a few weeks later. Did BB retreat from the adult world as some boarding-school teachers seem to? As in many children's writers you sense in BB's books a feeling of regret at the loss of childhood, and unhappiness in the adult world. 'We have left that world for ever and live in another of our own making, infinitely less lovely and as barren as a desert.'

He is a writer well worth discovering. His motto, which was printed inside all his books, came from a tombstone in the North Country:

---

[1] *Ibid.*

The wonder of the world
The beauty and the power,
The shapes of things,
Their colours, lights and shades,
These I saw.
Look ye also while life lasts.

The issue of BB as the countryman and the wider issue of killing animals for meat-eating should be addressed. He was happiest when out walking with his Labrador dog Honey and his gun, working the fields and hedges of Northamptonshire for pheasant or partridge. He also went to the salt-marshes of Scotland and Norfolk to shoot wild geese. Throughout his life he shot wildfowl for the pot, but his mantra was that you should never kill what you don't intend to eat.

'One thing I unblushingly own. I have devoted more than my allotted span of pages to wildfowling. This is a luxury I have allowed myself, because of all the forms of shooting this is, to my own tastes, the finest. It is the last real "wild" hunting that is left to us, with the exception perhaps of deer stalking. It is also the most unpopular form of shooting, and I never cease to give thanks for this fact. Wildfowling is no game for old men; it calls for the best physical condition, a sense of woodcraft, or should I say "marshcraft", a clear eye, sound wind, and a total disregard of cold and wet. Above all it requires patience, the inexhaustible patience of the coarse fisherman, who, like the wildfowler, more often than not returns empty-handed.'

To modern sensibilities this seems cruel, but it seems a more honest relationship with nature than ours, which ignores the mechanised murder of thousands of creatures destined for the supermarket. Why shudder at the sight of a bone if you're not prepared to kill and eat an animal yourself? I suppose it's what you're used to. My father lodged our family in a farmhouse in Lincolnshire which was, effectively, still living in the 1800s. Smelly game hung from the rafters in the 'dead room' and Mr White the farmer made cheese from his own cows. We often ate the harvest of the gun. Later on in the seventies, in Rutland, my friend Paul used to poach pheasants with his small .410 shotgun (using a much lighter shot than BB). Late at night we would walk quietly along the hedges, looking up against the sky for the huddled shape of the game birds. Once spotted, a torch-beam would highlight the head, which would be raised in alarm. The shot would kill the bird immediately and Paul and I would have to grab the corpse and run for cover as the sound of the shot would alert the gamekeepers.

One night my best friend Duncan took me out to net wild salmon in a river in north-west Scotland. He slid quietly into the freezing water with a long net. Then he waded across, chest-deep, and circled the pool. Together we hauled out a thrashing heap of writhing wild salmon. As we got them onto the bank we heard the bailiffs, grown men with clubs, running downriver to catch us and beat us up, so we had to crouch in a ditch with our haul. Local hotels would buy the wild salmon in the dead of night for cash, no questions asked, or we would eat it ourselves. The wild flesh was very different from the slimy, artificially coloured, pink jelly that passes for salmon in the supermarkets.

There are some odd village names around here. The village of
Wootton Wawen, which lies just to the west of the canal, gets
its name from the Saxon lord Wagen and his 'wudutun', or
woodland village. Here stands Warwickshire's oldest church, St
Peter's, which dates back at least to the 900s. We see a good
sign aimed at getting reluctant kids out this spring: 'Telly off.
Phones down. Boots on!'

Spring is a stressful time for the female mallard duck, and
we see some interesting duck behaviour in the canal near
Wootton Wawen. This particular female appeared to be feeding
quite happily with a male drake when two other drakes arrived
and started some aggressive behaviour. It looked like an
attempted rape. Her male fought back. In the end she had to
escape down the canal, taking off and flying low and fast over
the water.

She would have selected her mate back in the autumn and
has probably just laid her eggs. The male leaves around now to
join other males to await the moulting time, which begins in
June. These other males have probably not paired up but are
still sexually active and are looking for females who have lost
their eggs. They try to catch females who are isolated or unat-
tached. This was clearly not the case here and her drake
protected her by attacking the intruding drakes.

These males are insatiable and also attempt to rape males of
their own and other species. A Dutch researcher, Kees
Moeliker, recorded a case of homosexual necrophilia when a
mallard drake copulated with a male he was chasing after the
victim died having struck a glass window. This window
belonged to the Rotterdam office building in which Mr

Moeliker was working. He rushed out and observed the behaviour. 'When one died the other one just went for it and didn't get any negative feedback – well, didn't get any feedback.' The paper that described this, 'Homosexual necrophilia in the mallard *anas platyrhynchos*', won the 2003 Ig® Nobel Prize in Biology awarded for improbable research.[1]

Spring is a very hard time for the female as she has to lay more than half her body weight in eggs and then protect them in a safe nesting site away from predators. She will have laid around a dozen eggs, which are incubated for a month and then she has to look after the ducklings for two months. They can swim as soon as they hatch and we've seen these tiny fluffballs following their mother all along these canals. They follow her every move, learning where to find food and snuggling up if it gets cold. When they're able to fly they will somehow learn about their migration routes.

Mallards are also targeted by brood parasites, occasionally having eggs laid in their nests by other mallards, but not cuckoos. These eggs are generally accepted when they resemble the eggs of the host mallard, although the female may attempt to push them out or even abandon the nest if the parasitism occurs during egg-laying. The most dangerous predator around here is the fox. The ducklings are preyed upon by grey herons, herring gulls and even pike, striking up at the tiny fluffy morsels from below. For all that, mallard ducks seem to be doing very well on the canals we've walked along.

We walk under the M40 motorway on the canal, feeling very distant from the hurtling cars above us. The astonishing speed and racket of the opposing flows of traffic,

---

[1] www.theguardian.com/education/2005/mar/08/highereducation.research

closing at over 140 mph, is soon gone and we're out into
open countryside again. At Kingswood junction the
Stratford-upon-Avon Canal meets the Grand Union Canal
and we take the latter, turning west for Birmingham. We
walk for a few miles to Haslucks Green, where the canal is
carried across the River Cole by an aqueduct. The Cole
(which means hazel trees) flows from the north under the
canal, coming down from the Birmingham plateau where it
rises at Forhill to the south-west. It looks as though there's
a good walkway alongside the river and it's heading in the
right direction, so we drop down to the river and head north
for the city centre.

Birmingham was a big surprise. We wanted to walk through a
city to see what happened there in the spring, but we didn't
expect to find so much greenery and so many beautiful spaces.

Birmingham has seen a meteoric rise throughout history. It
was once a tiny, miserable settlement in the ancient forest,
recorded in the Domesday Book as worth only 20 shillings.
Before that the heavily forested plateau served only as an
impediment to the invading Roman forces, so they built a fort
at Edgbaston to suppress the natives. In 1166, a hundred years
after the Norman invasion, the lord of the manor, Peter de
Bermingham, managed to get a charter to hold a market at his
castle and in so doing founded one of the most significant
cities of the world.

Metal-bashing is what the locals call it, but in fact what
grew up in Birmingham was highly-specialised manufacture

employing well-paid craftsmen. During the central years of the Industrial Revolution, 1760 to 1850, Birmingham citizens registered three times as many patents as any other British city, and it became known as the workshop of the world; something like China today.

On this fine spring morning we're walking along a green lane that follows the River Cole towards the city centre. Suddenly we spot a scrapyard. Much of my youth was spent roaming around our local yard and like this one it was an ex-railway siding, abandoned after the Beeching cuts and then stacked with the rotting carcasses of 1960s Austin 1100s, Minis and Ford Granadas. It was owned by an Italian family, exotic by Rutland standards. But there were other even more exotic things in there: bits of railway engines and aircraft parts from the east of England American air force bases. There was always the chance of finding treasure.

I approached three Asian lads standing inside the gates of the Birmingham scrapyard and got into a chat about the possibility of putting a Subaru engine in the back of a Porsche. Car enthusiasm knows no boundaries, and soon we got talking about life in the car salvage business and in Birmingham in general. At the end the boss gestured towards Gina. She was standing in a pool of sunlight, very fair, and dressed rather like an explorer in hat, rucksack and climbing boots. 'I knew you two were foreigners as soon as I saw you.'

The English countryside is nearly a whites-only zone, an unspoken apartheid country. We saw few brown faces on our walk through the rural parts of Dorset, Hampshire, Wiltshire and Gloucestershire. In the Lake District, photographer Ingrid Pollard said she 'wandered lonely as a black face in a sea of white'. There are only a couple of black farmers in the whole country, despite the many Afro-Caribbean and Asian residents who immigrated here from farming backgrounds. One of the two black farmers, David Mwanaka, is such a rare sight that three times in five days he found himself being questioned by police who accused him of stealing crops. On one occasion, he claimed, four patrol cars turned up at the farm where he grows maize, pumpkins, sweet potatoes and sweetcorn. He said that he had been reported by people 'who are not used to seeing a black man working in a farmer's field'.[1] Presumably they would have felt more comfortable with the sight in Carolina in the early 1800s. I asked one Asian family out on their rambles what they thought of the English countryside and they said they liked it but didn't feel particularly welcome, which is shameful. In Birmingham itself we saw plenty of locals of all shades and genders happily walking in parks, so walking is not the issue. It's the chilly welcome.

Walking into Birmingham is a surprising pleasure. We're still following the greenway along the River Cole and it runs straight into the city centre with barely a sign of houses or factories. We're looking for Sarehole Mill, originally a grain mill driven by the River Cole, and older than Shakespeare. It was once in a hamlet in the long-ago Forest of Arden, and the name suggests this is where service trees grew. There were once great oaks standing around the mill pond, too. And here it is. Now there's a road roaring in front of it and brick

[1] www.dailymail.co.uk/news/article-1059780/Black-farmer-quizzed-police-THREE-times-suspicion-stealing-field.html

suburbia presses in from all around, but the atmosphere in the grounds is still tranquil. Sarehole is another one of our literary destinations that was important to an English author, because near here the young John Ronald Reuel Tolkien lived during his boyhood, and the mill features in *The Lord of the Rings* as the mill in Hobbiton. Here is how Tolkien remembered Sarehole Mill as a boy in the early 1900s:

'It was a kind of lost paradise . . . There was an old mill that really did grind corn with two millers, a great big pond with swans on it, a sandpit, a wonderful dell with flowers, a few old-fashioned village houses and, further away, a stream with another mill.'

Here, again, is an author's remembrance of lost time, a 'lost paradise'. The young boy was distraught when his favourite willow tree was felled at Sarehole Mill. Correspondingly, at the end of *Lord of the Rings*, Sam is grieved to find that the Party Tree has been cut down by Saruman's men during the Scouring of the Shire. All this boyhood experience fed into the fantasy novel that became the world's bestselling children's book. One day, bored during examination marking and confronted with a blank sheet of paper, Professor Tolkien had started writing the words 'In a hole in the ground there lived a hobbit . . .'

Because he wrote the story just for his children the manuscript almost disappeared from history. But then, by a series of lucky accidents, it came in front of the publisher Stanley Unwin; it was accepted and eventually sold 140 million copies, with its adult sequel, *Lord of the Rings*, selling 150 million. In 2003 *The Hobbit* was voted Britain's favourite novel of all time.

Spring is the setting for the beginning of *The Hobbit*, as it is for so many archetypal hero-journeys. Gandalf the wizard arrives in spring, which represents new beginnings, rebirth and

renewal. Bilbo Baggins, the protagonist, is reborn into his
Took nature, and during the journey in summer grows in
maturity and capability, needing the help of the Gandalf/parent
figure less and less. In autumn he fights the dragon Smaug,
and winter represents the death of his old Baggins self: he is
now an adventuring hobbit, presumably with a 1,000-yard
stare.

Spring is important in *The Lord of Rings*, too: when the
White Tree of Gondor comes into leaf Isildur, the King of
Gondor, is healed of his wounds, and in the enormous store-
house of Tolkien's mind the season of spring continually
resurfaces as the time for renewal. Tolkien was a professor of
Anglo-Saxon literature at Oxford University at the time of
writing *The Hobbit*, and undertook a translation of *Beowulf*, the
Old English epic poem which deals with legends and does not
differentiate between real events and fantasy. Beowulf slays the
monster Grendel, who has been attacking the mead hall of his
host, Hrothgar, king of the Danes. Tolkien said the poem was
among his most valued sources. The second great influence
was William Morris, whose poetry and prose romances Tolkien
wanted to emulate.

Tolkien's father, a bank manager, had taken his young family
to Africa from England to run the head office in Bloemfontein.
His family returned to England when the young Tolkien was
three but his father died unexpectedly before he could rejoin
them. After this early death the impoverished family had to
find somewhere cheap to live: 'I was brought back to my native
heath with a memory of something different – hot, dry and
barren – and it intensified my love of my own countryside. I
could draw you a map of every inch of it. I loved it with an
intensity of love that was a kind of nostalgia reversed. It was a
kind of double coming home, the effect on me of all these

meadows. I was brought up in considerable poverty but I was happy running about in that country. I took the idea of the hobbits from the village people and children. They rather despised me because my mother liked me to be pretty. I went about with long hair and a Little Lord Fauntleroy costume. The hobbits are just what I should like to have been but never was; an entirely unmilitary people who always came up to scratch in a clinch. Behind all this hobbit stuff lay a sense of insecurity.'

The insecurity may have been based in his father's death, the family's straitened circumstances after his death or the fact that the Tolkiens were originally German immigrants who had to swiftly become more English than the English. There's something of the passion of the convert about his love of Deep England. As an Oxford University lecturer he had a strong sense of entertainment. One of his former students remembered how he would begin a lecture:

'He would come silently into the room, fix the audience with his gaze, and suddenly begin to declaim in a resounding voice the opening lines of the poem in the original Anglo-Saxon, commencing with a great cry of *Hwæt!* which some undergraduates took to be "Quiet!" (It is actually the traditional beginning of many Old English poems.) It was not so much a recitation as a dramatic performance, an impersonation of an Anglo-Saxon bard in a mead hall, and it impressed generations of students because it brought home to them that *Beowulf* was not just a set text to be read for the purposes of examination, but a powerful piece of dramatic poetry.'

In later years his student W.H. Auden wrote to Tolkien and described the impact made on the young poet by his readings of *Beowulf*: 'The voice was the voice of Gandalf.'

Tolkien's Middle Earth legendarium was not on another

planet, as some adult readers assume, but in a past described in the Middle English epics. It is the earthly realm between the ice in the north and the fire in the south, above hell and below heaven. This imaginary land was deeply rooted in his boyhood haunts: Moseley Bog behind the mill provided inspiration for the Old Forest, and the giant brick-built towers of Perrott's Folly and Edgbaston Waterworks inspired the Two Towers of Gondor, Minas Morgul and Minas Tirith, in the second volume of *The Lord of the Rings*.

Once again there is a sense of loss of the countryside, the infiltration of the creeping suburban housing that eventually surrounded Sarehole. He had a recurrent nightmare throughout his life which involved a tsunami engulfing the English countryside, and anxiety seems to lie under much of his writing.

Some accusations of racism in Tolkien's depictions of the invading Orcs are probably mistaken. The Tolkien family were immigrants and knew about being outsiders. Because he was born in Africa, Tolkien knew more about the realities of racism than the critics and dismissed those accusations with: 'I had the hatred of apartheid in my bones.' His neo-Nordic monsters have more to do with the industrial proletariat of Birmingham and the nightmarish creatures of *Beowulf*.

A more reasoned criticism might be that Tolkien has the same distrust of technology as his predecessor, William Morris. The result is a backwards-looking view towards a Deep England of thatched cottages, cream teas, village inns and Morris dancing (the reality included incest and diphtheria). The hobbits are rather like rural smiths or millers: 'A well-ordered and well-farmed countryside was their favourite haunt. They do not and did not understand or like machines more complicated than a forge-bellows, a water mill or a hand loom,

although they were skilful with tools.'[1] No doubt Tolkien
would claim that if the English working class had been content
with these rural technologies the whole world would be a
better place. This attitude might have been fine for a pre-war
Oxford don, but the fact is that we are now in a brave new
world of runaway digital technology and we can't stuff the
genie back into the bottle. Embracing the best of technology is
surely the only way forward, although Morris and Tolkien
would no doubt disagree.

It's dawning on me as we walk through this literary spring
how crucial childhood imagination is to writers. Around here
Tolkien invented a language called Nevbosh, and as an adult
writer he invented Elvish. The Brontë children, who we'll meet
later on this spring walk, wrote their Gondal Sagas. And children's stories seem to develop from older stories: *Lord of the
Rings* from Middle English sagas, Arthur Ransome's *Swallows
and Amazons* owes much to *Bevis*, and even *Thomas the Tank
Engine* is suspiciously like Rudyard Kipling's steam engine in
his short story *.007*, where steam engines have the power of
speech and run off to have adventures. Or was that number
borrowed by Ian Fleming?

For my money, Tolkien's Middle Earth palls somewhat when
read as an adult. There are a few too many elves and the
hobbits are somewhat cloying. All the magic raises some
awkward questions, too; why not just wave away your problems? *Beowulf* is a darker, more muscular adult epic, and BB's
fantasy world is deeper rooted in the close observation of the
English countryside, and more believable.

We're now walking away from Sarehole Mill, which gave so
much, now drowned by a sea of cheap brick houses. It was

---

[1] Preface to *Lord of the Rings*

even instrumental in the birth of the Industrial Revolution, which brought the creeping suburbia that Tolkien so loathed. Here, after water-powered corn milling became uneconomic, Matthew Boulton (business partner of 'steam-engine' James Watt) used the mill for metal-rolling. By the young Tolkien's time the mill had changed use again. Unable to compete with factories, it had turned to bone-grinding (not the corn of Tolkien's recollection). The miller's son, George Andrews, used to be covered in bone-dust and John Tolkien and his brother Hilary nicknamed him 'The White Ogre' because he used to chase them out of the yard. An angry miller duly appeared in several of Tolkien's stories. George Andrews remembered the boys only too well, and gave them a memorable non-literary epitaph. 'The two of them were perishing little nuisances.'

Further along the River Cole, Gina spots a path named Blackberry Way, and we sing some of the Move's lines written by local singer Roy Wood. The Move was a Brum Beat band and this song was Roy Wood's answer to the Beatles' 'Penny Lane' and 'Strawberry Fields Forever'.

> Goodbye Blackberry Way
> I can't see you
> I don't need you
> Goodbye Blackberry Way
> Sure to want me back another day.

We continue our walk into the centre of Birmingham. Much to

my surprise there are plenty of places to plant my oaks alongside the path. Thanks to enlightened landowners around here
who left land uncultivated on condition it wasn't built on, and
a conservation-minded council, there are now 150 miles of
Birmingham Greenways. Here you can walk or cycle beside
rivers, along canal towpaths and across parks. The result is
that the city is remarkably green and pleasant – when viewed
from the paths. When we take a bus along the A34 we see a
different story. Jammed with traffic, thick with exhaust fumes,
crowded with markets and pedestrians, it looks like a third-
world thoroughfare. Yet two streets away there's a parallel
universe of deserted parks and empty canals. We hop off the
bus and walk into Shirley Park, right next to the main thoroughfare. There are rare small-leaved lime trees planted here,
which will give a home to insects such as the lime hawk and
hook-tip moths. These trees used to be called lindens, and the
fine-grained white wood was favoured by Grinling Gibbons,
probably our best English wood-carver. He surely had the best
name. He carved wooden garlands for St Paul's Cathedral and
Hampton Court Palace at the end of the seventeenth century,
and his light touch was legendary. He even carved a wooden
cravat for Horace Walpole, who said of him: 'There is no
instance of a man before Gibbons who gave wood the loose
and airy lightness of flowers, and chained together the various
productions of the elements with the free disorder natural to
each species.'

There's quite a bit of free disorder in the street-markets
here, and the exotic smells and colours in the spring sunshine
are exciting after weeks of countryside. A bit further on there's
some wetland in Shirley Park, which apparently was becoming
difficult to mow, and some interesting wetland plants were
emerging. So instead of draining it the conservationists from

Solihull council have encouraged the spring plants and so we spend a pleasant half an hour spotting them with the guide book. Before modern medicine it was vital to know what local healing plants could do. Here's yarrow, a fern-like herb looking like a long green feather. It was known as soldier's wound-wort or the nosebleed plant, because it could staunch bleeding. Nearby is self-heal, a mint-like plant with a square-section stem. It was used against inflammation in infected wounds. We know this one, red clover, seen in lawns and used for coughs, and here's another familiar plant we've seen a lot of lately, meadow buttercup. This was crushed up; flower, leaves and all, and sniffed for headaches. Even more effective against head-aches is willow, growing over there near the river with its cascade of leaves like a feathery umbrella. This tree gave medi-eval medics a form of aspirin from its bark which could alleviate the symptoms of ague, a frequent ailment of the wetlands. This fact gave support to the Doctrine of Signatures, a theological notion that God showed Man which plants would be useful by placing them close to the causes of illnesses.

Meadowsweet is also growing here, and it became the origin of the name for aspirin because it provided a safer version of salicin which caused less digestive upset than pure salicylic acid. The new drug, formally acetylsalicylic acid, was named aspirin after the old botanical name for meadowsweet, *Spiraea ulmaria*. This herb grows over 6 feet (2 metres) in height and smells so sweet that it was strewn on the floors of houses to freshen the air.

Then there's great burnet, a 3-foot (1-metre) high plant with a blood-red head. The root of this was used in cases of bloody dysentery, and the lovely blue-flowered Devil's bit scabious, against scabies (from *scabere*, Latin for scratch) and the sores caused by the bubonic plague. The short black root of this plant was supposedly bitten off by the devil, enraged by the plant's ability to cure these ghastly buboes. We've seen it before as butterfly food in the Cotswolds.

All of these appalling ailments are making us feel a bit queasy, so we squelch back to the canal path and head for the skyscrapers in the distance. On the way we see another water park, Trittiford Mill Pool, and it's so big you can go sailing within a couple of miles of the city centre. There's a heron, head shrugged down below his shoulders. No fishing then. We get talking to a guy at the sailing club here. He's clearly retired and has the time to talk. No, he doesn't have any dinghies for sale. People just don't bother with sailing any more. He doesn't know why. I've noticed the accent has changed again, from the received pronunciation of the posh Cotswold villages to Brummie. This accent is popular abroad as it is easily understood, despite the bad press it gets in England. England has more accents per square mile than any other due to the waves of Germanic, Norse, French and later immigrants, and English people are adept at classing you as soon as you speak. The Irishman George Bernard Shaw wrote in *Pygmalion*: 'It is impossible for an Englishman to open his mouth without making some other Englishman hate or despise him.'

We emerge just a couple of miles from the city centre, and look for the Bullring. After the market was established in the twelfth century this area was a corn market known as Corn Cheaping. The Bullring was a hoop of iron mounted on the green to which bulls were tied before slaughter. Then they were baited, which means tortured and tormented.

Spring was when calves were born, and bulls were put in with their cows about six weeks after that. An old bull was surplus to requirements and would be killed and eaten. Before that he was often the victim of the sport of bull-baiting. This was a blood sport involving dogs, for which purpose the English bulldog was bred, with a short stature and huge, powerful jaws. Once their teeth are sunk into flesh they never let go. The bull was free to move on a length of rope, and pepper was blown into the poor creature's nose to enrage it. The dogs crept close, then dashed in to try to seize the bull's snout and hang on. The bull would attempt to impale the dog on his horns and toss it into the air. And so on. There were similar events in English market towns up and down the country. In Stamford, Lincolnshire, there was a tradition of bull-running since the 1200s, whereon one day every year a bull was released into the high street which was blocked by wagons parked cross-wise. The animal was tormented for a whole day by tricks such as a man rolling towards it in a barrel, plus jabbing and jeering from the crowd. Finally, it was chased by men on horses across the Bull-meadows into the River Welland, where the poor creature was killed. No doubt similar antics went on here at the Birmingham Bullring. Frederick the Great said 'The more I see of men, the more I love my dog.'

Bull-baiting wasn't only done for sport. Market towns like Birmingham had by-laws regulating the sale of meat, and it was believed that baiting the bulls tenderised their flesh, so laws were passed which stipulated that bulls should be baited before they were slaughtered and the meat put on sale. As the bull-beef was sold to the poor in Stamford at a cheap price this seems merely a justification. These by-laws continued in operation throughout the eighteenth century, but the good news is that in 1835 the Cruelty to Animals Act put a stop to all this.

Now high-rise buildings glitter all around the Bullring, and the city looks clean and modern. I become aware that we're getting some odd looks from the city folk trotting past in their skimpy city clothes. We're wearing outfits that were quite practical on the Cotswold Way: hats, Berghaus jackets, Craghopper shirts and clumpy boots. I still have a map and compass hung round my neck. We feel as if we're exploring a strange city in a far-away land, filled with exotic peoples with their own traditions.

As we approach the centre we hear distant music and jingling bells. There's a huge crowd of shoppers and a glimpse of dancers. Morris dancers! We push through the crowds of awestruck faces and get a glimpse of the Old English spring pagan fertility dance in the wild.

It looks fantastic fun. There are about a dozen men wearing white shirts and trousers with blue bands crossed over their backs. On their heads they're wearing straw boaters woven with spring flowers. They're performing an intricate dance to the music of a fiddle, a line of four men facing another four, and they're thwacking long sticks together with enormous energy. 'Hey-yah!' Thwack! We creep closer, and I'm reminded of David Attenborough's encounter with the mountain gorillas: 'Sometimes they allow others to join in . . . although they may play games you don't forget that these are the rulers of the forest . . . the great silverback is the king of the whole group . . . he's so enormously strong that he need fear nothing . . . '

During a pause I approach the biggest silverback and ask him some questions (he's actually called the Squire). How old is this dance? What does it mean? Apparently the name Morris dancing comes from 'Moorish' dancing. It's first mentioned in around 1445, but it's thought to be associated with English May Day rites, crowning a May Queen and dancing around a maypole. This is a pre-Christian tradition deriving from the pagan Anglo-Saxon customs held during

'Þrimilci-mōnaþ', or 'Trimilki-month'. This is the Old English name for the month of May, meaning the month of Three Milkings (because of the nutritious spring grass). He thinks it's the way that the younger men of the Anglo-Saxon villages demonstrated their fancy footwork and strength to the maidens. There are women performing the Morris dance here as well. They're dressed in black trousers, yellow tops decorated with a cascade of tumbling ribbons in brown and black. They seem to be having fun, too.

If this form of ancient dance was encountered in a Bhutanese village it would be described with reverence by a travel TV presenter who would intone awed praise in a hushed voice. The fertility motifs would be respectfully deconstructed and lovingly filmed. Yet our own native dance form is dismissed as a bunch of boring old men prancing around with handkerchiefs. This seems a little unfair.

What's surprising is that Morris dancing is suddenly becoming cool. Just as it seemed to be dying out there's a revival underway. There are sides (or teams) that are more urban in character, with The Pack in Black, a mixed male and female side from Kent who mix Goth elements into their all-black costumes. Their style of dance pushes the men to the edge of exhaustion and injury, while the women are more graceful with a hint of menace. Then there was a weekend event at the South Bank, in London, put together by the artist David Owen. It was a rebuke to Sebastian Coe who, when asked how London would compete with Beijing's Olympic opening ceremony, sarcastically replied: 'Five thousand Morris dancers.' This gave the event its name. It featured music from nu-folk revival bands, Morris-themed art and films and performances by Morris sides from all over England.

The last time this style of dance nearly died out was at the

24th March. Salisbury plain up ahead. Only 500 miles to go. © Gina Waggott

19th March. 'Two black lambs, full of mischief'. © Gina Waggott

4th May. A moorhen's nest under a willow. © Gina Waggott

20th April. A tree coming into bud. © Gina Waggott

20th April. Fields of rape on either side, smelling of coconut. © Gina Waggott

8th May. The heavy goods vehicle of the canal system.
© Gina Waggott

12th June. Two mushrooms: *Parasola plicatilis.* © Gina Waggott

6th May. The sandstone bridge at Shenstone, the weed waving like mermaid's hair. © Gina Waggott

15th May. The ex-factory flagstones of the Pennine Way. © Gina Waggott

28th May. A rare survivor of voracious sheep. © Gina Waggott

10th June. So hot that the sheep seek shade. © Gina Waggott

28th May. Public art near Marsden. © Gina Waggott

12th May. St. Helen's church at Darley Dale. © Gina Waggott

10th June. The 'Water Cut' sculpture, revealing the River Eden. © Gina Waggott

16th June. A fine oak at Ullswater, near Wordsworth's daffodils. © Fabrice Fleurot

15th June. Tree rings: a century at a glance. © Fabrice Fleurot

12th June. The last of the bluebells. © Gina Waggott

7th June. Lady Anne's Way.
© Gina Waggott

15th June. We spot a dipper
in the stream. © Fabrice Fleurot

7th May. Ducks at Chatsworth.
© Gina Waggott

16th June. Foxgloves contain heart medicine.
© Fabrice Fleurot

16th June. Another acorn is planted. © Fabrice Fleurot

15th June. A beautiful place to get lost: the Eden valley. © Gina Waggott

end of the nineteenth century, but it was spared when a music teacher, Cecil Sharp, saw a side of Morris dancers at the village of Headington Quarry near Oxford (it's now part of Oxford). He was another admirer of the other Morris we've already met: William. Excited by his find, Sharp toured Cotswold villages to record more dances and songs, avidly scribbled down notes and published them, and before long a revival was underway. He bowdlerised his transcriptions of the lyrics as these were heavy in erotic double-entendres. As a result of the near-death of the dance there's no continuous tradition and no one knows where the form originated. But there are clues. Dancers have always blackened their faces and this could be to disguise them from the local priest when pagan practices were being discouraged. Or it could refer to a Moorish (Morris) origin of the dance, as the dancing may have been brought back from Spain by John of Gaunt in 1387 when his army returned from the Spanish Wars. Whatever the origin, there seems to be a desire for a folk-tradition song and dance form in this country, and the only way it will survive is to mutate once again.

We're now travelling away from the centre of Birmingham, roughly following the route of Icknield Street, or Ryknild Street, the Roman road we have been following, off and on, since the Cotswold Way where we crossed it just north of Broadway. Just now we're following a more modern route, Cycle Trail 535. This follows traffic-free paths and canal towpaths from the centre, dives under Spaghetti Junction, the infamous motorway intersection, and ends up in Sutton Park. Once again we're impressed at the appearance of Birmingham from these greenways. A lifetime driving through the city would never prepare you for this view of it. The canal towpaths are deserted on the whole, just as the English countryside seems to be. We only saw an average of one other walker per day over the whole spring. The crowds that are killing the countryside live in the cities.

There's not much sign of spring on these towpaths. There are a few ducks, that's all, and some blades of grass. Does Birmingham really have more canals than Venice, we wonder? The simple answer is yes. There are 35 miles (56 kilometres) of canals within the city boundaries, whereas Venice has only 26 miles (42 kilometres) but you can hardly compare the two cities. Venice is smaller and has a higher concentration of canals, as there are no streets. Robert Benchley, the society drunk, when sent on assignment to Venice cabled back 'Streets full of water. Please advise.'

If you calculate water volume and depth, Birmingham has more cubic metres of water in its canals than any other city in the world, and in their heyday these carried the life-blood of Victorian trade in the middle of England. Every day there was a tidal surge of water as fleets of barges converged on the collieries. To enable 24-hour operation, gas lighting was installed above the locks and barges were built without cabins to maximise loading volume (I wonder: where did the crew sleep?).

It's wrong to dismiss old technologies as outdated and inefficient. The US Energy Transportation book calculates that one US gallon of fuel can move a ton of cargo 533 miles (857 kilometres) by barge, 209 miles (337 kilometres) by rail, or 61 miles (98 kilometres) by truck. Air freight can manage less

than 20 miles (32 kilometres). An eighteenth-century canal
horse could pull a 30-ton load at a steady 2 miles per hour
with no noise and only the occasional pollutant, which could
be used to fertilise the fields. This was around a hundred times
the horse's own body weight and about fifty times more than it
could manage using a cart on ancient roads. This payload is
remarkably similar to the average modern lorry load. The
barge would glide along with minimal friction, and little
energy was wasted. The end result was an extremely efficient
way of supporting huge loads in water and moving them using
the energy contained in a few handfuls of grain fed to a horse.

This is why there was such an explosion of canal building
in the eighteenth century and why there were still horse-
drawn barges up until the 1960s. When the Bridgewater Canal
opened it reduced the price of coal in Manchester by nearly
two-thirds within just one year of opening. Horses pulled coal
to the steam-engines that drove the Industrial Revolution.
Competition became so fierce that right here in Birmingham
we have just walked beside two canals that ran alongside each
other only seven feet apart. I wonder if some kind of canal
transport could ever return, maybe using robot technology.
Removing just some of the thundering herds of trucks from
the roads would help to bring back some peace to the English
spring.

The path is now dead straight and we're walking through
the leafy suburb of Handsworth Wood, the most desirable area
of Birmingham, with large Victorian houses and huge gardens
equipped with Elizabethan electric gates. As unkempt walkers
we don't feel particularly comfortable along here.

In contrast, just a few streets away to the west of us is
Handsworth, a different kind of suburb. Handsworth is where
Benjamin Zephaniah was born. He calls it the 'Jamaican capital

of Europe', an inner-city area which has also produced Joan
Armatrading and many other Afro-Caribbean artists (I worked
with him on BBC poetry programmes in the eighties). Here's
part of 'Nature Trail', one of his poems which might apply to
the Handsworth gardens we're passing. Imagine his voice:

> At the bottom of my garden
> There's a hedgehog and a frog
> And a lot of creepy-crawlies
> Living underneath a log,
> There's a baby daddy long legs
> And an easy-going snail
> And a family of woodlice,
> All are on my nature trail . . .
>
> My garden is a lively place
> There's always something happening,
> There's this constant search for food
> And then there's all that flowering,
> When you have a garden
> You will never be alone
> And I believe we all deserve
> A garden of our own.

Benjamin Zephaniah's poem seems simple, but like much of his
other poetry it points out that children don't need education to
learn and they don't need teachers to walk them round nature
trails, they just need to look in any urban wasteland. And
there's a lot of that in Handsworth.

There's been an uneasy history of racial tension and unemployment here. By 1985 fewer than 5 per cent of the black
school-leavers had found jobs. There was a lot of black

resentment at the way policing was enforced. An ill-judged arrest burst a festering sore and during the riots that summer in 1985 two Asian brothers, Kassamali and Amirali Moledina were burnt to death in their post office. But there were many whites in court over the following days, some who had poured in from surrounding areas and it seems that the causes were complex. The *Guardian* said: 'White or black, unemployed or fitfully employed, the rioters belong to the desolate, deprived underclass of modern Britain's urban ghettos. They are beyond the reach of conventionally organized politics.' The editorial continued, 'Their family life is a fractured nullity. Their homes are rundown hovels. Education has passed them by. They have no marketable skills. They are without immediate hope or immediate purpose in society.'

The police told a similar story: ex-West Midlands Police Chief Constable Geoffrey Dear said the root causes were down to five factors: massive social deprivation, inadequate housing, unsuccessful education, mass unemployment and racial discrimination. Figures showed unemployment in the area was running at 36 per cent, three times the national average, and the worst in inner-city Birmingham.

This country of England has been endlessly colonised by different peoples since the last Ice Age. After the exploring hunter-gatherers, Celtic and Pictish tribes were perhaps the first to put down roots, followed by the Romans, who sent black legionaries from the African part of their empire to guard Hadrian's Wall in AD 250. These were probably the first black people seen in these islands. After the Romans, Germanic tribes sailed over the North Sea, and four hundred years after the Jutes, Angles and Saxons colonised southern England the Vikings arrived in the north and east. The Normans were next, descendants of Vikings who had invaded

France. Jews were invited by the Normans; West Indians and Asians in our times. Any ideas that England was ever populated by one homogenous race are mistaken.

Who's going to arrive next? There is gross over-population in England, particularly in the south-eastern corner, and there's already conflict over living space. That's what's behind the explosion in house prices.

We're now walking under the Gravelly Hill intersection, better known as Spaghetti Junction. We're on the towpath of the Grand Union Canal, and this is the meeting place of three canals, two rivers, two railway lines and two motorways: the M6 and A38 (M). There might even be a Roman road lost down here. There are an awful lot of gas pipelines and electricity next to the canal and over our heads there's a stream of high-speed traffic. The engineers had to place the motorway flyover pillars carefully so that they didn't foul the towropes of horse-drawn barges. It's all grey concrete and filth down here, the absolute antitheses of spring. I have nightmares sometimes that England will one day all look like this. I must have driven overhead a hundred times but never suspected what lay below. It's a relief to get back into the fresh air.

We've arrived at Sutton Park, where we're walking along a preserved section of Icknield Street, the Roman road, which has emerged from under the modern roads and housing. It's easy to imagine the African legionaries marching along this. Or Romans walking from Bath to Hadrian's Wall. The road is heavily cambered and has ditches either side of it. The surface is made of heavily pounded stones and gravel, whereas in other parts of the empire, such as Pompeii, the roads are made up of stone blocks. This roadway is driven straight through woodland and overcame whatever obstacle presented itself. We join it at the Royal Oak gate and march north until we get to

Streetly, the 'meadow by the paved street'. There were Roman coins found around here, perhaps dropped by a horseman.

This road would have been busy in spring in Roman times. The winter floods were past and supplies of fresh food would be funnelling up to the garrisons along Hadrian's Wall. These Roman roads were one of the defining features of the empire: all roads led to Rome.

We know now that the Romans probably drove on the left, like the English do now. The evidence for this was found at a Roman quarry near Swindon. The left-hand set of grooves in the road leading down and away from the quarry were much deeper than the grooves leading up to it, suggesting that the heavily-laden carts were leaving on the left. There's another good reason for driving on the left, which is that if you've ever led a horse you'll know that you tend to do it with your left hand, keeping your right hand free for a stick (or a sword). You would also want to walk along the middle, drier part of the cambered road and so you would probably choose to walk the horse on the left side of the road.

It's even claimed that the size of the Space Shuttle was dictated by Roman roads. These were wide enough to accommodate a horse harnessed into a cart, which was the width of the horse's haunches. The distance between the two wheels appeared to be about five Roman feet, and it would surely make sense to use a round number when calculating the length of a cart axle-tree. You can still see ruts this width on Roman stone paving in the streets of Pompeii. One Roman pace (Latin *passus*) was the same measurement: five Roman feet. One thousand paces gave a Roman mile, which was named after that distance as the *mille passus* and it's where our word for mile comes from.

This dimension became the standard wheel-track of the

English cart, because if they used any other measurement their wheels wouldn't ride in the old Roman ruts and the wheels would break. The pre-railway tramways and then the railways used the same track. If you calculate five Roman feet you come to around four feet ten inches, a figure remarkably close to the four feet eight and a half inches which became the standard railway track width (gauge) in England. The US railways were built by English expatriate railway workers and they used the same measurement.

When the Space Shuttle was built it used two rocket boosters on the sides. These were made in a factory in Utah and were not as big as the designers would have liked. The reason is that these boosters had to be shipped by rail to the launch site in Florida, the railway passed through a tunnel just a bit larger than the double tracks and so the boosters had to fit through the tunnel. So the most advanced vehicle ever built had its size dictated by the size of a horse's behind. Or so they say.

CHAPTER SIX

Sunny spring weather – oak and ash – a typhoon – Doggerland – a
tsunami – Dr Johnson – a water-vole – the great god Pan – beer,
Marmite and DDT – Silent Spring *– Deep Ecology*

This April has been the sunniest on record, according
to the Met Office. A weather station in
Northumberland has had its sunniest April of all its
110-year recording history, with nearly nine hours per day of
spring sunshine, which is almost double the April average. In
Northumberland! And the highest temperature this April was
recorded in Kent, at 25.6 degrees Celsius. In contrast, the clear
skies meant that the temperatures sometimes feel low out of
the sun. We've certainly had a wonderful walk so far, with
sunny days that haven't been too hot for walking.

We're crossing Sutton Park well away from the centre of
Birmingham now, and we're still able to plant an acorn every
mile. The oaks around here are just coming into leaf before the
ash, so according to the old English proverb we're in for only
light rain this summer:

> Oak before ash, in for a splash
> Ash before oak, in for a soak.

The only problem is that there are similar Norwegian and
German weather proverbs about oaks and ash that predict the

complete opposite. So who's right? Both tree species come into leaf around now but the timing of an oak leaf is determined by temperature, whereas ash leaves are more influenced by day length. As the climate changes, England is having warmer spring months and so oak trees are coming into leaf two weeks earlier, while ash trees are only a week to ten days earlier. Over the last forty-four years the ash has been first to leaf only four times and the last time this happened was nearly thirty years ago. In the race to grow woodland canopy first the oak is winning hands down and will shade out the ash. This in turn is going to mean big changes in the ecology of woodland as time gets out of joint for the wildlife living on these species of tree.

The two species are quite different when you get used to spotting the differences. From a distance an oak is like a sturdy great green cloud, while an ash is more erect, with the graceful branches visible through the lighter canopy of leaves. The ends of the ash branches turn upwards to the sky, like a ballet dancer's fingers. The bark of an oak is grey and rough, with vertical and horizontal fissures, while the ash tree's bark is much smoother, with a beige colour. The oak leaf is the familiar lobed shape, while the ash leaflets are oval and grow in pairs along the leaf stems, with six to twelve pairs per stem.

Which species live with ash trees? Ash trees have a light canopy and their leaves fall early so they allow enough sunlight through for wildflowers such as wild garlic and we've seen lots of this in ash woodland. Then there's dog violet (five violet petals, no scent) and dog's mercury (pointy leaves, foul smell), both of which encourage insects such as the high brown fritillary butterfly. There's enough light for hazel, too, which provides a home for dormice.

Birds such as owls, nuthatches, woodcocks and redstarts like nesting in ash trees, and bullfinches eat the seeds. Ash bark provides a substrate for lichens and mosses, and their leaves feed the caterpillars of many species of moth, including the privet hawk-moth, the coronet, brick and centre-barred sallow.

The consensus amongst climate scientists seems to be a prediction for drier summers in the future punctuated with spells of heavier rain, so our old English rhyme may yet have the ring of truth. Once again, this country seems to be at a slight advantage in the global climate change lottery, but we'll have to work hard if we want to keep our native species alive and thriving. Maybe I should have planted ash trees instead of oaks.

We've decided to try to follow Icknield Street, the Roman road, as far as Derby. One of the fun things about this walk is that we can change the route as we go, just as long as we head north. So we dive into the suburbs again north of Sutton Park, following a dead-straight street that gives the clue that it was once Roman. Once again there's a palimpsest of asphalt, tar, railways and houses overlaid on top of the ancient way. We get out into countryside with a feeling of freedom, but near Shenstone we're stopped in our tracks by a huge set of electric gates across the old Roman road emblazoned with '****Livery'. This is armed with CCTV and electric intercoms and is, apparently, 'A purpose-built secure gated premises' for the rich young daughters of Birmingham. I'm furious, and we have to detour around fields and difficult footpaths, cursing the greed and selfishness of the rich. The Roman legionaries wouldn't have been stopped by a bloody electric gate.

It's 6 May and we've paused to look at a lovely little

sandstone bridge to the north of Shenstone, with long green waterweed waving in the river below. A motorbike roars over the bridge and flits by this spot, so beautiful and so ignored. I'm reminded that Norton motorcycles were built here in Shenstone; they've been and gone while the bridge and water-weed remains.

We're trying to work out if the waterweed is an invasive species. We've been seeing the bamboo-like shoots of Japanese knotweed along the riverbanks around here, they zoom up in spring reaching 7 feet (2.1 metres) and flower in summer. Japanese knotweed is one of those introductions that have proved so disastrous to the host environment, rather like grey squirrels, rhododendrons and humans. Alien introduced species do better than indigenous species because they arrive without all their pests, predators and diseases in tow.

The botanist Philipp Franz von Siebold travelled to Japan in 1823, narrowly escaping being drowned in a typhoon. Millions of gardeners and homeowners might now wish the typhoon had tried a bit harder. He smuggled out of Japan the seeds of precious tea-plants, single-handedly starting the Java tea culture. Regrettably, he also took *Fallopia japonica*, the cursed knotweed. It was a popular garden plant in Victorian England as it looked like bamboo and could grow anywhere. Unfortunately, that's just what it did. Its extensive roots penetrated foundations and destroyed walls, drains and flood defences. The weed's very presence on a property is enough to make a house unsalable. And now there isn't a six-square-mile area in the UK that is without Japanese knotweed.

What if, one year, spring didn't arrive? If winter didn't loosen its grip, if the birds didn't sing, if the woods didn't come into leaf?

It looks as if this did once happen in England, and as amateur historians we wonder if this might have given rise to the giant calculator we now call Stonehenge and the flood myths of Noah and Atlantis. During the last Ice Age there was a vast sheet of glacial ice over all of Canada and most of North America, up to two miles thick (3.2 kilometres). We call it the Laurentide Ice Sheet, and when global warming caused it to melt vast lakes were formed, held in only by a steadily weakening ice dam. Just one of these lakes was the size of the Black Sea, and it was several hundred feet above sea level.

At that time some of our Mesolithic ancestors were happily living in what we call Doggerland, a large area of wetlands and undulating plain located where the North Sea is now. Sea level was a couple of hundred feet lower than today and Britain was a promontory of Northern Europe. Life would have been good for these people, as the complex meandering rivers and lakes provided an attractive habitat for fish, wildfowl and grazing animals. But when the ice dam finally burst, in around 6200 BC, an ocean of fresh water poured into the North Atlantic in a cataclysmic event of Biblical proportions.

This Great Flood resulted in an instantaneous sea-level rise of between 7 to 13 feet (2 to 4 metres), and shallow low-lying areas such as Doggerland were flooded in a tsunami-like wave. Anyone who survived was suddenly promoted to The First Britons, as the British Isles were cut off from the rest of Europe (this is reminiscent of the apocryphal 1930s *Daily Mirror* headline: 'Fog in Channel: Continent cut off').

Doggerland eventually disappeared in further melting, the Storegga Slide tsunami and sea-level rises. Even worse followed. The sudden influx of meltwater is thought to have affected the North Atlantic thermohaline circulation, which brings heat from the south-west Atlantic, making north-west Europe warmer than its latitude might suggest. The surge of fresh water diverted the warm circulation southwards. England experienced a sharp cooling, a drop in temperature of around 3 degrees Celsius, which is very significant indeed (limiting warming to no more than 2 degrees Celsius has become the de facto target for present-day global climate policy). To our ancestors it would have seemed that the seasons had stopped. Clouds covered the sky. The birds fell silent. Migrating birds didn't come. This cooling continued for two to four centuries and the effects on surviving Britons were catastrophic.

Imagine: these people were very similar to us, just as intelligent, just as keen to manipulate their surroundings to make life comfortable. They're only 320 generations distant, and they weren't just Stone Age brutes. Other peoples all over the world would have been experiencing the same sea-level rises and the same loss of low-lying habitat. No doubt they would have told stories to their grandchildren of long-lost happy lands of warmth and easy living, now sunk somewhere under the seas. Could these have been prototype myths of Atlantis and Noah's Flood? The nature writers we've met on this walk seem to have an atmosphere of loss ingrained in their work; could this be an intrinsic part of gloomy human nature or some kind of folk memory?

Furthermore, the advent of spring every year would have been eagerly awaited by our ancestors, as with the cooler climate there would be less food available. It would be very important to know when the sun stopped its inexorable decline in the sky and the days started to get longer. Could this be a motivation to build observatories such as Stonehenge which could predict the day of the spring equinox?

Global warming seems a joke today as we walk in sleet which for a moment turns into snow. We see dandelions and lesser celandine petals closed up against the cold. The lesser celandine can not only manage that trick but it can also turn its flowers around to track the sun during the day. This probably warms the flowers to attract insects inside to pollinate. This beautiful little yellow flower was William Wordsworth's favourite, not the daffodil. He wrote three poems about it.

We might assume that migrating birds come to England in spring, not prepare to depart. But in BB's novel *Manka, the Sky Gypsy: The Story of a Wild Goose*[1] we hear the call of the north:

'. . . those early days of spring coming to the hills were pleasant after winter frosts and hard days. There was a new song, too, in the reeds, not the dry, shivering rustle of starved and dead vegetation. The curlews had left the coast for their breeding quarters on the moors, and with them went the trim-spangled plovers and redshanks from the tidal oozes. One day three swallows came hawkering over the reeds, twittering with happiness and joy that England was theirs once more. Parties of geese were already beginning to leave, every day there were fewer on the Carse. They departed at night, secretly and without fuss, and one morning in early April the white goose and his companions did not take their usual flight out to the Sidlaws. Six thousand feet above the Earth, they were on their way to Spitsbergen, and no man saw them go . . . this was

---

[1] Denys Watkins-Pitchford, *Manka, the Sky Gypsy: The Story of a Wild Goose*, Eyre & Spottiswoode (1939)

Manka's world. The sky was his, the fields were his, the stars, the moon, the winds.'[1]

As in his previous book about a fox, *Wild Lone*, BB inhabits the mind of a wild animal in a way that few other writers can manage. Manka the albino goose becomes an existential spark flying high over the night ocean: '. . . the geese sped on in a moonlit world of unreality, darkness below and darkness above, the glitter of the moon on the sea, star dust above them.'

It's reminiscent of Saint-Exupéry's *Wind, Sand and Stars* (published later in 1939),[2] an account of a different kind of night-flying which, like night-sailing, puts you face to face with the universe:

'. . . the night flight with its hundred thousand stars, its serenity, its few hours of sovereignty.'

Watkins-Pitchford's illustrations for *Manka* are amongst his finest. The dust jacket has a skein of geese rising up from left to right in a great inverted V, their black silhouettes against a white cloud at the bottom left, with Manka the albino goose at the apex in white against a black sky. Inside, his illustration *'Heading North in the Spring'* again uses the black-and-white scratchboard style, but inverts the dust-jacket image. This time the skein is flying in the other direction against a huge white sky, and somehow the artist suggests a great bank of sun-lit pink clouds using only black and white. Cold hard mountains and a mirror-still lake lie beneath the geese as they fly to Spitsbergen.

On 29 and 30 April there was frost in England, a sharp snap to remind us that spring weather is changeable and all those delicate flowering plants had better watch out. I think of

[1] *Ibid.*

[2] Antoine de Saint-Exupéry, *Wind, Sand and Stars*, Reynal & Hitchcock (1939)

Coleridge's 'secret ministry of frost' in 'Frost at Midnight', a poem written for his baby son in the hope that he too would become a child of nature.

We see silver birch trees in leaf and remember that their name is Lady of the Woods. Their slender silvery trunks belie the fact that they were among the first trees to regenerate in Britain after the Ice Age. The blackthorn in the hedges is in full flower. The wood of this tough little tree makes good walking and riding sticks and was the traditional wood for Irish shillelaghs, the fighting club. The roots were considered the best for shillelaghs as they were less likely to split during use. The stick would be shaped with a knob at one end which would be hollowed out and 'loaded' with molten lead poured inside. The shillelagh would then be smeared with lard or butter and jammed up the chimney to smoke, or cure, which gave it the shiny black appearance. You can make sticks out of hazel, ash or holly as well, but they're best left to season for a couple of years.

After Shenstone we walk to Lichfield under the M6 toll road and pop out in the Roman staging post of Letocetum, at the significant crossroads of Watling Street, the Roman military road to North Wales, and Icknield Street, which we've been following all the way from Birmingham. The name meant Fort Greywood, and may refer to the elms and ash trees that grew here. This used to be an important place for important people hastening to tell other people what to do. As a result luxurious bath-houses and mansions were built for the politicians, and slums for the rest.

We walk up Claypit Lane into Lichfield. This town of ideas was the home of Dr Johnson, the author of the first English dictionary, and one of our greatest literary critics. *The Rambler* was his self-written journal that we would now call a blog. In his essay *On Spring* he urges young people to 'make use at once of the spring of the year, and the spring of life; to acquire, while their minds may be yet impressed with new images, a love of innocent pleasures, and an ardour for useful knowledge; and to remember, that a blighted spring makes a barren year, and that the vernal flowers, however beautiful and gay, are only intended by nature as preparatives to autumnal fruits'. Quite.

You might like to think of Dr Johnson every time you make your breakfast porridge. His dictionary definition is: 'Oats: A grain, which in England is generally given to horses, but in Scotland supports the people.'

His dictionary was a wonderful addition to the English language and sometimes makes amusing reading; here he is on tax:

Excise: A hateful tax levied upon commodities, and adjudged not by the common judges of property, but wretches hired by those to whom excise is paid.

Patron: One who countenances, supports or protects. Commonly a wretch who supports with insolence, and is paid with flattery.

Pension: An allowance made to any one without an equivalent. In England it is generally understood to mean pay given to a state hireling for treason to his country.

Politician: 1. One versed in the arts of government; one skilled in politicks. 2. A man of artifice; one of deep contrivance.

Stockjobber: A low wretch who gets money by buying and selling shares.

His thoughts on divorce were: 'We hang a thief for stealing a sheep; but the unchastity of a woman transfers sheep and farm and all from the right owner.'

Johnson described himself as a lexicographer: 'A writer of

dictionaries; a harmless drudge that busies himself in tracing the original, and detailing the signification of words.'

This extraordinary man was another writer who suffered from depression, but it now appears he also had undiagnosed Tourette's syndrome: tics, involuntary utterances and a wide range of physical ailments; so much so that Hogarth took him for an 'idyot'. He was in fact a man of robust good sense; his biographer James Boswell tells the story of their discussion about the theory of the non-existence of matter, and how hard it was to refute. Dr Johnson kicked a large stone and shouted 'I refute it thus!'

Of course, this is no argument at all, and only shows how little we humans really understand. Our scientists don't know where Dr Johnson's stone came from, pre-Big Bang (it was in Harwich churchyard in 1764, that's for sure). Nor do they know what constitutes the sunlight he saw it with: does light come in packets or waves? Nor do they know whether Dr Johnson had any free choice to kick it or not. It's no surprise that we don't even know what Stonehenge was really for.

Spring is now in full flood. It's 8 May and we're walking along another canal towpath, the Trent and Mersey, heading towards Burton upon Trent. Nettle flowers are out and the dandelion seeds are turning into clocks. There are big flower candles on the chestnut trees. There are soft new cones coming on the pines; instead of the rough, dry cones we're used to seeing on Christmas trees these are rubbery and green. The cow parsley flowers are out, too.

There's a flicker in the grass ahead of us: a water vole. It's a rare sighting because this little creature is the UK's fastest-declining mammal, down from 8 million to 220,000 in fifty years. Water voles are a bit like brown rats, but they're smaller, have rounder noses, little ears and furry tails. They're suffering from habitat loss, but the big problem is predation by an introduced species, the American mink – a vicious killer.

The water vole is an attractive little creature, sometimes only noticed by the V-shape of its passage through the water. In another favourite childhood book, *The Wind in the Willows* (1908), a water vole appears as 'Ratty'. Once again, it's spring at the beginning of a children's book and Mole is bored with spring-cleaning his hole (a hole rather like the hobbits', with furniture and whitewash). He sets off on an adventure to the River Thames, which he's never visited before, and meets Ratty, who is a rather cultivated and leisured kind of water vole. They spend their days boating together. 'There is nothing – absolutely nothing – half so much worth doing as simply messing about in boats' says Ratty. Mole wants to meet Badger, a gruff, wise old creature, and disappears off to find him in his cosy home in the Wild Wood. They all have a series of adventures with the egregious Toad of Toad Hall, a spoilt, loud and boastful creature who has inherited riches from his father.

So far, so anthropomorphic: all these animals portray easily recognised human characteristics and indeed social classes: Badger displays upper-middle-class Art and Crafts tastes in his interior furnishings while Mole has lower middle-class garden ornaments. Toad's vulgar nouveau-riche mansion would be recognised by any Edwardian child. All these animals appear to have attended a minor public school.

The one oddity of the book is the chapter 'The Piper at the

Gates of Dawn', a description of Ratty and Mole's encounter
with the god Pan. It's similar to the scene with Pan in *The
Little Grey Men*. It is a chapter which is usually dropped by
modern abridgers of the novel because it seems out of kilter
with the whimsy of the rest of the book, but the author
Kenneth Grahame thought it was crucial. He had retired in
1908 from an exalted position as secretary of the Bank of
England, and spent much of his time, like his characters,
simply messing about in boats on the Thames. As with so
many children's storywriters, he transcribed the stories he told
to his son Alistair. I think in his way he was another nature
mystic. In this episode Ratty hears the Pan-pipes and is transported onto another plane:

'Rapt, transported, trembling, he was possessed in all his
senses by this new divine thing that caught up his helpless
soul and swung and dandled it, a powerless but happy infant in
a strong sustaining grasp.'[1]

(It is worth noting that Grahame's mother died when he
was five.)

Mole hears the pipes, too, and the animals crouch before
their god, lay their heads on the earth and worship him. All
their senses become heightened; the colours of the roses are
intensified and the meadowsweet becomes more odorous and
pervading. At the end of the séance Pan erases the animals'
memories of their encountering in case the joy of the remembrance should overshadow the rest of their earthly lives.

This is pure nature-mysticism in play. The Edwardian period
was one filled with religious doubt and an uneasy awareness
that the good times of the Victorian era were gone with the
death of their queen. What looks, on the face of it, to be a

---

[1]   Kenneth Grahame, *The Wind in the Willows*, Methuen (1908)

nostalgic ode to lost childhood in fact appears more and more like a reluctance to face up to the uncertainties of adulthood. Unfortunately, water-vole Ratty's days are now numbered. He may need Pan's help once more. But is he still to be found?

One night I sat inside a wood opposite my house, just uphill from a badger set. Silently, one by one, three badger cubs emerged in the gloaming and started to play-fight. I sat entranced, unable even to breathe fully until the tumbling, squeaking creatures returned to their parents. It was a deeply moving experience and felt rather like an encounter with Pan.

We keep seeing moorhens on the nests today. These little black waterfowl have a white stripe along their flanks and a red and yellow beak. Their call goes something like 'Kwarrrrrrk!!', and it's an evocative sound of the English waterways, echoing along the water. Their nests appear to be floating rafts of twigs but in fact they're aground. We see one under a willow that must be a good 6 feet (2 metres) from the canal bank. Along the towpath we eventually come to the village of Alrewas, which is an Anglo-Saxon place name meaning 'alluvial land growing with alder trees'. (We ask locals how to pronounce it, assuming it's something like Arsefaceley, but no, it's just Al-re-was.) Right enough, we spot some alders in boggy ground just down from the towpath. These are a medium-sized tree with a dark bark that looks a bit like a smooth beech. You can spot them in spring by their long, yellow, dangling catkins and long, dark green leaves. They love this cool damp sort of place and they're a useful tree used for stabilising riverbanks. Otters like to nest in their roots. The wood survives well underwater, and much of Venice is built on top of piles made of alder trunks. These trees have an interesting relationship with a nitrogen-fixing bacterium: the tree provides sugary liquid in the root nodules and it gets fertiliser in return. The catkins are actually slim flowers that are usually wind-pollinated, and as a child I thought they only appeared on hazel trees. In fact many trees have them, such as willow, sweet chestnut and birch. Catkin is a borrowed word from Dutch meaning 'kitten', presumably because they look like a kitten's tail.

We pass a sign on the towpath for free-range eggs from 'Happy Girlie Hens' at Willow Wharf Farm (I'm relieved that the eggs aren't from boy-hens). The poor owners here had 180 hens stolen by low-life humans a few years back, but the farm seems to be thriving now. We have salad for lunch, together with a pork pie with pickle on top.

It's so good sitting in the grass in the sunshine without a care in the world, watching the canal flow past. Gina remarks that we're having our salad days, double-meaning that we're having the time of our lives but also that it's now feeling summery enough for cold meals. This is a Shakespearean line from *Antony and Cleopatra*: '. . . My salad days, / When I was green in judgment, cold in blood . . .' and it means the days when you're young and indiscreet. Well, she's young and I'm indiscreet.

This towpath walking really is wonderful. We're very slowly overtaken by a narrowboat steered by an older gentleman with lookout duties undertaken by his dog. They both give us a long appraising look, then stare straight ahead again in silence. They don't look very impressed. There is an Arabic proverb: 'The camel driver has his thoughts; the camel, he has his.'

As the spring warms up it's noticeable how many more narrowboats are appearing on the canals. A narrowboat is one less than 7 feet (2.1 metres); the reason for this is that locks and bridges on the canal system conform to this size: it was cheaper to build them narrow. Wider boats than this tend to be called barges, and they're restricted to the wider rivers.

There's an interesting sub-culture emerging in England to do with this eco style of living, and now there are around 15,000 people living on boats in the country: a small town's worth. We live on a boat during our holidays and know that being a live-aboard forces you to be aware of your consumption, or at least minimalist. You can't leave taps on when you have to carry 5-gallon jerry cans from the shore; you wet yourself down with the shower, turn off, lather up, turn on, then rinse off. You become averse to large amounts of packaging when every scrap of rubbish has to be carried off the boat. Electricity is carefully rationed when you have to make it yourself with a rattling generator. Fuel becomes an issue when you try to live minimally, diesel smoke stinks and so it's far nicer to burn wood on a stove on a cold April evening. Most of the narrowboats that we walk past have heaps of firewood on the roof.

The people living on these boats are from all walks of life. There are young couples who tell us they can't afford a bricks-and-mortar kind of house, and retirees who want to travel cheaply and safely. These people have traditional roses and castles artwork on the sides and wince-inducing names such as *Onion Bargee* and *Never Again, 2*. Living in a room seven feet wide and seventy feet long obviously was the inspiration for *Corri d'or*, and there was a line of optics in the window of *Cirrhosis of the River*. There was no sign of the crew.

Then there are the more serious eco river travellers who are deliberately pursuing an alternative way of living from the mainstream. Their boats can be recognised by more extravagant artwork, a dog and lots of metalwork on the owner. Most of the live-aboards have a 'continuous cruiser' licence from British Waterways, which means they can't stay in one place for more than fourteen days. However, we are walking past many boats that are boarded up with 'For Sale' signs. It's a hard life and the dropout rate is high. As we turn the corner, Burton upon Trent comes into view, and we walk under a metal bridge with these huge letters on it: *'The home of Marston's Pedigree'*. We echo it with a huge sigh of relief and head for the nearest pub.

Spring Ale is brewed by Burton Bridge Beers at the old Fox and Goose Inn, which was built in the late seventeenth century right next to the great 36-arch medieval bridge which finished just outside the front door. Remains of the first two arches are still there but are buried under the road. A Roman bridge probably crossed the river at the same spot. And there's good evidence that the Romans started the whole pub-sign thing. Their system of roads needed places to eat, drink and stay the night. Their *taberna* became our 'tavern', and originally meant a shop that sold wine, whereas an inn sold beer. Most people now call them both the pub (public house: a house open to the public). Today, an inn implies that accommodation is also available. As most customers were illiterate the Romans used to hang a bunch of vine leaves outside, and in cooler Britain a small bush of evergreen leaves was substituted. The Bush was therefore one of the first Roman pub signs, and may even be the origin of some modern-day pubs of the same name. If the establishment also brewed beer a long pole or ale stake, used for stirring the beer, was hung outside.

As with so much that I value about the English countryside,

the pub is also under threat. There are around thirty closing every week in the UK, a rate of decline that would suggest total extinction by the 2040s. It seems that we can thank the Black Death for the growth of the pub, as the few country workers left alive after the plague were able to command higher wages and thus afford to drink alcohol in a place of entertainment. It might be a little extreme to hope for another nationwide plague, but perhaps we can hope instead for a change of heart amongst those property developers devoted to buying up our favourite pubs and turning them into flats.

The brewing industry was hugely successful in Burton upon Trent, and at one point brewed a quarter of all beer sold in the UK. The reason for this was the quality of the local water. The hills around the town are full of gypsum, calcium sulphate dihydrate (which is the stuff in blackboard chalk and plasterboard). The old brewers realised that if you used the water from these hills for making beer the sulphate made it taste pleasantly bitter. The sulphurous whiff of beer made from this water became known as the 'Burton Snatch'. The gypsum also helped to reduce the pH to the best range for enzymes converting starches into fermentable sugar. A greater proportion of preserving hops could be added, which in turn meant that the beer could be shipped further abroad. Burton developed India Pale Ale (IPA) which could survive the long, hot steamship voyage to India, and it was popular there.

The water quality is so precious to the town that chemical treatment to the surrounding open land is forbidden. Marston's Pedigree is one of the few beers that still contains water from the original Burton Well and the only beer that still uses the Burton Union system of brewing. Invented in the 1830s, the Union system involves a line of wooden casks with a trough running across the top of them. The barrels were connected to the trough by a series of header pipes. Any excess yeast foam (the bready-smelling barm) would be expelled from the casks without leaving wasteful head-space, and any expelled beer could be returned to continue fermentation.

Burton also gave us Marmite, which was invented in the late Victorian period by the German scientist Justus von Liebig (also the 'father of fertiliser', rather disturbingly). He discovered that brewer's yeast could be boiled with salt, sieved, concentrated, bottled and even eaten (I love the stuff, but it's an acquired taste). The used yeast was supplied by the Bass Brewery in Burton, and the first Marmite factory was built in this town. And the whole place smells delicious.

In the rain we see swifts feeding on a hatch of flies on the still canal water. The bluebells are in flower, but apparently they've only been out for a week here. It feels a little cold and damp. We follow the canal through Burton and splash through some muddy puddles on the towpath.

A local man remarks that 'it's a bit mucky' and we notice that the accent has changed again to east-west Midlands, with a bit of north. The ducklings are feeding themselves here; apparently they can feed as soon as they leave the nest, just ten hours after they hatch. They are the tiniest balls of fluff imaginable, a pike's TV snack. The laburnum's long cascades of yellow flowers are out and we wonder again why so many spring flowers are coloured yellow. Daffodils, lesser celandines, pansies, buttercups, broom, gorse: all yellow. The whole of the laburnum tree is poisonous and it was used by various murder-mystery authors as a convenient cause of garden death. The seeds were used as a plot device by Daphne du Maurier in her novel *My Cousin Rachel*.

Also coming out are the rhododendrons and the cow parsley, and we notice in one street that the cherry blossom has already fallen in a great pink carpet onto the pavement: the first sign of the mortality of spring. Rhododendrons have large attractive flowers in the spring in pinks, reds and purples. These make the mountainsides in the Himalayas a colourful place to go trekking before the summer monsoon but their thick foliage kills everything underneath and *Rhododendron ponticum* has become an invasive pest in England. It is difficult to eradicate as its roots can make new shoots, and even though this species was here in the British Isles before the last Ice Age it never returned until humans reintroduced it.

The great plant-hunter Frank Kingdon-Ward was responsible for introducing many rhododendrons to England. In the winter of 1924, Kingdon-Ward and Lord Cawdor undertook an Indiana Jones-style adventure following the unexplored Tsang Po river gorge from Tibet to India. Their expedition not only solved the mystery of the course of the river, confirming that it became the Brahmaputra, but Kingdon-Ward also collected many significant plants including the flower that made his reputation; the Himalayan blue poppy. He also collected half a dozen more rhododendrons and took them back to England.

We decide to take a gamble with the route from Burton to Derby. We want to see the arrival of spring on the verges of a motorway, but it's unsafe (and illegal) to walk along the hard shoulder of these roads. The A38 trunk road between Burton and Derby is the next best thing as it has a walkway protected by a safety barrier and its landscaped verges are much like those on the motorway system, so we decide to go this way. We leave the peace and quiet of the canal towpath and climb up a steep embankment. We hop over a fence and jump into the maelstrom. The pavement is just feet away from trucks blasting past at 56 mph and cars doing over 70. Their slip-streams batter us and the noise is incredible. We set off in the direction of Derby.

Here the A38 is built over Icknield Street, the Roman road we've been following off and on; from well south of Birmingham. It joined the two Roman forts of Wall and Derventio, and this was a front line between two warring peoples. The lands north of the River Trent were occupied by the British tribe of Cornovii, the people of the Horned God, and in AD 50 the Roman army under the governor Aulus Plautius were using this road to control the lands to the south. Romans to the right of us, Britons to the left of us. I wonder what would they have made of modern traffic?

Just off the main double carriageway we poke around in the grass verge and find a vestigial, single-track A38 from the 1950s, built on top of the old turnpike road, built on top of the original Roman road. There is also evidence that the Romans built on top of a Bronze Age trackway hereabouts. And so the layers of our countryside go deeper and deeper. Surely we're bound to take to the skies in future, and these vast strips of asphalt will one day be blistered with weeds and young trees.

Fast-food detritus, flung from passing cars, decorates the verges. Styrofoam coffee cups, fried-chicken boxes and hamburger wrappers predominate with, surprisingly, quite a few beer bottles. The Lincolnshire farm of my early childhood was on the side of the A1 Great North Road and I once found a note tossed out of a car from a bored child. It led to my first correspondence, and since then I've regarded roadside rubbish as a magical source of unexpected messages from passing strangers. Here the messages are of appeased hunger and boredom.

Hovering above the dual carriageway's embankment is a kestrel, Hopkins' wind-hover. It's a true bird of prey in the narrow definition of the phrase in that it has exceptionally good eyesight, with strong talons for grasping the prey and a powerful curved beak for flesh-tearing. It's a raptor, which means to seize or take by force, and like other raptors it grabs its prey with its feet then transfers it to the beak. So owls are birds of prey, seagulls are not, despite appearances to the contrary.

The Victorians exterminated every bird of prey they possibly could, so much so that the marsh harrier, white-tailed eagle, goshawk and osprey were virtually eliminated from the British Isles. Boys used to steal eggs for their collections (girls didn't seem to do this much). Then in the 1950s and 60s organochlorine pesticides, in particular DDT, were used, which resulted in concentrations of these poisons in the bodies of the top predators. For various other complicated reasons birds of prey died in their thousands.

Swiss chemist Paul Hermann Müller won the Nobel Prize in Physiology or Medicine in 1948 for his discovery of the high efficiency of DDT as an insecticide. It proved spectacularly effective against all the bugs that farmers love to kill, and they sprayed it indiscriminately. The stuff itself appears benign, being a colourless, tasteless crystalline powder. The name also seems inoffensively dull: dichlorodiphenyltrichloroethane, but in fact DDT was persistent in the environment and lodged in the fatty tissue of animals. As they themselves were eaten, the DDT became more and more concentrated in the bodies of the predators in the process called biomagnification. At the top of the food chain the birds of prey were receiving huge doses at the same time as losing their prey species, because they in turn were losing their food. And so they died.

Silent Spring was published in 1962 by an American biologist, Rachel Carson, and her book was surely one of the most effective ever written. She dedicated it to Albert Schweitzer, quoting him: 'Man has lost the capacity to foresee and to forestall. He will end by destroying the earth.' This apocalyptic message continued throughout the book, starting with a description of an idyllic American township poisoned by pesticides. Carson went on to describe the effects of indiscriminate DDT spraying on the environment, particularly on birds: hence the title of the book. Chapters headed 'Elixirs of Death', 'Rivers of Death', 'And no Birds Sing' drove the message home. Her prose is eloquent and elegant, with unexpected, delightful descriptions of wildlife and nature. Her arguments are made clearly and dispassionately. It's a great read and she was a great writer. It is even more powerful when you know she was dying of cancer at the time of writing *Silent Spring*.

The book caused an outcry, and it was probably the seminal event in the modern ecological movement. President Kennedy authorised an inquiry which led to the banning of DDT in agriculture in the USA in 1972. This in turn was a major factor in the return of the bald-headed eagle (the national bird of the USA).

A major problem with all of this is that DDT is also effective in reducing human deaths due to malaria, by spraying the mosquito breeding grounds, and this ought to be weighed in the balance against environmental concerns. The debate has continued until today, with James Lovelock, the inventor of the Gaia concept, suggesting in his 2014 book *A Rough Ride to the Future* that we're not valuing the human lives spared by DDT highly enough. 'Neither Rachel Carson, nor the green movement – nor the US government seemed aware of the dire human consequence of banning the manufacture of DDT and its lookalikes before substitutes were available . . . In 1963 malaria was about to become effectively controlled. The insecticide ban led to a rise in malaria deaths to 2 million yearly, plus over 100 million disabled by the disease.'[1] (But, as some point out,[2] there is no ban on the use of DDT in malarial control.)

Carson also writes that no amount of lethal chemicals can control the entire world's insects, Nature alone can keep the balance: 'The trouble is that we are seldom aware of the protection afforded by natural enemies until it fails. Most of us walk unseeing through the world, unaware alike of its beauties, its wonders, and the strange and sometimes terrible intensity of the lives that are being lived about us. So it is that the activities of the insect predators and parasites are known to few.'[3]

She writes powerfully, but her critics complain that she overstated her case. So do some other environmentalists when making theirs. This only serves to weaken their arguments and gives ammunition for those who would make profits out of pesticides, pollution and all the other unthinking stuff that humans do to ruin the world.

And the last word goes to John Moore: 'It is not entirely out

---

[1] James Lovelock, *A Rough Ride to the Future*, page 127, Allen Lane (2014)

[2] www.theguardian.com/environment/georgemonbiot/2014/apr/24/james-lovelocks-book-genius-defence

[3] Rachel Carson, *Silent Spring*, Chapter 15 'Nature Fights Back', Houghton Mifflin (1962)

of the question that despite man's ingenuity the insects might
beat us in the end. If they do it will be because we haven't
used our biological knowledge, but instead have employed
chemists as our hired assassins to kill our fellow creatures in
their cave-man fashion, ignorantly, wantonly, wastefully.'[1]

Since Carson and Moore's time the banning of DDT in
agriculture and the Wildlife and Countryside Act 1981 seem to
have turned the tide for birds of prey in the UK.
Reintroduction schemes such as the white-tailed eagle on the
island of Rum in Scotland and the red kite near here in the
Derwent Valley have been a huge success. You'll see the red
kites circling in the thermals above the M40 in Oxfordshire.

Silent Spring's dedicatee, Albert Schweitzer, was interested in
the apocalypse. He points out that Christianity started as a
Jewish apocalyptic movement, arguing that the historical Jesus
was an apocalyptic prophet and really meant it when he said
he would die and return to judge the world before the end of
his generation. Word-weaselling Bible scholars have been
trying to explain his inconvenient non-return for 2,000 years,
trying to suggest that 'coming quickly', 'near' and 'soon' could
somehow mean some indeterminate time in the future. Most
religions promise an End of Times, sometimes tomorrow and
always to the detriment of unbelievers. Islam, Mormonism,
Jehovah's Witnesses, the compilers of the Mayan Calendar and
many others have predicted imminent death and judgement.

---

[1] *The Year of the Pigeons*, John Moore, Collins (1963)

The problem with this human tendency is that a disregard for the future of nature is implicit within it. *Silent Spring* serves as a warning to those who care about the future.

My last big project with the BBC was a series of films about world religions. I was struck by the absence of nature-based religions in the world today, and the preponderance of the Abrahamic religions: more than half the world's population subscribe to Judaism, Christianity or Islam, all based on a vindictive god who demands the death of Abraham's son as proof of allegiance. All these religions treat life and nature as resources to be exploited. And being religions, of course, no one is allowed to question these beliefs in a spirit of scientific enquiry. However, other philosophies are rising from the green movement: Neo-Paganism, Wicca and Deep Ecology.

Deep Ecology maintains that never-ending economic growth is impossible and that we will destroy the beauty of the world in our attempts to make everyone wealthy. It recognises that humanity is part of a complex ecosystem that we damage at our peril. In this complex web, developed over millennia, all species are dependent upon one another, no one part of this web can be considered as superior to any other, and any idea that this environment has been created for us and our prosperity is delusional. This natural web appears to be related to Lovelock's notion of Gaia, but there is more to Deep Ecology: a spiritual dimension. We know from indigenous people (and I suspect our own Stonehenge builders, too) that our relationship with nature is not just physically sustaining, it is also spiritually sustaining. It can be seen in their rituals and heard in their prayers. In our own culture we feel this spiritual nourishment in the countryside, and I too have felt a sense of wonder this spring in the power and beauty of the English countryside.

This isn't valued in any economic measures of our progress. How do we attach a non-monetary value to the English spring? There is a huge danger in letting politicians put a price tag on, say, an acre of Green Belt. There will always be a fudge, someone will always pay the money, and houses will be built over English countryside that belongs to us all. Once built over it's gone forever.

We can dismiss these concerns as the new-age beliefs of hippies, but just take a look at the organic food movement. It was originally dismissed as uneconomic and idealistic but now most commentators regard it as economically and environmentally sustainable. In his book about money, *Sacred Economics*, Charles Eisenstein writes: 'When we must pay the true price for the depletion of nature's gifts, materials will become more precious to us, and economic logic will reinforce, and not contradict, our heart's desire to treat the world with reverence and, when we receive nature's gifts, to use them well.' I fear that it will be much too late by then.

Refreshing as always, James Lovelock suggests that we are not near the end of times, but instead at the brink of a new form of electronic life that will preserve and tend Gaia for millennia to come. Our minds may one day exist as a shimmering haze of electrons instead of living in brains made of meat in profligate bodies. Ray Kurzweil agrees. A futurologist, he is now director of engineering at Google. He looks forward to a time when humans combine with computers and cease to be biological organisms. If so, the English spring can sing on peacefully without us.

CHAPTER SEVEN

Verges – a yacht delivery – the River Derwent – Cromford Canal – Industrial Revolution – Mongolia – The Compleat Angler *– the Golden Fleece – Curlews – blanket bog*

The roadside verge is a great place to see the spring as you drive along in a car. It's probably the most observed habitat in the country, giving millions of people the chance to watch the season as it changes every day. For many of them it might be the only contact with nature that they have as they go on the school run or drive to work. You might catch a glimpse of orchids or cowslips amongst the various species of grasses. There are rare flowers to look out for, too: in East Anglia you might see sulphur clover with its fluffy upright yellow flowers, or purple-flowered crested cow wheat. In the south-west you might spot bastard balm with its pinky-white flowers. Then there's oxeye daisy, with the big cartoon-like cow's eye (this one has become an invasive weed in the US and Canada but it's welcome here). Ragged robin is a lovely pink meadow flower that's had to find a new home in the verges. Then there's the bright blue meadow cranesbill, which we'll look out for later, in June. You'll almost certainly see a bird of prey hovering above, watching for the flicker of a vole's tail.

If you add up all the rural country road verges in the UK they amount to an area bigger than the Dartmoor National Park, over 100,000 hectares – and that's half of our remaining

priority grassland reserve. You could argue that this resource
should be treated as a national park. If so, the National Car Park
would have the biggest number of (high-speed) visitors by far.

We've walked along a couple of hundred miles of English roads
and paths now and we've seen how wildflowers are being driven
to extinction by prairie farming, and how the bees and birds that
depend on these plants are also suffering. With 97 per cent of
meadows gone since the 1930s, grassy verges are becoming the
last refuge for wildlife. We saw that on the wet day in Wiltshire
where the only wildflowers to be seen were on the verge,
squeezed between the fields of monoculture and ribbons of
tarmac. We know how useful motorway and railway embankments
are as corridors for wildlife to migrate up and down the country,
undisturbed by walkers. They cut across a wide variety of geolo-
gies and habitats and they join up a countryside fragmented by
modern agriculture. Cars, trucks and trains act as vectors of
dispersal, sweeping insects, seeds and pollen along in their wake.

The roads authority, Highways England, is rightly concerned
that ordinary roadsides shouldn't be allowed to grow too high
as driver visibility at junctions would be obscured, so the county
councils mow back the growth in the spring, often using huge
flailing machines. Ditch-clearing is also done by machinery.
Sixty years ago these jobs were done by a man with a scythe
and spade who knew his stretch of roadside and treated it like
his own garden. He would be careful to let wildflowers such as
cowslips set seed, and he might let the cow parsley flower before
cutting it back. He would make sure holes and burrows were left
on the side of the ditch and not just torn open by an excavator.
This is not considered cost-effective today, but the man on a
digger listening to music on headphones can't be expected to be
sympathetic to the creatures crushed under his bucket.

If the verges could be treated as hay meadows they would

become havens of biodiversity instead of clumps of rank nettles. Most of our natural wild flora only grows to a height of about a foot so it shouldn't obscure sightlines. Anyone who objects with the argument that this would cost too much might care to look at Dorset council. As we saw when we started this walk, the Dorset road verges are well tended and the reduction in mowing may actually save money. It would certainly give millions of us something beautiful to look at as we drive to work in the morning. Maybe future technology could help by giving us robot workmen to dig around plants sensitively.

Verges are under pressure, though, as we're seeing along this section of the A38. Although it's well planted with a variety of trees there's lots of rubbish to be picked up and it's a difficult place to work. Without any management, coarse vegetation grows unhindered and turns eventually into scrub and woodland, losing the flower-rich habitat. Budgets are being cut back. When councils stick to a few basic principles, though, the results are encouraging. It's something that's working.

These flowering plants that look so attractive on the edges of the road need to have time to grow up, flower and set seed. Then they can be mown down between mid-July and September. If they're cut down before they flower, insects that depend on them are deprived of nectar and pollen. If the grass cuttings can be collected this mimics the pattern of traditional meadow management. Rabbit grazing helps, too.

Newer motorway and trunk-road verges are much better managed by people who have clearly given careful thought to the subject. You'll see trees of different sorts planted carefully, and wildflowers coming into season. It is clear that these road-sides are becoming some of our best-managed conservation areas. It's heartening to see. So how did this come about?

Twyford Down, not far from where we began our walk, was

the site of pitched battles between road-builders and conservationists in the early 1990s. There were beatings of protesters
by police and security officers. They were fighting over a
proposed extension of the M3 through an area of high chalk-
land south of Winchester. It was a beautiful, rolling,
ecologically rich stretch of grassland, home to the chalkhill
blue butterfly. The Battle of Twyford Down shows what
happens when pressure of over-population and traffic collides
with natural beauty. The politicians, police and road-builders
won, of course, and now a great, white, mile-wide trench
drives through the Down (instead of a tunnel which could have
been built for £75 million). The protesters gained a great deal
of national attention in the media, though, and in many ways
they swung public opinion in their favour. There's been more
resistance to indiscriminate road-building since.

One irony is that just as work was getting underway in
1994 a government committee concluded that more roads just
encourage more traffic, and that congestion and pollution were
better controlled by other methods. Twyford Down is now
part of the South Downs National Park – with a whacking
great motorway driving through it.

One good thing that came out of the debate was that road
schemes now include a great deal of thought about conservation. At Twyford Down large areas of intensively farmed land
were turned back into downland by stripping off the topsoil to
make the ground less fertile. This means that new wildflowers
wouldn't be swamped by nettles and rank grasses. Then
different species and sizes of wild plants were sown; vetches,
cowslips, thyme, rock-rose and clustered bellflower. These were
grown from local seed, not imported. A chunk of water meadow
that was going to be destroyed was physically moved to a new
island site in the River Test that had become species-depleted.

So far, so commendable, but aren't we just making a pretty garden out of England? I would argue it was ever thus, and we just have to make the best of it. As we've seen, after the Ice Age most of this country was covered by thick forest, but ever since humans came to live here we've cut down the trees and completely changed the land to suit ourselves. The archetypal patchwork of fields that resides in the national mind as 'the English countryside' is manmade. But it's still beautiful to walk through and we've seen how effective conservation really is.

It doesn't need to cost too much. The Highways Agency, which presides over 75,000 acres of motorway and trunk-road verges, were criticised for planting non-native trees and areas of grass of no conservation value. Some of their activities were polluting rivers with run-off. Stung by the criticisms, they decided to do something about it. In one small example, in 2002 they announced a ten-year action plan to biodiversify some of their land. They consulted conservationists, who came up with 25 species and habitats. The plan was for 150 ponds for newts, including the creation of 25 wetland features for other wildlife, five new chalk grassland sites for the Adonis blue butterfly, and five new sites each for the Deptford pink and the western ramping fumitory butterflies. The plan only cost around £15 million, about as much as half a mile of motorway.

We suddenly stumble across a heavy drift of burger cartons along the side of the A38. There might be an interesting calculation involving location of fast-food joint, average speed of vehicle, eating time and speed of descending electric window.

No doubt the Roman legionaries also tossed food and rubbish into the hedges. As we have seen, here they had a nasty job to do; they had to subdue a British tribe. It is likely that these people worshipped the Lord, the Old One, the horned nature god, Pan. The Romans built a fort here to protect the crossing of the River Derwent. The name means 'valley thick with oaks', and it was a dangerous front line, the woods filled with savage native people. This was a Roman Heart of Darkness, reminiscent of the nineteenth-century European conquest of Africa. The Derwent Valley was a deep thrust into the underbelly of the Peak District, where the Romans knew there was a precious metal, lead, to be had up in the mines called Lutudara, possibly at present-day Matlock Bath. The Roman Empire depended on lead, it was their thermo-plastic; it was easily melted into complex shapes for plumbing (*plumbum*) and drinking vessels. What they didn't know was that it was poisoning them for centuries. Ingots have been found here stamped with the words 'Socii Lutudarenses', possibly the company name. We follow the old path along the river.

We're now walking past the site of the Roman fort Derventio Coritanorum, next to the River Derwent, in Derby. Here our Romans might have found somewhere safe to stay for the night. This was injun territory, and the next day they would have to head up the river towards the lead mines where much of the wealth of Britannia was being extracted.

The river now looks much the same as it did in those Roman days. Having powered the first mills of the Industrial Revolution and then been polluted, it's now been cleaned up and is becoming the home again for one of the world's oldest fish. Lampreys are spawning here this spring, demonstrating that the water quality is now back to where it was in the early 1800s.

The lamprey is a snake-like fish that grows up to a metre long, in the case of the sea lamprey. They are the world's oldest living vertebrate and were 200 million years old when the dinosaurs were around. They don't have a mouth as we know it, but instead have a sucker and a ring of razor-sharp teeth. They attach themselves to their prey and suck hard, like a sort of English piranha. They're not the most attractive creature, but the much smaller brook lampreys in the Derwent indicate that the health of the river is good.

The flesh of lampreys is more like meat than fish and was much prized as a luxury during religious fasts when only fish was permitted to be eaten. They have been eaten (along with snails) by Romans, lightly poached in red wine, and by British monarchs, baked in pies. Lamprey pie also featured in the *Game of Thrones* TV series.

We take a short break from our spring walk at this point. There's a boat delivery to do from the west coast of Ireland to Bristol, a yacht on which I hope to sail to Spitsbergen in the late summer to visit the breeding grounds of geese. Waiting for the tide in Kilrush I'm reminded that spring tides, which happen around the full and new moon, are not named after the season: these high tides happen every two weeks or so throughout the year. The word derives from the Old English *spring* (a noun), from *springan* (a verb) of Germanic origin 'jump, burst forth, rise'. The Old English word originally referred to the source of a well or stream, the place where a flow of water rises naturally from the earth. Then the English started using 'spring' in the context of the first sign of something, as in 'the spring of the day', 'the spring of the dawn', and 'the spring of the year'. These expressions were used from around 1380 to 1600: between the times of Chaucer and Shakespeare. From the middle of the sixteenth century 'the spring of the year' became shortened to spring as the name of the first season of the year. Before that the season had been known as Lent, or Lenten, another Germanic word which referred to the lengthening of days that happens in spring. Now that word only refers to the period of fasting and repentance between Ash Wednesday and Easter.

Once out of the Shannon estuary the long, grey Atlantic rollers break endlessly on the foot of the Irish crags. I feel a bit queasy in the rough conditions but once round the Fastnet rock the sun comes out. By the time we're approaching England the wind has dropped completely and sun-lit fog surrounds us. The only way of knowing where we are on the chart is by checking the same Garmin GPS I've been using to mark the oaks. Out of sight of land the sea is timeless, and I realise that I'm seeing just what the Roman mariners would have seen as they felt their way up the Severn estuary. The feeling continues as the fog clears, revealing gorse bushes flowering yellow along the shore. When we turn into the narrow muddy entrance of the River Avon I see great masses of dark green foliage ahead just like Conrad's Congo. Maybe to the Romans this land seemed a heart of darkness, too, filled with savages and strange gods.

Back in harness, we're walking up along the Derwent to the next town. This place has the distinction of making the harmonious French original name of Beaurepaire, meaning beautiful retreat, into an English name which is rather less lovely: Belper. It's a pleasant, friendly town though and today we feel that we're back in the north of England. The footpath takes us through some private grazing and we meet the horse and owner walking up to the field. She's a robust character, a no-nonsense northern horsewoman. Once she's established we're not about to steal her darling and sell it to a supermarket she's very informative about horses in the spring.

They shed their coats in February, and when they're put out on grass they get excited and 'fizzy'. That's because spring grass is growing five times faster now in May than in September, and it's full of fructans, a type of sugar. It's like putting a child out to graze on a diet of Krispy Kreme doughnuts. Given too much of this, the horse can develop laminitis (a horrible hoof condition) or colic.

Horse owners have to watch out for other evils: ragwort is one that is coming out now. It's another yellow wildflower of the spring, but taller than most, sometimes growing over 6 feet (2 metres) tall with a woody stem and big florets 1 inch (2.5cm) across. You'll see them on grassy verges standing out high against the other foliage. Ragwort's other names of 'stinking nanny' and 'mare's fart' refer to the sharp smell of the leaves, caused by alkaloids. These can cause liver damage to horses, but only if fed dried in fodder, as the sharp taste of the fresh plant deters horses in the field. Ragwort is a vital plant for many insects, including the cinnabar moth, which is totally reliant on it, so once again there is a conflict of interests between humans and insects.

John Clare, the Northamptonshire peasant-poet, loved ragwort's intense yellow colour:

Ragwort thou humble flower with tattered leaves
I love to see thee come and litter gold . . .
Thy waste of shining blossoms richly shields
The sun tanned sward in splendid hues that burn
So bright and glaring that the very light
Of the rich sunshine doth to paleness turn
And seems but very shadows in thy sight.[1]

On my mother's Scottish Isle of Arran there was a Gaelic
story of the fairies living on the knoll. When the king of the
fairies wanted them to fly to Ireland (which is just visible on a
clear day), each fairy would jump onto a ragwort and fly over
the waves, 'every knee of them'.

Just upriver of here is a wetland reserve: Wyver Lane Pool. It's
important because it's one of the only areas of wet grassland
in the mid-Derwent Valley. We walked around quietly and saw
a large number of waterfowl. Waders such as curlew and
common sandpiper stop here in spring, and redshanks and
lapwings will stay to breed. There are residents such as
Canada geese, tufted duck and little grebes, and there's enough
room for widgeon to come down from Iceland and Russia and
over-winter. They're a duck with an attractive chestnut-
coloured head. Wyver Lane is within the Derwent Valley
World Heritage Site and it's a pleasant contrast to the mills
further upriver. There are frogs and toads here, too. Gina has

---

[1] John Clare, 'The Ragwort' (1832)

been hunting for frog spawn and has spotted some. Apparently toad spawn is laid in long chains like pearls whereas frog spawn comes in clumps. Here there are froggy tadpoles emerging with just a tail.

Along here we see two black lambs, full of mischief, herding an irritated-looking goose. We also see one of the ducks from the nature reserve flying steadily along the canal (a common sight) and, without missing a wing-beat, headed straight into a dark tunnel (an uncommon sight). We wondered if it came out all right at the other end. We also watch a swan carefully pushing one of her eggs back into the nest after it had rolled out onto the towpath.

We're walking along the Cromford Canal towpath, and the over-arching trees turn into a sun-lit tunnel. It's like walking into paradise. But Cromford is the unlikely birthplace of the Industrial Revolution, which has so changed the world, for it was here in 1771 that Richard Arkwright built his first water-powered cotton-spinning mill. It was swiftly copied in Lancashire and abroad, and the revolution began. The new process was completely unregulated and labourers had no protection whatsoever. By 1833, reformers like our friend William Cobbett were arguing that the daily hours worked by children in the new satanic mills should be reduced from twelve to ten. Their political opponents expostulated that this would bring the economy to its knees overnight, rather like the complaints about the minimum wage in 1999.

You wouldn't dream that so much started here because Cromford Canal is now an idyllic waterway. My first thought was that we have tidied up the mess remarkably quickly, but apparently we've just exported it, as far away as Mongolia. Bautou is the largest industrial city in Inner Mongolia, and is one of the biggest suppliers of rare earth minerals in the world.

These go into our green technology, such as wind turbines and electric cars. It is dominated by a huge, artificial lake filled with toxic waste. The skies are thick with smoke from coal-fired power stations, which are built next to vast apartment blocks. The roads are black with coal-dust, and the 2.5 million inhabitants are exposed to cripplingly high levels of pollution. It all looks something like Sheffield in the 1930s, which George Orwell called the 'ugliest town in the Old World'. Similarly, Bautou was recently billed by the BBC as The Worst Place on Earth (perhaps Sheffield and Bautou could organise a twinning). But the rare earths are not particularly rare, and the reason why China produces 90 per cent of the world's rare earth minerals is because they are prepared to take the levels of pollution that we in the West have refused and exported to the other side of the world. As a result Cromford Canal now looks like paradise. But where on earth can China export their polluting industries? There's no more planet left to export them to.

As we've walked through England this spring we have passed under maybe a hundred Victorian railway arches, and I always look up and appreciate the brickwork on each one. There's some very clever stuff up there. When an old road or canal and a new railway intersected at right angles the brickwork was fairly straightforward: the builders put up a wooden framework and built a regular arch of bricks laid side by side parallel to the abutments (the substructure at either end of the bridge). So if you look up you'll see the bricks all in line with the road beneath, perpendicular to the faces of the bridge. This meant that all the loads were fed directly to the abutments, without side loads tending to make the bricks slide sideways.

Very often, though, the railway had to cross the road or canal at an angle, and this is where the Victorian engineers had a problem. The faces of the arched bridge were not at right angles to the abutments, and therefore the plan view of the bridge was a parallelogram, not a rectangle. A regular arch of bricks just would not do: sliding side loads would be introduced, the arches would bulge and the bridge would collapse.

The answer took a while to calculate, but it was solved by a succession of English engineers. Using complex geometry they developed the skew arch, which can be thought of as a spiral quadrilateral solid wrapped around a cylinder, like a square-threaded screw (imagine wrapping a long piece of square-section liquorice in a spiral around a can). In appearance it's like the rifling inside a gun barrel. The first skew-arch bridges were constructed out of stone blocks, each one chiselled by masons to a unique shape, with no two edges either parallel or perpendicular. These were very expensive. Soon, though, these extraordinary engineers developed a geometry that enabled the use of mass-produced bricks. There was a vigorous battle conducted in the *Civil Engineer and Architect's Journal* between these men, who accused each other of stealing ideas, but the fact was that they were all brilliant and all immensely resourceful. Every time I walk under a skew bridge I mentally take off my hat to those engineers and their craftsmen builders. The spiralling brickwork, as one of them wrote, 'is elegant and pleasing to the eye'. Modern concrete bridges, made out of frozen porridge, are not.

The Cromford Canal fell into disuse due to the expansion of the railways. In 1849 the Manchester, Buxton, Matlock and Midlands Junction Railway was built alongside the canal and killed the business stone dead. The same happened to the Somerset Coal Canal. Then in turn railways fell victim to the rise of the motor car and thousands of miles of English branch railways were closed in the Beeching cuts of the 1960s.

There is a lesson from history here. Disruptive technology is ruthless. The British government is about to commit the folly of building a railway line from London to the Midlands: HS2. According to a study by the Institute of Economic Affairs the total cost will come to £80 billion, costing each household in the land £3,000. But the cost to the English countryside will be far higher: 33 ancient woodlands will be ruined, with 34 affected by pollution and noise: over 21,000 homes will suffer from extra racket. HS2 will also wreck the 29-mile-(47-kilometre-) wide Chiltern Hills area of outstanding natural beauty, the Colne Valley Regional Park on the outskirts of London, and other areas of Green Belt. It will be a great ugly scar ripped up the belly of England.

What no one in government is seeing is that this is using nineteenth-century technology to solve a twenty-first-century problem. HS2 will be obsolete before it is completed. The disruptive technology coming along is the driverless car: this is going to be as much of a revolution as the railways them-selves, and if handled wisely could benefit the English countryside.

Self-driving cars use GPS, sensors and lasers to navigate our roads with extreme precision. There are prototypes up and running now, with 400,000 miles travelled so far by Google's cars without an accident. As 90 per cent of crashes are caused by humans there will be fewer casualties and better use of the road space. This is the interesting bit for the countryside: platoons of cars would be able to travel on motorways like train carriages, each one a few feet from the car in front and maintaining over 100 mph. Five times as many cars will be able to use roads that can have narrower carriageways. Why would you want to go to the railway station when you can catch your own carriage outside the door, request your destination and then work, read or sleep all the way there?

At Sainsbury's supermarket in Matlock we go in the entrance, follow our footpath straight past the checkouts, then continue out of the exit. We get some odd looks in our clumpy boots, rucksacks and hats. Outside at the station we see a steam engine, then we head up onto the cliffs and walk through deciduous woodland. At the top we look down on the Derwent and the A6 road, hundreds of feet below. I'm glad we came this way up into the Peak District rather than across the moors: it's a beautiful part of England. We still have miles to do along the Pennine Way on moorland and time is beginning to get tight: spring ends on 20 June.

At Darley Dale there is a wonderful old church: St Helen's. The south wall of the chancel has a glorious muddle of architectural styles. There is a blocked-up Norman door with a round arch. Then there's an Early English lancet window, thin enough for lepers to listen to divine service without infecting the congregation inside. To the right of it is a Decorated buttress, and over the chancel door is a window in Perpendicular style. In the porch are stone Saxon coffin lids, suggesting there was a Saxon church here before this building. One depicts a wolf, common around here in those times.

I wonder, not for the first time, if churches were partly built as a sort of village fortress in addition to their main function as a place of worship. Consider this; they were built of stone when most houses were little more than wooden hovels. They usually featured a strong door, narrow windows and a tower like a castle, often with battlements also like a castle, where defenders could hide behind the merlon (the square upright bit) and chuck dung and stones at their enemies through the crenel (the square hole). They could accommodate the whole population of the village, as they did every Sunday. Our local church in Chapel-en-le-Frith was used as a prison for some of the defeated Scots from the Battle of Preston in 1648, showing that the concept could work in reverse. I ring Julian with my theory, which he says is absolute nonsense.

We wander into the churchyard to look for the 2,000-year-old yew tree said to be one of the oldest in Britain. There's a gravestone inscribed for 'Daniel Dakeyne of Toad Hole, 27 February 1819'. Apparently he was one of the many mill-owners hereabouts and Toad Hole is a village. We find the yew near the south side, an immense tree surrounded by iron railings and at least 33 feet in circumference. This would have been a sapling before the Romans forced their way up the Derwent, and maybe even before Jesus of Nazareth was working as a builder apprenticed under his father, Joseph. The conclusion is obvious: these ancient trees pre-dated Christian churches. There are yews in Welsh and Scottish churchyards up to 5,000 years old. So what did they represent? We know the churches were often built over the pagan sites to obliterate them. Their Christian priests turned the Horned One into the Devil. But who worshipped this tree?

The gate creaks and the rector of St Helen's arrives. He lets us in to the church and shows us a Roman cremation stone leaning against the building, a stone lid looking rather like a millstone. The artefacts here seem to be getting older and older, and the oldest one is still alive: the yew tree. I feel the centuries collapsing together in this place: the yew outside has seen British tribes, Romans, Saxons, lepers, lovers and two thousand springtimes.

The rector, Stephen Monk, was once a Catholic hospital chaplain, perhaps demonstrating a bit of nominative determinism. Despairing of the Church's rigid approach to medical ethics, he moved away from Rome towards the Church of England, an unusual step. He shows us a fine Burne-Jones window from the nineteenth century – fresh as yesterday – and the stone sculpture of Sir John de Darley, a thirteenth-century knight, a comparatively modern interloper. Bizarrely, he holds his stone heart in his hands as he suffered a massive heart attack during a session with his mistress. His legs are firmly crossed. Why? Is this crossing a symbol of a Crusader (as thought by some), or of a humiliated wife?

I walk away from this church feeling rather stunned by the shrinking of the years. Our tribe roars past in their shiny cars, soon to be gone, yet the yew tree still stands.

Later on, treading through the sun-dappled woods towards Rowsley, I swear I catch a glimpse of a clean-limbed figure fleeting ahead. A dryad? Why not? We had a perfectly useful home-grown religion in this valley before the Church, before the Romans, before whatever exotic cult is next, when the yew tree was young.

At the Peacock Inn, Rowsley, we see a party of anglers returning from the fishing boats with all the apparatus of their sport. It's a lovely time to be fishing the river, with the leaves coming out and the brown trout rising. Their great predecessor, Izaak Walton, used to fish these Derbyshire rivers. His book, entitled *The Compleat Angler, or the contemplative man's recreation: being a discourse of fish and fishing, not unworthy the perusal of most anglers*, is the second-most reprinted book in the English language after the King James Bible, and has been in print since 1653. Oddly enough Walton never used a reel and knew little of fly-fishing.

The Compleat Angler is much more than a handbook of a sport, it's a discursive, pastoral account of the fun that can be had with a bunch of friends just fishing. Angles were what we now call hooks: thus 'angling'. Walton throws in verse and a bit of philosophy, too. He's another writer who finds that contemplation of nature leads to feelings of timelessness. This description of an elderly friend's poem gives a flavour of his style:

'. . . he sate quietly in a Summers evening on a bank a fishing; it is a description of the Spring, which because it glides as soft and sweetly from his pen, as that River does now by which it was then made, I shall repeat unto you.

> This day dame Nature seem'd in love:
> The lustie sap began to move;
> Fresh juice did stir th'imbracing Vines,
> And birds had drawn their Valentines.
> The jealous Trout, that low did lye,
> Rose at a well dissembled flie;
> There stood my friend with patient skill,
> Attending of his trembling quill.

> Already were the eaves possest
> With the swift Pilgrims dawbed nest:
> The Groves already did rejoice,
> In Philomels triumphing voice:
> The showrs were short, the weather mild,
> The morning fresh, the evening smil'd.'[1]

Izaak Walton also was a fine biographer, writing lives of the notable poets John Donne (who he knew very well), and George Herbert. He was a man of action and a man of reflection.

Gina and I miss the bus but manage to hitch-hike back to Matlock from outside the Peacock Inn. We had no luck hitching back to our accommodation in the southern counties in previous weeks, but here, up north, people seem to be either more trusting or more generous, or both.

The next day we pick up our walk by the same group of anglers on the Derwent. They're posh gents wearing thigh-length waders and sweaters and jackets in expensively subdued greens and browns. They tell us they're after brown trout in the spring. The fish isn't a fighter but it's strong and full of guile. Yes, they've heard of Izaak Walton. Did I know he stayed here at the Peacock Inn? Once again I get the little jolt when we visit a place that I've read about: the manifest connection between imagined and perceived.

We tramp off upriver, leaving the anglers to their convivial sport. There is a perfect haze of bluebells in Lindop Wood, looking like low-lying wood smoke, and the weather is so lovely that we sit down and have our lunch on the riverbank opposite the huge palace of Chatsworth House. Started three

---

[1] *The Compleat Angler*, Izaak Walton (1653)

years after Izaak Walton's death, it has since then been considered one of the noblest residences in England. It has managed to make a living for its owners during a time when most great houses bankrupted theirs. Here I am attacked by a female duck whom I am taunting with an orange biscuit. Quite right, too.

We see a tufted duck here, and a pair of widgeon. Before setting out on this trip I wouldn't have recognised a widgeon if it fell on me, but on consulting our bird book I read that they belong to the 'dabbling' family. That means that this colourful duck feeds on the surface instead of diving for its food. We always laugh at the mallards as they up-end themselves to gobble up food on the river-bed. All we see is a comically waggling tail and a pair of waving webbed feet. They always bob up again as dry as when they went in.

Packing up our lunch we stroll on upriver to Calver Weir, a great dam of stonework which was built to hold the River Derwent back to drive the mill here. Now it contains a large area of ferny woodland which is the home to willow trees and alder, and on the ground there's another yellow flower of spring; yellow loosestrife. The name refers to the use of the herb for quelling truculent oxen. The smell is odious to the flies and gnats that torment cattle and so if it was wrapped round the shafts of carts it would drive the insects off, making the animals more tractable. Once again I'm struck by the many uses our ancestors found for the plants around them.

We're curious about the great crested newt which, it's hoped, is going to return here. We've all heard about planning decisions being settled in favour of these protected creatures, but neither of us has ever seen one. They look like miniature dragons about 6 inches (15cm) long, and go on hunting expeditions up to half a mile away from their home pond. If one is found in a pond earmarked for development there will be a

delay of a year while specially trained newt hunters capture
them and transfer them to new ponds. Meanwhile, developers
fume about conservation. We don't see any great crested newts,
nor any of the brook lampreys which are supposed to live here.

It's getting hilly up ahead, the first sign of serious heights
since leaving the sea at Christchurch in Dorset. We arrive at
the Sir William Hotel in Grindleford. We're not sure why he
was named after a hotel but it seems a good place to wait for
our friend Mark Vallance, who is giving us a lift. We're now in
the Peak District National Park and Mark was a ranger here
before starting a company making mountaineering hardware.
He tells us over a pint how he started working on the first
youth opportunity programmes, training youngsters how to
build drystone walls. For many of them it was the first contact
with the English countryside. For him as a ranger the arrival
of spring was signalled by bluebells and wild garlic. When he
goes climbing in Cornwall in the spring it's well ahead of us
up here in the park.

The Peak District only has 38,000 residents but 10 million
visitors from the surrounding conurbations of Manchester,
Sheffield, Derby and Nottingham, so it's under considerable
pressure. The paths across the moors have had to be paved
with stone flags to cope with the erosion of so many feet.
Mark suggests that we don't take the Pennine Way all the way
to Scotland if we want to see spring, it's high bog most of the
way and we'll see more trees and wildlife in the valleys. He
loans us another one of his inventions, a British mountain map
of the Peak District made of polythene which is impervious to
rain. His party trick is to scrunch it up, stuff it into a bucket of
water and then pull it out. A child is then invited to stand in
the centre of the map, which is then lifted into the air by four
men. These maps can be used as emergency bivouacs, sails and

even for navigation. Ordinary paper maps turn to papier mâché in the first rainstorm.

Having said that, for those who want to navigate their way through the English spring countryside the Ordnance Survey Explorer maps are the *sine qua non* of national mapping. I just wish they were made of polythene like Mark's. They chart the whole of Britain in 403 orange-bound beauties and they show a world of fascinating detail at a scale of 1:25,000. We've been following them all the way and the scale is sufficient to show which corner of a field we should strike out for when navigating off footpaths, but they are still big enough for us to walk across in three days. And yet our government is plotting another attack on a precious institution: the sell-off of the Ordnance Survey. The maps only bring in 5 per cent of revenues, so you can be quite sure that the bean-counters will cut them out. Quite how a party in government that presents itself as Britain-loving can do this beggars belief. It makes me mad.

In Lewis Carroll's *Sylvie and Bruno Concluded* there is a map that had 'the scale of a mile to the mile'. Mein Herr, a voyager from a distant land, says there were difficulties with this map as farmers complained that it blocked out the sun, so 'we now use the country itself, as its own map, and I assure you it does nearly as well'.

We're not far from home now, where we're going to take a few days off. The next leg is from Grindleford to Edale, walking beside the River Derwent across large flat meadows lined with oaks. The hills are steadily rising on either side as we walk into the Peaks. When we set off I realise I've forgotten my acorns. I usually have a pocketful of these and every single mile through England so far I've looked for a suitable place for an oak, stopped, dug a hole and planted an acorn. We'll have to come back from home and fill in the gaps.

I feel bereft, and cross with myself. It's 14 May, so we've managed almost two months without missing one oak per mile.

A few fields upriver we see temporary sheep-shearing folds being erected. A group of up to eight men called a shearing gang will come in soon and work through the entire farmer's flock. It's another sign of spring in these parts. Each sheep will be glad to be rid of her hot, itchy fleece when summer comes and the farmer will be relieved of the worry of fly-strike – a nasty condition caused by flies laying eggs next to the sweaty skin under the thick fleece. When the maggots hatch out they burrow into the flesh and start eating the sheep alive, from the inside out.

Shearing is highly skilled and physically hard labour. The gangs are paid around £2 per fleece and a good shearer can get through over 200 sheep a day. You can tell any bad shearers by the number of blood-stained sheep that are standing around, bleating piteously. When they're finished in the UK the gangs fly out to Norway, the US, the Falklands and then New Zealand in each of those countries' spring and carry on working. They're doing a sort of spring-surfing; seeing the best part of the year in each of these countries, one by one. It's a hard-drinking, tough life but a fun way to get close to a lot of sheep.

The shearing costs more than the fleece is worth, which seems bizarre when you consider the wealth of England was once largely based on the sale of wool. The lord speaker even sits on a ceremonial woolsack in the House of Lords because King Edward III commanded that his Chancellor should sit on a bale of wool to symbolise the vital importance of wool to England's economy. In 1938 it was discovered that the woolsack was in fact stuffed with horsehair. The English have always been masters of hollow ceremony.

The wealth of Bronze Age Knossos, in Crete, was also sheep and wool related, and the largest group of their Linear B tablets are an archive of sheep breeding and shearing records. The Greek myth of the Golden Fleece appears in the story of Jason and the Argonauts. Jason steals the fleece, symbolising kingship, from a sacred oak defended by bulls and a dragon, and escapes with it on his ship, *Argo*. As with much Greek mythology the story appears to have its origins in real events. In the land now called Georgia, to the east of the Black Sea, there is an ancient method of trapping gold from streams. A fleece, still incorporating its sticky lanolin, would be stretched on a wooden frame and immersed in the gold-bearing water. Upstream the miners would agitate the gold-bearing strata and flecks of real gold would cover the fleece, which was then hung in a tree to dry in the hot sun. The appearance of gold in the fleece must have been striking to any unemployed myth-writers wandering by. Strabo, the Greek geographer from near the Black Sea, writing at the time of Christ, has this:

'It is said that in their country gold is carried down by the mountain torrents, and that the barbarians obtain it by means of perforated troughs and fleecy skins, and that this is the origin of the myth of the Golden Fleece.'

Tim Severin, the British explorer, described in his book *The Jason Voyage* (1984) how he had a replica of the *Argo* built and followed Jason's route as described in the epic poem *The Argonautica*. He and his crew managed to row through the Hellespont and sail to Georgia. His findings corroborate Strabo's description. I believe that Severin's method of re-enacting historical events gives vital insights into historical truths not granted to his chair-bound academic colleagues. It was his example that led me to test George Mallory's clothing on Mount Everest to see if he could have climbed the mountain in 1924, and I recommend Severin's inspirational books to anyone with a drop of historical curiosity in their veins.

A bit further up the Derwent we see a strange duck, and spend some time watching it, trying to figure out what it is. It has a green head, yellow eyes, a white body and brownish flanks. It's a most colourful bird. Gina's smartphone tells us: a shoveller duck. She's been taking pictures of the information boards as we go through conservation areas. The shoveller has a big wide beak, hence the name, we suppose. Here the River Noe meets the Derwent and passes through the memorably named village of Shatton. Apparently the name means 'farmstead in the nook of land between two streams' and I am quite sure it has been the source of childish hilarity for years.

We leave the valley of the Derwent and follow the River Noe, striking north up into the hills through Hope village. Apparently lots of people around here live in Hope. A few miles upstream from this confluence the Derwent is held back by a dam to form the Derwent Reservoir. This was used in the Second World War by the Dambuster Lancaster bomber crews to rehearse their raids on German dams which took place in spring 1943, and I can almost hear the roar of the great V12 Rolls-Royce Merlin engines hammering overhead at this very spot.

Today a different kind of merlin flies these Peak District skies: our smallest bird of prey, a dashing little hawk with broad wings and a long tail. Now, thankfully, there's only the distant fluttering sound of a peacetime helicopter in the hills, and we spot one carrying a white bulk bag angling up to the heights. I wonder what's going on up there.

The great mass of the Pennines looks quite intimidating from the valley bottom: we have to climb over those mountains on our way to Scotland. A bit further on we hear my favourite bird, the curlew, high up on the surrounding hills. Have we caught up with the spring? Our altitude is increasing and we're walking further north, so we might have done. The lambs seem smaller and bluebells are in full bloom here. The dandelions are back in flower, whereas further south we saw them seeding. Gina suggests that we're doing a kind of time-travel; the season is going backwards.

Earlier I had noticed a man sitting in a car reading an Alexander Kent novel in a lay-by. Our eyes had met and I nodded hello. His car now appears from behind us, slows and he rolls down the window. 'Are you doing this for fun, or would you like a lift?' We explain that we have to walk every step of the way through England with no cheating, so he nodded and drove on. Again I think about the kindness of strangers.

Walking into the Vale of Edale we pass Tony Favell's house. I happen to know that he used to be the chairman of the Peak Park Authority and can answer some questions. I wander into his back garden and find him weeding. I admire the trees he has dotted around and he tells me that his father advised him to put them in when he bought the house 40 years before. 'He said you might be busy now but you'll appreciate them when you retire.' He paused and gazed around at the garden. 'Well, he was right, wasn't he?' Tony's very taken by the idea of planting oaks all the way up through England.

In other countries national parks are state-owned but here

the land is usually private. Tony pointed out that this means there's continual conflict between individuals trying to get planning permission to build houses or factories and planners trying to keep things the way they are. How did he reconcile these pressures on the park? 'Well, there are lots of points of view: one, that the park should be a nature reserve and access by people rationed; two, it should primarily be for visitors; three, it should be for farmers; four, it should be for retired people to enjoy; five, it should be an open space for 4x4 car drivers to explore; or six, it should be preserved in aspic!' His job was to balance these interests, and with a 35 per cent reduction in funding recently he thinks the park is now under critical pressure.

I ask about the project up on the moors, and we watch a white helicopter just taking off from across the valley. What are they carrying up? Apparently the bags contain fertiliser and plant materials for the biggest moorland restoration project in Europe. This is bringing back active blanket bog that was damaged by 150 years of pollution from the surrounding cities of Greater Manchester and Sheffield. Much of the moorland vegetation has been lost, leaving depressing bare peat and blanket bog, which is an important habitat as it supports rare wildlife. It forms in areas of high rainfall and low evaporation and covers the whole area, hence the name. Another name is blanket mire, which I prefer. Birds such as the golden plover, dunlin, short-eared owl and merlin are all dependent on it. It also provides clean drinking water to the surrounding cities, mitigates flooding and stores land-based carbon.

Nearly all of the Peak District National Park is farmed, and Tony says it's the hill farmers that keep the park looking the way it does. Employment law wouldn't allow them to work

such long hours if they were conventional employees. Most of
it is marginal land, or 'less favoured' in the euphemism, and
the work is hard. They have to draw the single-payment
subsidy but that is far more efficient than trying to employ
people to keep the fields tidy. 'Do you think we have too many
sheep?' I ask, 'they kill all the young trees.' Well, no, he thinks
that farmers do understand the value of trees and flowers but
their sheep can't co-exist with nettles. If the Peak reverted to
the wild it would just become scrub.

'Do you think our countryside is in danger?' Not really. He
quotes a John Ruskin remark about the Peak District's Monsal
viaduct, which Ruskin considered an eyesore:

'There was a rocky valley between Buxton and Bakewell,
once upon a time, divine as the Vale of Tempe[1] . . . You
Enterprised a Railroad through the valley – you blasted its
rocks away, heaped thousands of tons of shale into its lovely
stream. The valley is gone, and the Gods with it; and now,
every fool in Buxton can be in Bakewell in half an hour, and
every fool in Bakewell at Buxton; which you think a lucrative
process of exchange – you Fools everywhere.'[2]

Well, we two fools walked across this fine piece of Victorian
architecture recently and think that it now complements its
surroundings. You can look over the parapet and admire
Ruskin's rocky valley. A preservation order was placed on this
viaduct in 1970, and recently the Monsal Trail, which is
routed across it, was voted the UK's favourite National Cycle
Network route under thirty miles. So couldn't HS2 end up like
that? Unlikely, as it will destroy far more countryside than this
viaduct. So who's right? This is the eternal paradox of the

[1] The Valle of Tempe is a gorge near Mount Olympus, stuffed full of sight-
seeing Greek gods.

[2] *Praeterita*, vol. 3 (1889)

English countryside: we continually change it and then wish for what we had before.

Tony waves us goodbye and says we should talk to a farmer and a ranger if we really want to learn about the spring in the Peak District.

It's now 15 May. Walking through Edale village we see a cherry tree in full blossom with swifts whizzing around it and I think of the Ted Hughes poem:

> Fifteenth of May. The swifts
> Materialize at the tip of a long scream
> Of needle. 'Look! They're back! Look!' And they're gone.[1]

---

[1] Ted Hughes, 'Swifts', *Collected Poems for Children*, Faber (2008)

CHAPTER EIGHT

The Pennine Way – the Garland King – a warrior goddess – a
sunken hero – golden plovers and curlews – mountain hares – stone
flagstones – foxgloves – the answer to a question – wise women –
dropsy and digitalis – my meeting with Ted Hughes – a real-life
Heathcliff – 'The Thought Fox' – a fox hunt

W e're trudging up Jacob's Ladder, the first steep
climb of the Pennine Way, the footpath along the
spine of England. The beautifully built stone
staircase winds up the hill towards the bleak humps of Kinder
Scout. It was built by Jacob Marshall, who farmed here at
Edale Head in the 1700s. He cut these steps into the unre-
lenting hillside to help him get up to his sheep. We sit down
on one of the peat hags to draw breath, and shiver slightly in
the chill breeze. It's sunny though, and there's a fine view
down valley over Edale.

Just over Mam Tor to our south, with a Bronze Age camp
on top, lies the village of Castleton. In a fortnight's time the
whole place celebrates the ceremony of the Garland King.
This is held on Oak Apple Day, 29 May, which commemo-
rates the escape of Charles II from the Roundhead Army
after the Battle of Worcester by hiding in an oak tree (oak
apples are a type of spherical growth on the trees caused by
wasps). This led to many English public houses being named
'The Royal Oak'.

The 'King' rides on horseback at the head of a throng of village people through the streets of Castleton. He is completely covered in a pyramid of spring flowers, fastened to a framework. It looks like a classic Jack in the Green motif, together with the hidden face and vaguely disturbing undertones. A vital part of the garland is the 'Queen', a removable finial at the top which for some reason local Christians used to object to as pagan. Young girls dressed in white and carrying small maypoles perform a Morris dance at each pausing place. After touring the village the King rides to the foot of the parish church tower, where oak branches have been draped over the pinnacles. The garland is removed and hoisted to the top of St Edmund's church tower, where it is placed on the central pinnacle. The villagers then dance around a maypole and dance the crossover dance back to the pub.

It is probable that this whole tradition is pre-Reformation and maybe even pre-Christian, despite the Stuart costumes and the inclusion of the parish church in the ceremony. What may have happened is that the Puritans banned May Day celebrations and that the villagers simply transferred the ancient custom to another date. Local historian Peter Harrison explained that in the 1970s the carved stone head of a goddess was discovered near the Russet Well in the village. I have seen this, and it depicts an enchantress with a winking eye: left eye open, right eye closed. She has thick lips and long hair. This image belonged to the tribe of Brigantes who lived on Mam Tor 3,000 years ago, and who worshipped her as a goddess of fertility: their 'queen'. Tacitus refers to the Brigantes, under a woman's leadership, almost defeating the Romans.

Harrison suggests[1] that it is perfectly feasible for a long tradition to survive in a small land-locked village in a remote district such as this. It would be passed down by word of mouth, and by young villagers performing each year with their older relatives. It would be a vital part of the year-round tradition, necessary to ensure the return of spring. And if the spring duly appeared every year after the ceremony, who could gainsay them?

We're still sitting at the top of Jacob's Ladder, eating lunch. On the way up here from Edale we saw a cast-iron green sign announcing ominously: 'The Official Start of the Pennine Way. Kirk Yetholm 268 miles/429 kms.' The sign has two acorn motifs flanking the text, but I'm fairly confident the only acorns up here will be the ones in my pocket. It seems an awfully long way still to go, and I'm wondering if we will actually make it to Scotland by 20 June.

In the village we walked past crocuses in a garden and buttercups in a field, the first we've seen. There were swallows nesting in the eaves at Lee Farm, too. Then crossing a field I noticed rooks waiting, watching a Derbyshire Gritstone sheep that was walking around awkwardly. They seemed to know that she was going into labour. I wondered what they were hoping for. The nutrient-rich after-birth? Or perhaps a still-born lamb? Or maybe both. It seemed very

---

[1] http://castletonhistoricalsociety.madewithjam.org/assets/b2/766d61c9404e4
62dd79d4a67859999/Garlands_Day_a_History.pdf

late for a lamb to be born, but we're high and cold up here.

After a picnic lunch in the sun I scout around for some-where to plant an oak, but there's absolutely nowhere on these bare moors safe from sheep. It seems pointless burying an acorn in the acid peat. It will just be nibbled.

Peat damaged by industrial pollution can have the same acidity as lemon juice and nothing can grow on it (not even lemon trees). In some areas up here there are just big slabs of bare peat with nothing growing on it, but we see the first signs of the restoration project Tony was talking about: rows of giant white shopping bags filled with lime. The original plant life up here had been killed off by the smoke of thousands of coal-burning factories in Manchester and Sheffield, so first the peat is being neutralised by the spreading of lime, then 200,000 fresh plants are being planted out by hand. These are heathers, grasses and cloudberries, which produce a gorgeous little orange berry later in the year, bilberries, crowberries and cotton grasses with their bobbles of tufty cotton. A clever way of propagating new sphagnum moss has been developed: they chop it into fragments and spray it onto the bog in a nutrient-rich gel from backpacks. As a result the moors are greener and less intimidating. The question is: which past landscape is being recreated? There were trees up here after the glaciers retreated, and if reintroduced they would soak up excessive rain and help prevent disastrous flooding in the valleys. Are householders subsidising the wrong conservation up here?

The first day on the Pennine Way from Edale is brutal and

in my opinion badly designed. Big walks like big climbs should start gently and build up to long days but here the neophyte walker is expected to stagger sixteen miles over bleak moors on day one. There is no accommodation en route either, so our hopeful walker has to do this hike with tent, food and bedding in a huge heavy pack.

The bard of the Lake District, the immortal Alfred Wainwright, clearly loathed this part of the Pennine Way. In his *Pennine Way Companion* he described his traverse of the national footpath and he doesn't pull any punches. You get the impression that he was walking it on sufferance. At times it seems he doesn't even want to start the day's walk: 'better a postponement than a post-mortem'. At one point hill-walking literature nearly lost its greatest hero when he got off route and his 16-stone bulk sank slowly into a bog near Black Hill. Only a chance encounter with a passing walker saved him. 'The worst part of the journey is behind you,' he intones grimly, 'from now on the Pennine Way can be enjoyed.'

We're enjoying it more than Wainwright; the path itself has now been much improved by paving whole sections across the worst bogs with stone flagstones. There are miles of these on the Pennine Way, and clearly some of them have had a previous life in the very factories that caused the sphagnum moss to die off. You can see rust stains and square recesses chiselled into the stone where machinery has been mounted. They've been carried up here by helicopter, too.

The altitude means that spring has gone into reverse. Temperature drops as much as 3 degrees Celsius every 300 metres of height, and so plants and animals have to adapt to survive. When the moorland warms up at the beginning of the year some birds fly up to these heights to spend the spring and summer then descend again to winter on the lowlands.

Meadow pipits, skylarks and snow bunting are all altitudinal migrants and don't have to travel far.

On the other hand the Arctic Tern flies up to 44,000 miles (70,811 kilometres) from the Antarctic to the Arctic and back again each year. Those that breed in England arrive in the Farne Islands in Northumberland in spring. I've seen these birds at sea and was surprised to learn that they're ferocious and will attack sailors, pecking heads with their red beaks. The Arctic Tern rests on land from time to time, but the record-holding migrating bird for one continuous flight is a female bar-tailed godwit which was recorded by her satellite tag flying from Alaska to New Zealand, a journey of 7,145 miles (11,500 kilometres) across the Pacific Ocean, in a single hop. Why didn't she run out of energy? I don't know.

But why migrate so far if all you want is to be a bit warmer? The shortest bird migration that we know of is that of the mountain quail in North America, which simply descends a few hundred metres from its mountaintop summer home to pass the winter in the valley below. It doesn't even bother to fly: it waddles downhill on foot. Somehow I feel that the mountain quail has the easier life. But maybe not: nature sets her boundaries at the limit of what each creature can endure.

A few miles further on we stop again, sit and look closely at the tiny plants and creatures amongst the heather. Although this tree-less khaki expanse looks devoid of life, if you stop and look you see a profusion of tiny plant life. We spot a

round-leaved sundew, which is insectivorous. Gina finds some
water boatmen in a puddle of bog water. And there are spiders
here, too, clinging to the plant stems. As we sit, wait and
watch the featureless bog seems to come alive.

A few miles further on we're treated to the surreal sight of
cars zooming across the bog, and so we plod up to the A57,
the Snake Pass road between Glossop and Sheffield. We've had
enough for one day and I stick my thumb out. Amazingly,
considering we are covered in mud and heather, a car that had
passed in one direction screeches to a halt, turns in the middle
of the road and picks us up. It turns out that the driver is
ex-army and had done a fair bit of yomping himself. He reckons
that the best age for long-distance walking is twenty-five. He
takes us into Sheffield where we catch the train back to Edale
and so back home.

I'm interested in how the British Army train their men to
walk long distances, so I speak to General Sir Peter de la
Billière, with whom I had collaborated on a project. He was
once the director of the SAS, commander of British Forces in
the Falkland Islands and later commander-in-chief of the
British Forces in the 1990 Gulf War. During the Falklands
War the British soldiers had yomped 26 miles (42 kilometres)
carrying 140-pound (63-kilo) packs. How did they do it? Well,
his answer is that you build up to it slowly by training, by
doing similar walks beforehand. You should walk fifty minutes,
then rest for ten, being careful not to get cold from being
sweaty. Walk up to five or six hours a day, no more than 20 to
25 miles. Slow drinking of water and salt will replace that lost
in sweat (we use rehydration sachets). New boots must be
broken in. He was interested in our base-camp system: in
Malaya in the fifties his SAS team used the same technique to
avoid carrying their entire camp on their backs during their

daily patrols. It's a shame Gina and I don't have re-supply from the air, as he did.

The next day we pick up the trail at exactly the same spot on Snake Pass and set off for Crowden. We resume our walk along the Pennine Way, crossing Doctor's Gate, the old Roman and packhorse way from the Roman fort at Brough near Hope to the Melandra fort at Glossop. This bleak plateau must have felt like the ends of the Earth to those legionaries. Dr John Talbot of Glossop paved part of the old Roman road, which is one version of why it's named the Doctor's Gate. Another tale has it that the Devil once pursued a Longdendale doctor on his horse up here, but failed to catch him. I would guess that, like Tam O'Shanter, a fair amount of spirits conjured up Old Nick, in his case maybe surgical spirits.

Today it feels like early summer across the rolling heath. We see a curlew nesting and it wheels around us with an alarm call, which seems to be the first part of its haunting cry without the long bubbling finish. It's a big bird and its long curving beak is clearly visible. We see a skylark on the nest, but avoid disturbing it. We hear a lost lamb across the moor, look for it but it falls silent, reunited with its mother. There are flying beetles, mating flies, water boatmen. There are mosses and water weeds in the river: so much life if you have the time to sit and watch. We're lying down eating lunch out of the wind beneath a bank of heather and see a red grouse flying past with its mad cackle. It doesn't seem to notice us. Remaining absolutely still we are visited by a wren. We can smell the warm peat and the heather in the gusts.

We see only two other parties of humans today: a group of youngsters carrying full packs and going our way, and a mother and daughter coming from the north. We swap notes on the paths ahead. The father is a bookseller, still at work, and they show polite interest in this book. As we descend towards the valley of Longdendale the lowland birds return: a wood pigeon clatters away and then a magpie cackles. Ahead of us lie a series of five reservoirs all the way down the Longdendale Valley. On Torside reservoir, right below us, we can see the first tentative dinghies of the season setting out from the sailing club.

We both feel strangely uneasy descending Torside Clough; Gina thought there was something watching us from the declivities below and I had a vague sense of impending doom. We only found out later that this is thought to be a haunted valley: lights have often been seen above the path we follow down to the reservoir, and the Glossop mountain rescue team has been called out time and time again. These spooklights are said to be the ghosts of the Roman legionaries, and many a time locals have been misled across Bleaklow by the will o' the wisp. I suspect that these may be the product of hostile surroundings and anxious minds, like Shackleton's Third Man and the many accounts of high-altitude climbers who encountered imaginary companions. We descend to Crowden and are picked up by a neighbour, Bryan McGee, a man who loves England and books of high adventure. Our walking trip must seem rather tame to him.

'Spring's arrived when you can step on ten daisies at once.' So says another neighbour, John Hearnshaw. I'm sitting outside in his garden with him and his wife Myra, looking over his land. They've farmed here in the Peak District National Park since

1953 and have seen a fair few springs in their time. They must be in their eighties now but they look twenty years younger. Myra is a keen gardener and they eat their own produce, and they seem remarkably healthy on it. John had a milk round for twenty-nine years as well as the farm.

The first signs of spring for them are snowdrops, then daffodils, crocuses, coltsfoot and aconites. On the pasture there would be violets and lesser celandines, buttercups and then the daisies. Every year they take part in our local Peak District spring festival of well-dressing, using flowers such as these. This is an ancient tradition of giving thanks for the purity of water drawn from springs or wells. A wooden frame is packed with clay mixed with water and salt. A design such as dancers around a maypole is traced onto the wet clay and then filled in with thousands of tiny flower petals, mosses, beans, seeds or cones. I saw John one year doing this work, delicately pressing each individual petal into the design. It needs more patience than I can muster.

This is marginal land, difficult to farm. John remembers how a farmer used to walk 100 mountain sheep down the main road from Snake Pass to his father's farm near Baslow in the 1930s to over-winter them. He collected them every spring and walked them back up to the hills. This would be unimaginable today with the weight of traffic. Winters were much harder then, with great drifts of snow along Curbar Edge in 1947 burying and suffocating all the sheep. John's twenty acres of hay used to be turned by hand – that's about eleven football pitches. Then it was all hand-loaded into a cart.

John specialised in sheep, but there are some cows around here. Another local farmer used to put his cows out onto the spring grass every 12 May, unless it was a Friday. Fridays were unlucky. The cows would kick their heels with delight all the way across the field, just like the dairy cows we saw down in the West Country a whole month earlier. That's how late spring is up in the hill country.

Myra's first jobs in spring are pruning and weeding. It's her favourite season because everything's new and there's summer to come. Both she and John think that the global warming debate is rather exaggerated: the winters are getting easier but they don't think the springs are much earlier up here in the Peak.

Just as I leave I ask Myra, a wise woman, if she knows why so many spring flowers are yellow. 'Oh yes.' She points to her evening primrose. 'The yellow stands out in the evening light, more than any other colour. It's so that the insects can find them in the twilight.'

'The first signs of spring that I see up here on Bleaklow are golden plovers and curlews.' The speaker is Gordon Miller. He's a tough, bearded character, looking like a sort of super-rambler. He's an Edale man who was a National Park ranger here for thirty-four years. And he's not just any ranger; he was president of the International Ranger Federation and travelled all over the world supporting his colleagues in Uganda and Congo, where they have to deal with gun-toting poachers and have to wear body armour.

I point out that there's no safe place for me to plant my oaks away from sheep and he nods: 'They are terrible on trees. But since we've started taking sheep off the moors we've noticed that trees are coming back, like birch. It's a severe climate, what you see is leaves waiting for a good spell and then they suddenly come out.' He doesn't think my oaks would do well up here, though. Best to drop down off the Pennine Way and follow the valley bottoms.

Gordon clearly loves his park but isn't optimistic: the Peak District small farms just aren't viable any more and there's no future for young people in the area. There are no jobs and they can't afford to buy a house here. It's just retired people who live here now. 'We need these parks. They're a beacon for all the English countryside. And after 911 happened in the States people poured into their national parks for their sanity.' What does he think the park will look like in a hundred years? He grunts. 'It'll be a zoo or a museum.'

As we part ways Gordon tells us to keep a lookout for mountain hares on the way to Black Hill, but I don't see a single one, which is a bit disappointing. Gina spots one still in its white coat but I just miss it.

In the spring mountain hares should be easy to spot because they still have their white winter colouring, which shows up against the light brown heather after the snow melts. The moult into their winter fur is initiated by the day length and then influenced by the temperature (which makes me wonder if we humans are still influenced by these things). Their ears are quite a bit shorter than those of their brown hare cousins, and their bodies are smaller and more compact.

Pliny, the Roman author of *Naturalis Historia*, wrote that the mountain hare turned white because it ate snow (a supposition which could have been tested if only he had a hare and some snow). Furthermore, he claimed that anyone who ate hare flesh would look fair, lovely and gracious for a whole week. Local hares would be looking nervous by now, especially if they read his next bit which claimed that eating various parts of hares would improve male potency, conceive boy-children, firm up young virgins' breasts and make older women fertile. By now I was beginning to suspect that Pliny the Elder ran a hare-farm, but in fact he was a rather important fleet commander, governor and naturalist who came to a sticky end at Pompeii, despite tying a pillow to his head to shelter from the rain of pumice stones from the eruption of Vesuvius.

Mountain hares are actually native to England, and bones have been discovered going back as far as 130,000 years. They probably died out around 6,000 years ago when scrub and woodland began to extend northwards in the post-Ice Age landscape, then they were reintroduced in the northern Peak District in the nineteenth century for hunting. These are the only mountain hares in England; there don't seem to be any in the Lake District. They live above 1600 feet (500 metres), feed on young heather and do well on these grouse moors where the heather is burnt in small areas to encourage new growth. This means there's a patchwork of burnt areas and new heather at different stages of development, which gives them a perfect habitat with fresh growth for eating and long heather to hide in. Which they are clearly doing today, as I keep looking for one. They like this kind of heather moor, mixed moor, wet heath, blanket bog, areas of mixed heath and grassland, and at several sites below the rocky moorland edges (great for human rock-climbing) they live on mat grass. Their numbers are increasing and there can be as many as 60 per square kilometre in heather and half that density on grassland, so I can't imagine where they're all hiding. It's frustrating, but at least Gina saw one. That's wildlife spotting for you.

From Black Hill, the scene of Alfred Wainwright's near-submergence, to Marsden we have a downhill walk. To our left front is Saddleworth Moor, where the child murderers Ian Brady and Myra Hindley buried their victims in the mid-sixties. We follow the course of Shiny Brook, where the still-undiscovered body of 12-year-old Keith Bennett is thought to lie. He was murdered on 16 June 1964. There still seems to be a chill hanging around this moor.

Unexpectedly we're hearing a woodpecker as we dip down towards Marsden. Green woodpeckers have been doing well in England in recent years, perhaps due to a warmer climate. One individual was photographed just a couple of months ago in a London park flying with a small weasel clinging to its back. Far from giving a little friend a lift it was trying to shake off a murderous attack. The image went viral and attracted enormous attention. Richard James, a wildlife advisor for the Royal Society for the Protection of Birds, said: 'These are an incredible set of images. Weasels are ferocious predators and often attack prey much larger than themselves. In this case the weasel appears to have targeted the woodpecker due to the fact the green woodpecker often spends a lot of time on the ground eating ants so is very susceptible to attack. If this had been a weaker bird I'm sure the attack would have been successful but this woodpecker was strong enough to take flight with the weasel on his back. It was pretty fortunate to escape.' The internet's meme-machine went into overdrive and a manipulated image of a miniature President Putin riding bare-chested on the weasel's back, riding on the woodpecker, promptly appeared.

I'm very impressed with the stone flagstones on this section of the Pennine Way. It makes the walk an absolute pleasure, especially when you see the bog alongside is so wet and deep. Some of the stones are so big they took six men to manoeuvre them into position, even though the helicopter dropped them in roughly the right place. The wide scars from the previous path across the bog are now fading, and ground-nesting birds are left in peace. Altogether it's another conservation project that's working well. I remove my hat to the National Trust volunteers who came up here to do this.

We see a common lizard basking in the spring sun, and there are some strange holes in the tussocks of grass with curious rodent-like squeaking emerging, possibly harvest mice? There's a tiny little brown bird which I think is the twite; a finch which breeds up here and over-winters on the east coast. It eats only seeds in the wild, and I make a mental note to put more seeds out in the bird-feeder at home. Feeding birds in winter can make a surprising difference to numbers; the blackcap has increased enormously in the last fifty years for this reason, choosing to over-winter here rather than in the Mediterranean (I know which one I would prefer). Their favourite delicacies are animal fats and sunflower hearts. Their fluting song has given rise to their other name: the northern nightingale.

A bit further down the path we see deer enclosed in a field, quite tame. Gina finds a beautifully made nest on the ground, cushioned with moss and white hair, and takes a photograph. My acorns are still hard to place, though; just by the stream there is a badly nibbled young tree which is probably going to die. There are tell-tale wisps of wool on the splintered branches: another victim of greedy sheep. There's a public art installation here: an empty picture frame on a tripod framing the landscape. The inscription reads: 'Many people look but only a few see', in that slightly irritating, revelatory tone that pervades the art world. The point might have been made better without the exhortation to 'make people think'. We drop down past Wessenden Head reservoir, and at the sight of the town ahead I break into a grateful shamble: it's been a long day walking over the hump of the South Pennines.

At first sight Marsden seems a grey place but actually it's an interesting little town that lies at the foot of the moors. There's a canal here, with a narrowboat-based theatre company, and the town has a strong theatrical tradition. Each year the town holds a spring festival, complete with costumes and dancing. Marsden's Cuckoo Day festival was on 25 April this year. The Green Man (spring) is seen to conquer Jack Frost (winter). It's named Cuckoo Day because of a local legend. In centuries gone by the people welcomed the cuckoo because it represented the arrival of spring and good weather. They tried to keep hold of these by building a tall tower around the cuckoo to imprison it. However, as the last course of stones was being laid the cuckoo flew away, taking with it the season of spring. And as the old-timers said of the tower: 'It were nob-but just one course too low.'

'The first sign of spring round here is snowdrops. We had them at Christmas this year, and people see them in flower and they want to buy them.' The speaker is Sheila Ranson at the Longdendale Nursery in Blackbrook. We're sitting in her huge greenhouse, surrounded by hardy perennials. 'We do sell snow-drops out of our woodland, but people should buy them in bud, or the previous autumn.' Sheila specialises in hardy plants that will survive the altitude and cold winters of the Peak District. Here she grows plants outside in big two-litre containers and they stay there all winter, so they'll survive a cold spring. 'I cannot understand why supermarkets insist on selling vulner-able plants in early April, it's criminal to see them being sold so early.' People plant them out, there's a cold snap and the tender plants promptly die. She thinks that people just don't know anything about gardening any more, despite TV programmes and the internet. They're unaware of the seasons and are just paving their gardens over for parking. Sheila's father loved gardening and she started potting up plants herself as a small child.

As I leave I try her on my idea of robot gardeners tending the beautiful gardens of the future, but she seems unconvinced. It's great wandering back through the nursery, looking at the young trees, herbs and perennials. I wish they were all in my garden.

It's nearly the end of May and it's blustery, and wet under-foot. I see Sheila's point about it being a cold spring up in these parts, despite all the sun we had when walking further south in April. We've been seeing lots of tree-planting around Scammonden Water; rank and file of white tubes. We have a look; each tube contains a tiny sapling, safe from the nibbling woolly parasites. There is a lovely walk through mature trees here, seeing green hairstreak butterflies in the bilberries. By standing on a hillside above a horse-chestnut tree I can see their remarkable flowers, the 'candles', from very close up. They look like a great big flowery ice cream. I used to think they were pink; in fact the flowers are white, each with a little red spot. They stand up in conical groups of twenty or so, called a panicle. Later on in autumn these trees will provide chestnuts for the English childhood game of conkers. There is sad news for horse-chestnut lovers, though: a combination of leaf miner moth and bleeding canker means that we may lose most of these beautiful trees in the next twenty years or so, the biggest change in our landscape since the loss of our elms to Dutch elm disease in the seventies.

There's an abandoned medieval village here, too. Then we dive into a surprising footway tunnel under the M62 motorway which is eerily quiet, considering there are so many tons of hurtling metal just overhead. The walls seem to be made of dripping wet corrugated iron, and I hope it doesn't rust away.

Just along the motorway here there is one of the more famous sights of the northern road system: the carriageways split apart and where you might expect to see a central reservation there is instead Stott Hall Farm. This stood here alone on the moors for two hundred years at 1100 feet, surrounded by miles of bleak bog, until the M62 arrived. Instead of demolishing it the two carriageways parted and were built on either side of the farm: a decision driven by ground stability rather than sentiment. Now the two streams of traffic part around the buildings and rejoin on the far side, giving surprised drivers a glimpse of a rural past.

We see horses and sheep shedding coats now. There are calves at Ripponden. And at last the foxgloves are coming out.

Foxgloves are some of the most exotic-looking English flowers of spring. Their tall stalks of purple flowers are welcome to bees and their name refers to the belief that foxes would slip the soft, glove-like flowers onto their paws before raiding a hen-house. The leaves contain digitalis, a drug which is used to control atrial fibrillation, a rapid and erratic beating of the heart. This caused what was called in the eighteenth century 'dropsy', a terrible condition in which the patients' bodies swelled up, their lungs filled and they drowned in their own fluids. The only cure was a potion brewed up by the folk-healers of England which contained an extract of the leaves of the foxglove, *Digitalis purpurea*. The dean of an Oxford college afflicted with dropsy went to a Mother Hutton from Shropshire, whose tea made from the foxglove alleviated his symptoms. An open-minded young doctor, William Withering, saw the beneficial effects of the potion, and decided to investigate. His paper: 'An Account of the Foxglove and Some of Its Medical Uses', ensured his fame, but not that of Mother Hutton. The active chemical which regulated the heartbeat was identified and named digoxin.

Another name for the foxglove was 'dead man's bells', because if an overdose is administered it can stop the heart. Digitalis kept my father alive for a while. Here is his spring poem to the foxglove:

> On climbing the shoulder he came to a gully
> Gashed by brown water from a high loch
> Where in the long shade let fall by the hill
> The foxgloves amongst hints of bog myrtle and honey
> Swayed like wands fastened in the bleak rock
> Clustered with the fiery wings of moths.

Finding them unbroken there despite gales,
The slash of rain and the raw kisses of the frost-
He idled amongst them, just aware
They had something to tell
If he could hear.

Next month, smothering,
With the main red pulse
Awry in the core of him,
He was brought
A smooth white pill.[1]

We're on the towpath of the Rochdale Canal, built in 1799 just as poor Dr William Withering was dying of self-diagnosed TB, not dropsy. We're on the way to Hebden Bridge and we've caught up with the spring again after our high-altitude bog crossing. The wild garlic is in flower once more and there are smaller ducklings than on the rivers further south. We see a turtle in the canal, or maybe it's a terrapin, which are native to Florida, so you would think that West Yorkshire would be a bit chilly for them. There was a craze for these snapping, biting smelly reptiles as pets after the popularity of the Teenage Mutant Ninja Turtles, but many were released into the wild after they grew too big for domestic fish tanks. Conservationists say this is a Bad Thing and should be stopped. Yes, Dudes and Dudettes, major-league butt-kicking is back in town.

---

[1] Michael Hoyland, *The Bright Way In*, Free Man's Press (1984)

We meet a hippie lady on a narrowboat live-aboard in Hebden Bridge. It's been a cold spring, she says, and she's had to buy extra coal for her stove. She likes the narrowboat life and enjoys seeing people's gardens from the canal. She recently saw four male ducks kill a single male competitor. I ask her what she knows about the spring, 'Never cast a clout till May be out,' she says, 'it's the last day of May tomorrow.'

On the face of it this old saying means 'don't take off any winter clothes before the end of May', but it could also mean 'the may', another name for hawthorn blossom. It's ambiguous, as indeed Shakespeare seems when he wrote this in Sonnet 18, his ode to immortality through verse:

> Shall I compare thee to a summer's day?
> Thou art more lovely and more temperate:
> Rough winds do shake the darling buds of May,
> And summer's lease hath all too short a date.[1]

Are the darling buds belonging to the month of May, which is in spring, or is it a reference to the hawthorn? Experts seem to incline to the first meaning in both cases.

We're now at Mytholmroyd, the birthplace of Ted Hughes, the English nature poet who was rated by *The Times* as fourth on their list of the 50 greatest British writers since 1945 (Larkin,

---

[1] William Shakespeare, Sonnet 18

Orwell and Golding were at the top of the list). He grew up hunting and fishing and acting as a retriever for his game-keeper brother who shot rats, magpies and (unbelievably) owls and curlews. He was another child immersed in English nature who then became a writer. I met Ted Hughes after a university reading in the seventies and was deeply impressed by him. Being a soft Midlander I was struck by his terse Northern vowels and his delicate verse. His tall, dark, brooding appearance brought Heathcliff to mind. Like him, Hughes looked to me like a wounded beast.

What I didn't know then was that his first wife, the talented poet Sylvia Plath, had gassed herself as he slept in his lover's arms. A depressive genius, her unhappy life fluttered against the bell jar of their marriage and spiralled down to a Greek tragedy. Hughes's later partner, Assia Wevill, chose the same method of suicide. Making a point was easier then: household gas contained lethal carbon monoxide. Some feminists loathe Ted Hughes, blaming him for both deaths, and someone defaced Sylvia Plath's gravestone near Hebden Bridge, removing her husband's name.

Ted Hughes read out his first poem, 'The Thought Fox', a poem about writing a poem:

> Cold, delicately as the dark snow,
> A fox's nose touches twig, leaf;
> Two eyes serve a movement, that now
> And again now, and now, and now[1]

---

[1] Ted Hughes, 'The Thought Fox', *The Hawk in the Rain* (1957)

'You, there, d'you see where the hinds went?' A large red man on a large sweating horse was pointing a riding crop at me. This was the early seventies in Rutland, when people still spoke like that. Even as a boy I didn't like being addressed in this fashion. The cascade of hysterical yelping, slavering hounds had actually burst through the village up towards the churchyard, so I mutely pointed the other way, up Clay Lane, where I knew a great grey-green, greasy Limpopo of mud awaited the unwary. More feverish clattering horses arrived, snorted and galloped off up Clay Lane, and I ran for cover.

I've had an uneasy relationship with fox-hunting ever since. Instinctively I loathe chasing small furry creatures and tearing them to bits, but I also know that galloping across country is about as exciting as life can get. And so it was with a sinking heart that I agreed to my ex-wife's suggestion that we 'ride out' with our local hunt. There would be no hunting, just a ride. We arrived one spring morning in a large pub car park filled with Range Rovers and horse-boxes. Various hearty types stood around quaffing sherry with huge brutes attached to them by thin leather straps. As Oscar Wilde remarked, these were indeed the unspeakable in pursuit of the inedible.

We had only ridden a short distance when the Master of the Hunt rode alongside to check me out: accent, riding ability, likely income. He was to be sorely disappointed on all counts. His horse was a prissy chestnut with an arched neck and a prancing manner caused by him riding with a short rein. The whole ensemble looked extremely showy: the red coat, the black velvet riding hat, the glossy boots.

Unfortunately I was riding the horse of my ex-wife, a psychopathic animal with a charming appearance. I knew something awful was about to happen when her ears went flat and her mad eye rolled back to take in the apparition jigging beside us. Without warning she let fly an almighty kick with both back hooves: a double-barrel. The chestnut grunted, staggered and nearly fell. The Master desperately clasped his hat to his head and gave me a murderous glare. The pair of them limped off and thankfully I was never invited to a fox hunt again.

Every spring, on the third weekend of April, the annual Mytholmroyd World Dock Pudding Championships are held here in the Calder Valley. Just now we're walking right past the community centre where it all happens. The main ingredient of dock pudding is the leaves of bistort, or gentle dock, mixed together with oatmeal, nettles and onions. It tastes of spinach or crispy seaweed and is sliced and fried with bacon.

There is a serious reason for eating this weedy stuff: in previous centuries after a long winter subsisting on preserved and salty foods the populace were desperate for green vegetables as a source of vitamins. The dock leaves were among the first to appear and so they were prepared in this delicious dish. They are boiled with oatmeal and onions then strained, left to set, cut into slices and fried. The dock is *Polygonum bistorta*, a purple-flowered plant, not the common cow dock leaves that we use to rub on nettle stings. In the Lake District the similar Easterledge pudding contains tasty young nettle-tops.

In the Second World War the German propagandist Lord Haw-Haw gloated that food rationing was so severe in the United Kingdom that in Yorkshire the population was reduced to eating grass. Haw-Haw's real name was William Joyce, an unpleasant anti-Semite and a member of the British Union of Fascists under Oswald Mosley. Although born in America, he and his family had returned to Ireland and he had applied for a British passport. He harboured ambitions to become Viceroy of India under a Mosley government. Escaping to Berlin at the outbreak of war, his broadcasts began with '*Germany calling. Germany calling. Germany calling.*' He struck fear into his listeners' hearts, seeming to know everything that was going on in the United Kingdom (including the eating of dock pudding). After his capture his post-war conviction for high treason was contentious as he was born an American citizen (high treason is criminal disloyalty to one's government). Joyce had few friends in court and despite an appeal to the House of Lords he was found guilty and sentenced to death. He met his nemesis in the shape of executioner Albert Pierrepoint. Drowning in dock pudding would have been too good for him, you see.

CHAPTER NINE

The real Wuthering Heights – Brontës or Brontés? – the Yorkshire
Dales – an Ole Timer – Himalayan balsam – camping – Malham
Cove and abseiling over the edge to see cliff-dwelling plants – the
Settle to Carlisle Way – a 100-mph unicycle – faithful dogs – rabbits
– a swarm of bees – a Gypsy caravan – Rose, the Gypsy princess – an
ice-cream van guitar hero

It's the last day of May and we have only twenty-one days
left to get to Scotland before the end of spring. We walk
up the A6033, a horrible, dangerous road with no pavement out of Hebden Bridge, dodging motorbikes ridden by
lunatics. There's a whole stream of born-again bikers pouring
past us towards the racing B-roads of Ribblesdale. I just hope
they're carrying their kidney donor cards. We turn off, to our
relief, onto Haworth Old Road. And then we find Wuthering
Heights.

It is mid-winter at Thrushcross Grange and 18-year-old
Catherine is delirious and dying, locked in her bedroom.
Miserably married to the vapid Linton, she still loves her
childhood sweetheart, the saturnine Heathcliff who has
returned to the area, now as rich as he was once poor.
Flinging open the window she gazes up at the far hills and
imagines she can see her childhood home, Wuthering Heights:
'Look!' she cries eagerly, 'that's my room with the candle in it,
and the trees swaying before it; and the other candle is in

Joseph's garret. Joseph sits up late, doesn't he? He's waiting till I come home that he may lock the gate. Well, he'll wait a while yet. It's a rough journey, and a sad heart to travel it; and we must pass by Gimmerton Kirk to go that journey! We've braved its ghosts often together, and dared each other to stand among the graves and ask them to come. But, Heathcliff, if I dare you now, will you venture? If you do, I'll keep you. I'll not lie there by myself: they may bury me twelve feet deep, and throw the church down over me, but I won't rest till you are with me. I never will!'

She knows the end is coming soon: '. . . they can't keep me from my narrow home out yonder: my resting-place, where I'm bound before spring is over! There it is: not among the Lintons, mind, under the chapel-roof, but in the open air, with a head-stone; and you may please yourself whether you go to them or come to me!' She dies on 20 March, the first day of spring, giving birth to her daughter Cathy as she does.

At times the novel treads dangerously close to the edge of melodrama, but what keeps it rooted in reality is the solid Yorkshire landscape, its people and their houses. The layers of unreliable narrators and the complex themes of identity and longing make it eternally puzzling. Are Heathcliff and Catherine actually half-brother and sister? Is their love therefore unnatural but compulsive? She is identified with nature and the seasons; she dies at the end of winter, giving birth to Cathy on the first day of spring. Is Catherine's rejection of the moors and marriage to Linton therefore symbolic of our own failed relationship with nature? Those of us who love *Wuthering Heights* find the story unutterably tragic and moving.

The Brontë sisters had to disguise their gender, like fellow writers George Eliot and Harper Lee: 'We had the vague impression that authoresses are likely to be looked on with prejudice', so she and her sisters became Currer, Acton and Ellis Bell: Charlotte, Anne and Emily. The first reviews for *Wuthering Heights* were what publishers called 'mixed': here's the *Graham's Lady's Magazine*: 'How a human being could have attempted such a book as the present without committing suicide before he had finished a dozen chapters, is a mystery. It is a compound of vulgar depravity and unnatural horrors . . .' It's the kind of review you dream of.

Most of us now agree that the woman who wrote it was a rare genius, it was her only novel and it has become a classic of English literature. Emily Brontë died the year after it was published, aged just 30, and grown very thin with tuberculosis. In a strange echo of Catherine's own 'narrow home' (the grave), the author's own coffin was only 16 inches wide. The joiner said he'd never made a narrower one for an adult.

As a boy I graduated to romantic fiction at the age of fifteen, read *Wuthering Heights* and promptly fell head over heels in love with the book's author. It wasn't a match made in heaven: she was a dead 154-year-old Yorkshire woman with tuberculosis and strong opinions, and I was a shy bookish boy under the age of consent. It was more *Harold and Maude* than *Romeo and Juliet*. Later, at university, I studied the book again and made my first pilgrimage to Haworth, trying to get In Touch with Emily. After that I worked on BBC Radio 4, the local radio station for the Home Counties, and one thing they did and still do bugs me even now: they seem unable to pronounce Brontë correctly. The *Woman's Hour* programme is the worst offender; they incessantly pronounce Brontë to rhyme with pâté: Brahn-TAY. It's not! It's Brahn-tee to rhyme with Monty. The father, Reverend Patrick Brunty, was from a poor Irish background and wanted to disguise his humble origins. So he added the diaeresis to the e: ë, not é.

'Far from indicating foreignness,' said Ralph H. Emerson, an authority on the pronunciation of literary names, 'the dots on the final e are simply a quaint device for showing that the letter is to be said as a separate syllable . . . They alert the reader that *Bronte* ends in *tea* instead of being plain *Bront*.'[1] Emerson further explained that Bront-tee is still used in Haworth. And the rest of Yorkshire, Gina points out.

Does it really matter? I think so. If we are to get as close to the writers as we can, we have to try to see their world through their eyes, and hear their name with their ears. Let's find out how they spoke, find out where they walked, see what they saw. Writing is, as we have seen, thought transference and time travel. You might call it getting In Touch.

A couple of years ago Gina and I walked up to Top Withens, the house that the tourist board claim is the inspiration for Wuthering Heights, but it's nothing like the house described in the book. Indeed, a plaque on the wall stated it clearly: 'This farmhouse has been associated with "Wuthering Heights", the Earnshaw home in Emily Brontë's novel. The buildings, even when complete, bore no resemblance to the house she described, but the situation may have been in her mind when she wrote of the moorland setting of the Heights.'

Instead, today as we walked on Haworth Old Road we suddenly stopped and gripped each other's arm. 'Look! That's it!' For, up on the hill, there stood a long, low gaunt ruin of a house. We climbed up to it. This was far more like it. Here was a grander entrance, and here surely was Cathy's window, where her ghost endlessly calls to the terrified Lockwood: *'I'm*

---

[1] Ralph H. Emerson, *English Language Notes* (1996)

come home: I'd lost my way on the moor!' Down there, surely,
Emily had walked to Haworth to meet her brother Branwell
on the old road, not the new turnpike. She must have seen this
house. And yet, and yet . . . our attempts to find the 'real' location of fictional places are doomed as they only ever existed in
the author's imagination. All we can do is try to experience
what the writer experienced.

On the way down to Haworth we are mobbed by a lapwing.
Perhaps its nest is nearby. Haworth proves to be another one
of those literary towns where everyone is desperately seeking a
connection to the fame of the famous residents. There seems to
be a weariness amongst the café staff, a weariness of tourists.
It's Brontë-land everywhere you look. Brontë tea towels,
Brontë biscuits, Brontë babble.

That evening we check into a hotel and the receptionist is
clearly confused. I can see the thought-bubble forming above
her head: *Mmmm, age-difference couple. Father and daughter? Or
partners? Twin bed or double?* We've had this problem before.
Our boat, *Curlew,* was once chugging down a USA waterway in
the Deep South when we spotted a wooden fuelling station.
There was a dockside to tie up to and a single diesel pump.
There was also an Ole Timer sitting in a rocking chair,
smoking a pipe and watching the world go by. We tied up with
amazing efficiency and Gina leapt ashore to pick up the diesel
hose and dragged it aboard for me to start refuelling. Silence
fell, except for the lapping of water and the buzz of insects in
the afternoon sun. All the while Ole Timer was observing
every move, puffing his pipe, oblivious to the heavy fumes of
diesel. We fuelled up, paid inside the building, cast off the lines
and motored off the dock. As we left he removed his pipe and
sang out in a cracked voice: 'Sure is good ter see father and
daughter gitting on so good!' At this Gina grabbed my hair

and gave me a deep-tongue snogging. The last we saw of Ole Timer was a pair of boot-soles in the air and a cloud of pipe-smoke. I can't imagine why he should be surprised. Surely they're used to that kind of thing around there?

The weather on 1 June is vile: lashing rain and high winds, so we take the day off. Starting late the next day we miss the rain. We walk from Brontë-land to Cononley and get a bit battered. The wind was huge, breaking branches off the trees and flinging birds around the sky. The biggest gusts must have been around 60 mph. We notice that the bluebells are just finishing.

By way of contrast the next day we're having a lovely river walk along the Aire Valley towards Gargrave. It feels like summer, with deep grass, clover, buttercups and many curlews. We meet a farmer rather unexpectedly, and kindly, lawn-mowing the footpath. He tells us that the first sign of spring for him is hearing the lane next to his house humming with bees on the blackthorn. However, we soon have to leave our pleasant footpath as there is a Private Anglers sign. I get very irritated by these: what possible harm can a couple of walkers cause to a fishing beat? I will now, no doubt, be inundated by letters explaining exactly what harm we cause, written in green ink and capitals. We see another hare, walk along a disused railway for a short way and then an abandoned foot-path (or one not used very often). Then we wade through a field of thick grass, ready for the first mow, and it is hard going, like breaking trail in deep snow. I suspect I am slightly

lost, and get grumpy with Gina when she expresses some
reservations about my map-reading. Whenever she starts
feeling like this I see her smartphone come out and she'll say
something like 'Er, the next village is actually behind us and
we're walking south.'

Just along here we identify a tansy beetle, a rare leaf beetle,
with an amazing greenish metallic sheen. It looks like an
animated emerald. The tansy beetle only seems to live on the
tansy plant (which is about as short-sighted as a panda only
eating bamboo) and it's usually only found within 30 miles or
so of York. I'm glad to say that, this being England, there is a
group of people called the Tansy Beetle Action Group (T-Bag)
who are trying to save this little jewel of an insect. Himalayan
balsam is the culprit: it's forcing out the tansy plant.

This 6- to 10-foot (2- to 3-metre) high plant, *Impatiens glan-
dulifera*, with its pink orchid-like flowers is attractive but, like
von Siebold's Japanese knotweed, it's becoming a serious
problem in the English countryside. It was introduced in 1839
as a greenhouse plant and escaped out into gardens. Then the
worst happened: people liked it. In fact, they liked it so much
they started collecting seeds and spreading them all around
the country. A Mrs Norris of Camberley sowed seeds in her
local woods and sent them to Ireland. She also took them on
holiday with her to France and Spain. I'm sure they are now
very grateful. A Miss Welch took seeds from Sheffield in 1948
and sprinkled them alongside a river on the Isle of Wight.
Dozens of well-meaning people like this have spread this plant
all over the country, and it is now going to cost £300 million
to eradicate it: that's about as much as a brand new hospital.
Unfortunately, as with most introductions of alien species,
there are no natural competitors or parasites to control these
plants. Himalayan balsam has fruit pods which, when ready,

explode spectacularly, projecting around 800 seeds per plant, so they propagate incredibly fast. Because of this they have even been marketed to children as an exciting toy. So why not let nature take its course and allow the plants to take over the country? The problem is that they thrive in low-light conditions and take over riverbanks and wasteland in dense thickets, suffocating all other native plants. Then they die back completely in winter, leaving the riverbanks exposed to erosion.

So what to do? The first thing is to inform people that it is maybe not such a good idea to propagate alien species without first checking with someone who knows. The second is to find a natural enemy, and that's exactly what the people at the Centre for Agricultural Bioscience International (CABI) in Surrey have been doing. After eight years of work they have found and released a rust fungus which appears only to attack the dreaded Himalayan balsam. This is the first such deliberate release in Europe. So will this rust fungus totally eradicate this pestiferous weed? Over to Dr Robert Tanner, Senior Scientist at CABI: 'No, unlike herbicide it will not wipe it out, but make it a benign plant in the ecosystem, as it is in the Himalayas where it has all its natural enemies to control it. We want the fungus to do its work where you get balsam in large swathes along our river systems, where it's highly dense and abundant, and act a self-thinning agent.'

It will take quite some time for the fungus to spread and reduce the vigour of the species, he says. 'Over that time we hope to see the balsam reduce, especially where it dominates ecosystems, and see re-colonisation with native species. It won't disappear altogether, but will take its place among the nettles, willowherb and meadowsweet.' Which is no bad thing, as Himalayan balsam adds welcome colour to the riverbanks at a

dull time of year. Once again it strikes me that a little bit of
knowledge and a little bit of money can make huge improve-
ments in our English countryside, and make future
generations' springtime walks as wonderful as ours.

We've been seeing nettles all the way up through England,
and soon we'll see the tiny white flowers that appear on the
non-stinging variety. As with most native plants they have
many uses. The German army's uniforms were made from the
nettle's strong fibres when they ran out of cotton during the
First World War. Alcoholic nettle beer is a favourite in some
areas of England, and the young leaves make a very healthy
early spring vegetable, similar to spinach, as we saw with Dock
Pudding.

We've taken up camping as the weather is now warm enough.
The first site is Gina's dad's back lawn in Yorkshire. Equipped
with a kitchen and bathroom, this is the kind of camping that
suits us. There's a chauffeur service, too: we get a lift with
John and Gillian back from our furthest point each day. I'm
desperate to get to Settle, where we can use the famous
railway line to return to our starting point after every day's
walk. We only have two weeks left to get to Scotland and I'm
becoming anxious about it. Are we going to be finishers?

We've got back on the Pennine Way for a short stretch
north of Gargrave and we're walking along the lovely River
Aire on a fine sunny day. We see a pale brown hawk with a
fantail. Over a garden wall I spot a gardener at work and hail
him. His potatoes look particularly fine. They're Maris Peer, he

says, he planted them early but they got frost-nipped on 4 April. It was a cold spring this year. He's growing runner beans and all sorts of delicious vegetables. He recommended Town End farm shop at Airton, the next village, because there we could try Rhea's egg frittata. Clearly there are some serious foodies at large in North Yorkshire.

A few miles up the valley from where we are walking is Malham Cove, a spectacular limestone amphitheatre with a great overhanging cliff 260 feet high (80 metres). The Pennine Way ascends its west side by 400 steps. A couple of years ago we both worked on a BBC TV shoot here for *The Great British Countryside.*

Fiddling with the camera and without looking properly I stepped backwards over the edge of the cliff and suddenly the horizon tilted 90 degrees. I sank into my harness. This job involved having to abseil over the edge in a gut-churning walk backwards and down the whitish limestone cliff. I was filming Tim Emmett, a well-respected rock climber, who was climbing up the other way without any ropes at all. After about 30 feet down all of a sudden my feet shot forwards as I reached an overhang and I started spinning in mid-air.

Gibbering with terror, I still managed to notice that there were some rather interesting plants occupying the vertical landscape next to my ear. Later on I found out what they were: a little yellow star-like flower called biting stonecrop, and a white flower on a long stem called hairy rock cress. Somewhere two hundred feet below me on the steep scree were some critically endangered prickly sedge, one of only four tiny colonies in the British Isles, but as I was feeling quite endangered myself I didn't look too hard. Struggling back up the rope I noticed the strange transition that grasses and cliff-plants undergo in your mind as you move from the vertical landscape of the cliff to a steep slope, then to a flat ledge of safety: from things you would try to grab as you fell over to things you lie on gratefully. I was reminded of the plant-hunter Roland Cooper, who in 1942 was traversing a steep slope in Bhutan when he started to slide over the cliff. He grabbed the branch of a shrub as he went over and hung there in mid-air. As he waited for his companions to rescue him he studied the flowers on the branch and realised they were of a new species. Later they were pressed and described as *Buddleja cooperi*. This fascinating man called his serendipity 'Just plant-hunter's luck.'

We are having the worst walk yet over the moors from Kirkby Malham to Settle. This road is very exposed and the high winds are nearly blowing Gina over, again and again. She's actually running out of energy and I have to physically tow her along by the hand. I'm getting slightly worried that we won't make it to Settle tonight: there's miles to go. None of the cars whizzing past are aware of her exhaustion, nor are they aware of the unpleasant conditions. It's strange to see people sitting in their shirt-sleeves speeding by in warm glass boxes as we physically fight the battering wind. Luckily I remember that at the bottom of my rucksack there are a couple of chocolate bars for this very eventuality and I dig them out. She devours them and we manage to push on to Settle. Here we find an excellent campsite and collapse gratefully into our sleeping bags.

We've been looking forward to getting to the Settle to Carlisle Way. This is a 97-mile (156-km) walking route which follows the world-famous railway, and this means that you can stay in the same place every night if you wish, just by hopping on the train for a return ride to your tent, hostel or bed-and-breakfast accommodation. The railway was the last mainline in England to be constructed largely by hand, and it took 6,000 workers seven years to build it. It passes through some of the most beautiful scenery in England, over twenty-four viaducts and through fourteen tunnels. It survived two attempts to close it, one in the 1960s and one in the 1980s.

Unlike most 100-mile walks you don't need a bag-carrying service or any complicated pick-up logistics. It's one of England's great expeditions, and you can do as little or as much as you like. For us, getting to Carlisle would mean that we would be within striking distance of our goal, the Scottish border.

Spring has certainly sprung in our campsite in Settle, and after the tough day yesterday we enjoy a long shower then breakfast in the sunshine before setting off over a fence and through a hedge. Gina regards no walk with me to be complete unless we commit some act of trespass, get lost or covered in mud, and all three conditions were met within one hundred yards of the campsite. Soon, though, we're following the River Ribble up Ribblesdale on a proper footpath, and passing through Stainforth Woodland, a new plantation of no less than 5,631 native trees: oak, alder, rowan, willow and our old hedging favourites hawthorn, blackthorn and hazel. These are all providing a wildlife corridor for kingfishers, dippers and otters. We hope we spot an otter as we haven't seen one yet, but we do see a pair of dippers.

It's a lovely day of sunshine and blue skies and we are having a brilliant walk, meeting the Pennine Way again at a corner of a hillside track under the peak of Pen-y-ghent. This

is one of Yorkshire's Three Peaks, the others being
Ingleborough and Whernside, and all three being visible today.
Unfortunately there are more anglers' 'Private' signs stopping
walkers from using the safe riverside route, so we have to walk
on the road. For a while we try to walk on the B6479, but
there is a terrifying stream of motorbikes today, some of them
doing wheelies at insane speeds. Seeing a man coming towards
you balanced on a 100-mph unicycle with no steering is somewhat unnerving.

Once again we have to come off route and go the long way
round. It strikes me that there's a lot of recreational pressure
on this valley and just for safety's sake there should be some
thought about controlling motorcycle speeds and re-routing
walkers along footpaths. We found out later that a motorcyclist
had been killed in a collision with a road sign just four days
before, a mile away from where we had been walking. Poor
guy. Surely it would be better to use these fabulous machines
on a dedicated racetrack where everyone's going the same
way?

Somehow we manage over sixteen miles, mostly uphill, in
this one day to the famous Ribblehead Viaduct, a construction
I have heard a lot about and wanted to see. Frankly I was
rather underwhelmed. It has twenty-four arches and is 440
yards long (400 metres), but in my native Rutland the
Harringworth Viaduct is nearly three times longer and has
eighty-two arches. And near my Peak District home there is
the magnificent double bifurcating viaduct at Chapel Milton,
which changes its mind halfway across and splits in two. These
were all completed within ten years of each other, in the 1860s
to 1870s. Then I get the point: Ribblehead has better public
relations. There was a vigorous campaign to keep the Settle to
Carlisle line open, and this viaduct became the campaign

symbol. And good for them, too, because they succeeded. This is a wonderful line built through fantastic scenery. There was a camp for 2,000 of the navvies right here, at Batty Green. It was so dissolute that the Midland Railway Company paid for scripture readers to tour the camp. Eighty workers died here in a smallpox epidemic, and 200 died in the course of building the 74 miles of track, a death toll I hope no modern engineer would tolerate. This place feels haunted by these men. Old George Horner, who was former signalman at the remote Blea Moor box, once followed a man beside the tracks who didn't leave a single footprint in fresh snow. All in all, road and railway seem to have exacted an appalling death toll in this valley.

We jump onto a train heading back south to Settle, sit with our backs to the engine and review the walk we have just done, spooling backwards. It's an odd, time-reversing experience.

The next day I manage to get us seriously off-route. We return by rail to Ribblehead, and we set off northwards. We are lucky enough to see a steam engine on a special run crossing the Ribblehead Viaduct. However, we are about to get unlucky. The railway dives into Blea Moor Tunnel and I try to follow its route 500 feet underneath us. In my defence we are using another, inferior map which just shows the Settle to Carlisle Way and not one of the excellent Ordnance Survey explorer maps. So I get lost and we go too far west, going by accident along Craven Way, an old packhorse route. Never mind, we end up in paradise: Dentdale. This is a valley much lower than Blea Moor and spring is in full flood here; birds are singing, lambs are bounding and the River Dee glinting in the sunshine. Every now and then in England you chance upon a beautiful little corner of the country and just can't quite believe how lovely it is. There seems to be a vigorous community here, too, by the parish noticeboards.

One of the curious aspects of the Settle to Carlisle railway is that the stations seem to be nowhere near the villages they allegedly serve: Dent station must be a good 5 miles (8 kilometres) out of the village and up a steep hill at that. The reason is that the railway's surveyors hung on to all the altitude so painfully gained all the way from Settle, and were reluctant to let the tracks dive down again into the valley bottoms where the villages are. As a result Dent is the highest mainline station in England at 1,150 feet (350 metres), and there's an excellent snow hut and bunk barn attached should you want to use this point as a base camp to explore the surrounding countryside. We start planning a future weekend walking trip even before finishing this one: it's a compulsion, you see.

At this point we are both suffering from Mountaineer's Foot; the inability to put one in front of the other. But we plod on another few weary miles over high moorland to Garsdale Station, where we shuffle gratefully onto the train taking us back to Settle. Much to our surprise we find a life-size bronze of a border collie dog sitting on our southbound platform. It turns out that this is Ruswarp, who belonged to one Graham Nuttall, who was one of the founding members of the group that eventually saved the Settle to Carlisle railway from closure. The petition was signed by 32,000 humans and one dog with his paw-print: Ruswarp (pronounced 'Russup'). Dog and owner disappeared on a walking trip in the Welsh mountains and Nuttall's body was found eleven weeks later next to a mountain stream. His dog was found nearby, very weak but he had presumably stayed by the body for all that time.

Ruswarp was 14 years old but he survived long enough to be present at his master's funeral.

In *The Road to Little Dribbling*[1] Bill Bryson recounts the story of the sheepdog, Tip, who stayed by the body of his master on Howden Moors for fifteen weeks, near where we walked up the Derwent Valley. Bryson claims that the owner was lying on the dog's lead, but this may not be entirely true. Still, Tip got a bigger monument than the one dedicated to the Dambuster bomber crews who were also belting around over the moors.

This sad story invites comparison with Greyfriars Bobby, the Skye terrier who watched over his master's Edinburgh grave for fourteen years in the nineteenth century. There is a memorial to this faithful creature inscribed 'Greyfriars Bobby – Died 14 January 1872 – Aged 16 years – Let his loyalty and devotion be a lesson to us all.' Unfortunately the story is almost certainly untrue. Jan Bondeson's *Greyfriars Bobby: The Most Faithful Dog in the World*[2] reveals that there were many dogs around at the time who hung around Victorian grave-yards and who became used to being fed with scraps. After the story appeared in *The Scotsman* the local community benefited from increased trade and Bondeson believes that the original Bobby died and was replaced by another, which explains his extraordinary longevity. Dogs are good at reading human facial expressions and tonal variations, and they are wonderful companions, but their loyalty is on their own terms. And that means sausages. And then walkies.

[1] Bill Bryson, *The Road to Little Dribbling*, Doubleday (2015)

[2] Jan Bondeson, *Greyfriars Bobby: The Most Faithful Dog in the World*, Amberley (2011)

We take a little detour the next morning. On my sound recorder app I record that 'it's 10 June, the weather is stunning: it's sunny and the sky is blue'. I sound very happy. Garsdale is one of the wildest stops on the Settle to Carlisle line. The area has been designated as a red squirrel sanctuary, so we're on the lookout. There are several items of good news to report here, depending on how you feel about grey squirrels. One is that the greys are good at planting trees. The other is that a natural predator is on the rise which will reduce their numbers. Another is that after an 18-year cull Anglesey has just managed to get rid of all its greys, leaving 700 red squirrels, so culls do work if they are carefully co-ordinated.

Grey squirrels are squeezing out our native reds and they are another one of those pesky Victorian introductions. They are native to North America and were first released in the UK in 1876 in Henbury Park, Cheshire. Like most exotic introductions they arrived without the checks and balances of their home environment and so they have undergone a population explosion. They cause a great deal of damage to trees by stripping bark and the Forestry Commission reckons they cost the UK £6 to £10 million a year.

Grey squirrels don't actually attack and kill their red cousins; they are just more effective at competing for food. They also spread the squirrel pox virus, a disease they rarely die from but which is fatal to reds. There is some evidence that the native red was in decline anyway due to habitat loss caused by humans, and disease. They had nearly died out in Scotland by the 1800s and so in 1844 Lady Lovat of Beaufort Estate, near Beauly, succeeded in persuading the government to reintroduce the red squirrels to the Highlands. They were seen as a rather cute adornment to large country estates. It was all part of the Victorian obsession with all things tartan: Queen Victoria had just made her first visit to the Highlands with Prince Albert. So successful was this policy that by the 1900s the red squirrels had spread to the stands of conifers around the estates and were becoming a pest. So the cute-sounding Highland Squirrel Club was formed in 1903, composed of fifty-six estates, and by 1946 their gamekeepers and workers had killed 102,900 squirrels and paid out over £1,500 in bounties (this compares with only 140,000 reds left in the whole of the UK today, of which 85 per cent are in Scotland). The tails were sent to the secretary as proof of kills, a box of 523 arriving one day by train. Ironically, Lady Lovat's Beaufort Estate recorded the most red kills – a total of 22,766. And now these very same estates provide a haven for most of the red squirrels in the UK.

There are a number of interesting conclusions to be drawn from this story. Introductions are nearly always a really bad idea. Next, the law of unintended consequences nearly always applies: if you reintroduce, then exterminate, then promote a species all kinds of knock-on effects happen. But encouragingly, as we've seen again and again, if there is a reservoir population of species they can bounce back surprisingly quickly if given a chance.

So now there are around sixty-six greys to each remaining red here in England. What can we do? Feeding the reds with sunflower seeds can increase populations by up to 50 per cent, but any greys around would also benefit. However, there is a natural predator of squirrels which would prefer a fat grey squirrel lunch to a skinny red one: the pine marten. This attractive little predator is native to England and is a mustelid: it's related to otters, badgers and weasels. It looks like a little chocolate-brown cat, but it's vicious enough to take on and kill a grey squirrel, which spends a risky amount of the time foraging on the ground. Red squirrels, on the other hand, spend more time aloft in trees and are half the weight of a grey. That means they can retreat to the ends of thin branches where a pine marten cannot reach them. The pine marten is staging a comeback and there are plenty of grey squirrels for them to eat.

Grey squirrels are scatter-hoarders and will bury thousands of caches of food during a season. Acorns are a favourite food, unfortunately, but forgetful squirrels are responsible for planting many trees. According to American researchers working in the Midwest, seven times more walnuts gathered by grey squirrels germinate than walnuts collected by red squirrels, who gather their nuts in piles above ground where they dry out. So grey squirrels might actually be better for some of our woodland than we think. They practise a number of deceptions when burying their nuts, such as pretending to bury food when they think they're being observed, even to the extent of miming the action of placing the food in the cache and covering up the hole after digging. This suggests that they, like other animals, can put themselves in other creatures' minds and attempt to deceive them. Is it possible that animals are sentient like us? The consequences of such a discovery could be far-reaching. Would we have to stop eating them?

Beatrix Potter's Squirrel Nutkin also lost his tail, in his case to Mr Brown Owl, who didn't care for his impertinence: 'Old

Brown carried Nutkin into his house, and held him up by the tail, intending to skin him; but Nutkin pulled so very hard that his tail broke in two, and he dashed up the staircase and escaped out of the attic window.'

As with most successful children's books there is a satisfying amount of horror and near-death trauma, together with a lesson in manners. And for aspiring authors, Potter's success in self-publishing is inspiring. She was a talented watercolourist, natural scientist and author, and drew and painted her own animals ceaselessly. She also studied the spores of fungus and illustrated her findings with immense skill. Today she would have had hopes of rising high in the scientific world but then she had to fight the gender stereotypes of the age, rather like the Brontë sisters before her. As a result she failed to interest any publishers in her children's stories about talking animals and so in 1901 she had to self-publish 250 copies of her first story, *The Tale of Peter Rabbit*. Peter's father is killed, chopped up and eaten in a pie by the gardener, Mr McGregor, and of course (spoiler alert) Peter nearly suffers the same fate. This was an early snuff story for kids.

The book was beautifully illustrated by the author and was a runaway success. One of the publishers who had previously rejected the story now reconsidered, and by Christmas 1902 Frederick Warne had sold 20,000 copies. *The Tale of Squirrel Nutkin* followed and was another huge success. Amazingly, Potter had to resort to self-publishing again for *The Tailor of Gloucester*, but once again she was vindicated. All in all she produced 23 stories in this format. She also patented a Peter Rabbit doll and invented much other spin-off merchandise, such as board games, wallpaper painting and even a Peter Rabbit children's Wedgwood tea-set of miniature teapot, two cups and saucers, sugar bowl and milk jug. These were painted with text and illustrations. This extraordinary woman would have fitted in well with our internet culture of multi-skilling and portfolio careers. Not content with all of this she then became a wealthy Lake District landowner, sheep farmer and a leading conservationist.

Beatrix Potter was largely responsible for the conservation of the Lake District as we know it today. Together with her solicitor husband (who had insider knowledge of properties coming up for sale) she bought up sixteen farms and 4,000 acres of the most beautiful countryside. She studied the old methods of hill farming and bred Herdwick sheep. And at her death she left most of her land to the National Trust, the biggest bequest they had had until then.

We are now walking down into Mallerstang, the dale at the head of the Eden Valley, and I announce that our walk is going to be downhill most of the way to Scotland from now. Spring has reached these parts in the form of nesting lapwings. Compared to the Peak District of a couple of weeks ago the season has advanced: the grass seems greener and the trees are in full leaf. There is also some good news that Beatrix Potter might have been glad to hear: this lovely valley is soon to be in an enlarged national park. The Yorkshire Dales and Lake District National Parks are to be extended to meet in the middle, with only the West Coast main railway line and the M6 dividing the 1,750 square miles (4,500 kilometres) of protected countryside. The two parks together will be the largest area of national park land in the country, with the Yorkshire Dales growing by a quarter and the Lake District by 27 square miles (70 kilometres).

As a resident of a national park I know from personal experience there are some downsides, such as the difficulties in getting planning permission for even a bird-table, but the advantages outweigh mere personal considerations. Because of the planning restrictions the whole area is safeguarded from major developments such as roads, towns and factories. By creating areas where people can enjoy exercise outdoors they promote healthy bodies and minds, and give urban dwellers a sanctuary from the pollution and racket of modern city life. Furthermore, areas within national parks are more prosperous than similar rural areas outside: farmers benefit from subsidies and the towns near here, such as Kirkby Lonsdale and Kirkby Stephen on the outskirts of this bigger park, should benefit from the spending of visitors. It's altogether a good thing.

This Vale of Mallerstang, together with the upper Eden Valley, has been described by the naturalist David Bellamy as 'England's last wilderness'. We feel very far from civilisation, with only the sight of a rare 'special' steam engine on the Settle to Carlisle line to remind us of the rest of humanity. We could have jolted back a century in time and nothing would look much different from this. Next to a bridge crossing the River Ure, at Yore House Farm, we find an idyllic lunch spot on lawn-like grass, and sit down in bright sunshine to a lunch of hummus and carrot sticks.

Reluctantly getting up I promise myself to come back one day and camp at this perfect spot. There's even a waterfall just below the bridge. I'm becoming aware that some locations have a 'feel'. Whereas we both felt uneasy coming down into the haunted valley of Longendale, and sad at the site of the navvies' camp at Ribblehead, other places have a happy feel. It's utterly irrational and unscientific, but there you are.

At night we have a camp-fire. As we lie silently next to the embers after a late dinner I gaze up at the stars, which are being joined by our whirling red sparks. I remember lying in the snow at Camp Two on Mount Everest in October 1993 and gazing through the thin air above. As I watched, and much to my surprise, a space shuttle tracked across the sky, the vehicle clearly visible to my naked eye. Years later I saw a photograph from the spacecraft taken at that moment as I lay looking up. I didn't know then that Karl Heize, a former space shuttle astronaut, was to die a couple of days later at Everest's Advanced Base Camp on the other side of the mountain. It strikes me, lying next to the fire, that the more we look the more connections we find.

It's a lovely spring day and Gina points out that the drystone walls have changed throughout England; around here they have sticking-out stones like footsteps up the sides. The barns are the same. So is this to allow access to the roof or is it to do with using up those awkwardly long through stones? There's no one to ask. The country is deserted. Only the curlew calls break the silence.

We climb a little way up the valleyside and gain the Pennine Bridleway (so much for downhill all the way to Scotland). We then have a great walk for miles, completely unimpeded by gates or stiles. Across the valley on this perfect day is the great mass of Wild Boar Fell, and above us to the right is Mallerstang Edge, a high contour of over 2,000 feet forming the watershed of the Pennines. A raindrop falling on this side will flow eventually into the Irish Sea, and its companion falling just a few inches to the east will flow to the North Sea. One of the many watercourses bounding down the hillside is Hell Gill Beck, the source of one of England's most beautiful rivers: the River Eden. We straddle the rushing stream, just as we did at Seven Springs, and look forward to walking the entire river's length to the sea. We are now in Cumbria, the last of our English counties.

A strange shape hoves into view, completely unexpected in this wild place. It's the first in a series of sculptures placed down the course of the Eden. This one is called 'Water Cut', and apparently it symbolises the power of the river cutting through the underlying rock. It is composed of two adjoining vertical limestone pillars with the intervening space in the shape of a meandering river. Looking between the pillars you see the real river in the valley below. The outline of the two pillars refers to the shape of the viaduct arches on the railway below.

I am not a fan of public art on the whole, but this is a pleasant enough example of the genre. To me it detracts from the feeling of the natural scene by forcing another person's view upon it. I wonder at humanity's incessant need to impose meaning upon chaos. Just over the hill in Haworth Emily Brontë was busy at it as well: attaching meanings to houses and people and moors. Her novel is a tapestry of woven patterns that just would not occur in the real, experiential world.

In his book *How We Believe: The Search for God in an Age of Science*[1] Michael Shermer argues that we are all the descendants of the most successful pattern-finding humans. Our human brains are belief engines, highly evolved pattern-recognition meat machines that create meanings out of the chaotic world of nature. The problem is that sometimes observation A is connected to observation B and sometimes not.

---

[1] Michael Shermer, *How We Believe: The Search for God in an Age of Science*, Times (2000)

When it is truly connected, for example a trail of footprints leading to an edible animal, it helps our survival and reproduction. 'This process is called association learning,' he writes, 'and it is fundamental to all animal behaviour, from the humble worm *C. elegans* to *H. sapiens*.' When A and B are not truly connected we see patterns that are not there, such as UFOs and gods. As long as we recognise that artists who have something to say employ fallacious patterns in art and literature, that's all right. But these moors are essentially inhuman, like the rest of nature: utterly indifferent to our puny lives, and I prefer it that way. There are no meanings here, no order, no hidden code. Just the great 'is'.

It's feeling like a summer's day now, with a clear blue sky and so hot that the sheep are standing in the shade of the trees. We're on Lady Anne's Way, a 100-mile footpath from Skipton to Penrith. Lady Anne was a wealthy baroness who owned no less than five castles along this route. She used to travel along this green track, staying at each castle for several months at a time. She was also a well-informed writer and diarist. Bishop Rainbow said of her at her funeral 'Prime Wit (Dr John Donne) is reported to have said of this lady, that she knew well how to discourse of all things, from Predestination to Slea-silk.' (Slea-silk, or sleeve silk, is thread capable of being divided into finer threads for embroidery.) They breed remarkable women up here, as you can see.

I was thinking about Beatrix Potter and Peter Rabbit when we come upon four dead young rabbits strewn in a line along the footpath. We can't work out what killed them; they're undamaged but look emaciated. Maybe it was the cold spring, maybe lack of forage. Whatever it was, there will be plenty of replacements because rabbits breed like . . . well, rabbits.

These furry little darlings were introduced to England by the Romans as a food source, as were the edible snails. Rather surprisingly, rabbits are now regarded as an even more expensive pest than Japanese knotweed. Seven of them will eat as much as one sheep, and they cost England around £263 million every year (the total cost of all invasive species is around £1.3 billion: about four full-sized hospitals). As well as eating pasture they will ring-bark trees, nibbling all the way around the stem and thus killing the young sapling. They can also dig under foundations, destroying buildings.

This is as nothing to the cost of rabbits to the Australian economy: thousands of millions of dollars have been spent trying to get rid of the European rabbit. The man generally blamed for the introduction is one Thomas Austin, an English settler who arrived in 1831. Can I propose him as member of the Disastrous Introducers' Club, joining such luminaries as Philipp Franz von Siebold (Japanese knotweed) and Mrs Norris of Camberley (Himalayan balsam)?

Thomas Austin was in fact a member of the Acclimatisation Society of Victoria, a club devoted to trying to make Australia more like England. I can't imagine that would have many members now. One fellow settler complained that in Australia trees kept their leaves in autumn and instead shed their bark, the swans were black, the eagles white, the bees were stingless, some mammals had pockets, others laid eggs and it was warmest up on the hills. Austin agreed. He missed his weekend rabbit-shooting trips back in England and so he wrote to his nephew William back in the old country, asking him to send out twelve grey rabbits, five wild hares and seventy-two partridges (but not a pear tree). What could possibly go wrong? 'The introduction of a few rabbits could do little harm and might provide a touch of home, in addition to a spot of hunting,' he wrote. William obliged, helpfully adding some extra domestic rabbits. These copulated enthusiastically with the wild ones, creating a super-rabbit destined to take over Australia. Imagine the offspring of Russell Brand and *Alice in Wonderland*.

The result was the fastest-ever mammalian population explosion, faster even than humans. Australia was particularly well suited to the rabbit, with sandy soil and low vegetation creating perfect conditions for burrowing and feeding. The mild winters enabled them to breed the whole year round, and with a 31-day gestation period, one pair could produce up to 30,000 kits in a couple of years (that's a lot of birthday cards). There were no natural predators, or at least none that could keep up. The population exploded from around twenty-four in 1859 to 10 billion in the 1920s. The effect of all these rabbits was devastating to the Australian ecology, and is now considered the most significant cause of species loss in the country. Australia has lost more native mammals than any other nation, twenty-two species in all, and rabbits are implicated in these losses. They indirectly support populations of feral cats and foxes (also European introductions), predators of many Australian native animals.

We can't blame Thomas Austin alone for the rabbit plague. Six of them had also been brought with the First Fleet leaving England in May 1787, and there had been a localised population explosion of rabbits in Tasmania in the early nineteenth century. Other settlers were bringing in rabbits. However, those eleven ships brought another mammalian invader: 1,483 humans, including around 1,000 convicts. These, for similar reasons to the success of rabbits, thrived, multiplied and then exterminated many of the original human inhabitants: the aborigines. An even worse fate befell the indigenous Americans, north and south, when the Old World arrived at the shores of the New. And, looking at the larger picture, we humans are worse even than the Australian rabbit because we are going to overrun the entire planet and, unlike rabbits, we should really know better.

We've just arrived at Pendragon Castle, an atmospheric ruin built on the banks of the River Eden. We're experiencing another reversal of spring, maybe because we've got higher in altitude, or maybe because we're that bit further north. For whatever reason, we're seeing bluebells and wild garlic flowering again in the trees hereabouts. There are signs of tree-planting taking place and so I'm able to plant one of my own oaks amongst the new saplings, protected by fences from the ravening sheep. I do hope the farmer doesn't mind one extra oak. It's still sunny, and we also hear a cuckoo and get attacked by a lapwing when we unwittingly get too close to its nest. On our sound recording of this event I can hear the squeaks and squawks of the irritated bird.

This castle was supposedly built by King Arthur's father, Uther Pendragon, a legendary British king of the fifth century. He was said to have unsuccessfully attempted to divert the river around his new castle to form a moat, giving rise to a local verse: *'let Uther Pendragon do what he can, Eden will run where Eden ran*. We have already encountered one of the later owners, Sir Hugh de Morville, Lord of Westmorland: he was one of the four knights who murdered Thomas a Becket. The high point of the Mallerstang Edge is named after him: Hugh's Seat. Another owner was Lady Anne Clifford, whom we've also met walking between her five castles. Pendragon Castle was one of her favourites, and it certainly has a wonderful situation. She added stables, a brewery and a bakery, but it doesn't look much bigger than an MP's second home. I look agog at these kinds of ruins, imagining what spring was like around here when the castle was new. The surrounding hills looked much the same, I expect, but it seems such a wild valley. What on earth did they eat?

As we leave the castle we step carefully through a field of thriving buttercups and daisies, and Gina wonders aloud why the two flowers are always mentioned in the same breath? Apart from the fact that they co-exist happily in fields during the spring, they also live together in a risqué traditional song, 'Strawberry Fair', whose lyrics include:

> As I was going to Strawberry Fair
> Singing, singing buttercups and daisies
> I met a maiden taking her ware
> Her eyes were blue and golden her hair
> 'Kind sir, pray pick of my basket,' she said
> Singing, singing buttercups and daisies
> 'My cherries ripe and my roses so red
> O I have a lock that doth lack a key
> O I have a lock, sir,' she did say
> 'If you have a key then come this way
> As we go on to Strawberry Fair'

We glimpse a weasel along the next stretch of the River Eden, just beyond the castle. He's gingery-brown in colour with a white chest and belly, and is only about 8 inches long (20cm). In spring the males extend their territory, looking for females, so maybe this one killed the four young rabbits we saw earlier. The weasel is England's most numerous carnivore but the smallest, which is just as well as it is a ferocious predator. They specialise in murdering small rodents such as voles and mice, but they will take on young rabbits and birds. Their slender, sinuous bodies are able to creep down the holes and runways of their prey and they'll live in the nest after they've eaten the occupant. They generally get a bad press, and are the chief animal villains in *The Wind in the Willows* in which they take over Toad Hall.

Stoats are similar to weasels, also being mustelids, but they're about a third bigger and will kill adult rabbits. We've seen one scuttling along the verge ahead of us, carrying an adult in its teeth. In winter they grow a perfect white coat: ermine. This meant that stoat skins were prized by the fur trade and their expense meant that ermine was associated with the heads of the Catholic Church, royalty or those of the highest status. In England the robes of the members of the House of Lords are trimmed with ermine (or sometimes rabbit fur, presumably according to party: stoat or rabbit). Stoats give birth in spring, but the females are mated in early summer, even the female kits who are two to three weeks old, so implantation is delayed for nine to ten months. That means that the embryo doesn't implant into the uterus until conditions are right. And that means when rabbit is on the menu again.

Ferrets are a bit bigger still, are also mustelids, and are domesticated polecats kept as pets. There is a picture of Elizabeth I with her pet ferret which has been mislabelled *The Ermine Portrait*, as the creature is not a stoat. They were used in hunting rabbits, which they would chase out of their burrows into waiting nets, but I am unsure if the queen was into a bit of poaching. The collective noun is glorious: a 'business' of ferrets.

We keep passing stone lime-kilns along this river valley; squat boxes of stone built into the hillside with arches at ground level. Carts brought fuel and it was tipped in from the top. Chunks of limestone were burnt in the kilns with coal or wood to make quicklime: calcium oxide. This is intensely alkaline and will improve the fertility of the local peaty acid soils. It was mixed with water in an explosive reaction to make slaked lime, calcium hydroxide, and thrown on the fields. It was another of the back-breaking, dangerous, springtime jobs for the farm workers hereabouts.

We walk into Kirkby Stephen at ten o'clock the next morning and it's so warm I have an ice cream as we stroll down the high street. Suddenly there's pandemonium amongst the passersby and everyone starts hurrying away with their heads covered. A swarm of bees has filled the street, and there's even some polite screaming.

In fact, swarming bees are not very dangerous to humans: they're too busy finding a new home. It's a springtime phenomenon, and the earlier the better as far as beekeepers are concerned. The later it is in the season the less time is left to collect nectar from the spring flowers. There's a seventeenth-century English rhyme to do with this:

A swarm of bees in May is worth a load of hay;
A swarm of bees in June is worth a silver spoon;
A swarm of bees in July isn't worth a fly.

(This raises an interesting point: a load of hay must have been considered more valuable than a silver spoon.) Today's silver spoon's-worth of bees have left their hive with the old queen because the original colony is crowded: it's the natural way by which colonies reproduce. Over half the bees will leave and the swarm will hang in a temporary place such as a branch while scout bees excitedly dash around looking for a permanent home.

This is an anxious time for beekeepers as they stand to lose half their stock. If you ever have a swarm in your garden just ring a beekeeper and they'll be round in a flash. The prospect of retrieving their own bees or nabbing a rival's is just too alluring. I used to keep bees in my Somerset apple orchard. They usually swarmed on a warm sunny spring day and would find a branch to hang on. The buzzing mass is a little intimidating but the trick is to put a white sheet down on the ground beneath the swarm with a box on it and gently knock the swarm off into the box. Then you can tape it up and carry it to the new hive that you have already prepared. Oh, and it's probably best to wear a bee-suit and veil.

After Kirkby Stephen and its excitement we head out into England's Empty Quarter. This district of Eden has the lowest population density of any district of England and Wales, and most people would say it is one of the most beautiful parts of the country, too. We deliberately chose our walking route through England to avoid centres of population, only taking in Birmingham to look at springtime in a city. We didn't fancy walking through the Greater London conurbation with its 10 million inhabitants. Pushing through crowds is not our idea of fun.

In Islington, for example, there are 14,735 people per square kilometre. In Eden district there are twenty-five. Yes, you read that right: just twenty-five people. Per square kilometre. That's nearly 600 times less density of population than Islington. The Office for National Statistics has just calculated that between 2014 and 2039 the UK population will rise by nearly 10 million, from 64.6 million to 74.3 million. That's like adding the entire population of Sweden to ours (in fact, that sounds quite a good idea. Would they mind?). The next ten years will be the most stressful, when Britain will have to accommodate another 4.4 million people. That's the population of Dorset every twelve months. The ONS states that immigration will account for 68 per cent of the increase, partly because of the higher fertility rates amongst immigrants. The rest is down to the fertility of the present inhabitants. This is not anti-immigrant at all, some of the most motivated, resourceful and useful members of our society have come to live in this country. But they have to live somewhere.

One solution to the overcrowding in cities might be to encourage people to live in places like Eden, but country life is costly: you have to drive every time you need to shop or go to work and fuel is expensive. Heating costs more in isolated country dwellings. A study conducted by the insurer National Farmers Union Mutual claimed that there was a £2,000 premium to live in the country and that inflation in the countryside was running at 7.7 per cent over twelve months versus 4.3 per cent in urban areas (but they might just have an axe to grind). The simple fact is that there is little work up here and people pour into the south-eastern corner of England because that's where they want to live. Spreading us out into the countryside is not an option. So Cumbria will probably remain the Empty Quarter for the time being.

What is more worrying for those of us who love the English countryside is that there is a great deal of pressure to build on the Green Belts around our great cities. And the way the developers are going to get round the law is to put a price on nature. The government has now created a Natural Capital Committee and an Ecosystem Markets Task Force which will be able to attach a price to hills, valleys and fields. And as we all know, once a price tag has been attached to a field of wildflowers at amount £A, then an economic benefit of a new road or housing estate will be rigged at £A plus 1. Lawyers will be hired to calculate the sum in court and the field will be built on.

We shouldn't engage in this kind of calculation. The value of the English countryside is infinite. If you attach a price to our environment we will see the biggest privatisation since the Enclosures. As Oscar Wilde might have written in *Lady Windermere's Fan*: 'A developer is a man who knows the price of everything, and the value of nothing.'

What Wilde actually wrote was this:

Cecil Graham: What is a cynic?
Lord Darlington: A man who knows the price of everything, and the value of nothing.
Cecil Graham: And a sentimentalist, my dear Darlington, is a man who sees an absurd value in everything and doesn't know the market price of any single thing.

Well I'd rather be a sentimentalist than a cynic. The last word on this goes to the great conservative radical William Cobbett, on the eighteenth-century privatisation of land that robbed English working people of the means to support themselves. 'It took from them their best inheritance: sweet air, health and the little liberty they had left.'

It's early on 11 June, and we're doing well, striding along in the spring sunshine and putting away the miles. We've been seeing horse-drawn Gypsy caravans and travellers in the area and find out that Appleby's famous horse fair has been taking place. It's another one of the springtime events that we've been seeing up the country. It has taken place under the protection of a charter granted by James II since 1685 and is one of the most important dates for the Romani, Gypsy and travelling community. It attracts people from all over the country and is one of the world's biggest Gypsy gatherings: 10,000 of them attended this year, and they had the same wonderful weather that we've been enjoying. It was so hot that many horses were bathed in the River Eden, and 30,000 other visitors came to buy from market stalls in Jimmy Winter's field and watch the fun.

As we are walking towards Appleby we come across a traditional Gypsy caravan, with a cob mare in the shafts with her head buried in the hedge. She's enjoying the fresh spring herbage and Dan, her owner, is standing holding her reins until she's finished. We get chatting and he tells us all about the fair. Quite a few people wanted to buy Sally, his mare, but he doesn't want to sell her. The caravan is a real, traditional Gypsy caravan with a green body and yellow wheels, with a bale of hay on the back and a sack of hard feed, too. Sally seems to be fed rather well as she has a round belly. The caravan's worth around £30,000 and weighs three-quarters of a ton. Sally and he can manage between ten and twelve miles a day, about the same as us. Dan used to be a gamekeeper but got tired of it. He now does eco-logging, which is pulling out felled trees from woodland using horses instead of tracked vehicles, which tear up orchids and damage the land. He has five horses for this.

Dan's interested in the fact that we've walked all the way from Dorset, and there's something of a meeting of minds: the fellowship of the road. He's curious about where we stay every night, not having a caravan. He says he can't settle down, he likes living on the road. He's been on the road this time for five weeks. He asks if any of his friends are ahead of him on the way we've come: the universal wayfarers' question.

An ancestor of mine, John Hoyland, a Quaker, was so concerned about the living conditions of the Gypsies that he made a study of them and published a book. In so doing he fell in love with a 'black-eyed gypsy girl'.

One story that he must have heard, and which happened in the Rutland village where I grew up, concerned a tribe of Romani who were camped on common land near the heath. It was Christmas 1793, a cold, miserable time of year. Boswell was the name of the Gypsy king, and he had a daughter, Rose, the princess. She contracted tuberculosis in the damp conditions and couldn't be moved, so the tribe had to stay another two months in the same place. When the poor girl died the churchwardens in my home village wouldn't have her buried in the parish because she wasn't a Christian. However, these un-Christians were overruled by the curate and Rose was buried in the church of St Mary's, South Luffenham. You can still see the marble slab in the south aisle, bought by a general subscription amongst the Gypsy community. It reads:

'In memory of Rose Boswell, daughter of Edward and
Sarah Boswell, who died February 19th, 1794, aged 17
years.

What grief can vent this loss, or praises tell,
How much, how good, how beautiful she fell.'

The smells of spring are evident today in the fields alongside
our footpath. When the frosts are first gone in March you can
smell the rich, loamy aroma of the earth warming up. As the
sun dries out the wet leaves there is an added note of sweet
decay. Then a few days later there are top notes of grass
growing and buds swelling. And now, in late spring when the
first hay cut is taken, there is the pungent stench of manure
being spread on the short remaining grass. This will
encourage growth and the farmer will be able to take a second
cut of hay later in the summer. This hay is usually wrapped up
in those huge round bales you see standing around in fields
like sculptures.

When I cut open the great round plastic-wrapped bales of
haylage on my little farm in the winter I couldn't resist
burying my face in the crinkly compacted grass. Inside there
were all the smells of spring, together with a wonderful alcoholic appley-cidery aroma that I have never smelled anywhere
else. By then the animals were usually shoving me aside in
their haste to get at this delicious stuff. Honestly, if I could eat
it for breakfast I would.

These big bales are dangerous to handle. They're 6 feet
by 5 feet in size (2 metres by 1.5 metres), and bound tightly

in shiny plastic which keeps the air out. They weigh over a third of a ton (around 360 kilogrammes). Mike Edwards, the cello-playing founding member of the ELO, was killed by one of these bales when one rolled down a field, jumped across the A381 in Devon and landed on his van. He died instantly.

I was once taking a couple of bales down to the horses who were standing around a large pond at the bottom of the extremely steep hill. Somehow one of the bales got away from me and started rolling away down the hill (does this sound familiar?). I tried to trip it up, but no, it gathered speed, began to bounce, then started making terrifying leaps in the air, with me running after it shouting at the horses to move.

It must have been doing 40 mph when the psycho-mare saw what was coming: her ears shot up and she galloped out of the way. I've never seen a horse running backwards quite so fast. With one giant leap the damn bale vaulted into the air right over her and landed bang slap in the middle of the pond, where it sank slowly. It took a lot of getting out.[1]

On the footpath from Warcop we see some young calves and then spot a very young blackbird hopping around in front of us. These fledglings leave the nest when they're fully feathered but unable to fly. They remain flightless for a couple of days, but their parents are still looking after them for around three weeks. It seems a risky time for them. We look around, can't see the parents and decide to leave well alone.

Barnacle geese have an even tougher time when they leave the nest. They hatch out on cliff ledges in Greenland, hundreds of feet above likely predators such as Arctic foxes. As we know, geese eat grass, so the goslings' parents can't feed them. So,

---

[1] With a Tirfor winch and a tree, if you ever have the same problem.

unable to fly, they jump out of the nest and bounce down the cliff, where they land on scree and then have to avoid the hungry foxes.

Appleby is a pleasant little town built in a loop of the River Eden, and there's another of Lady Anne Clifford's many castles. What were her heating bills like? We wait at the bus stop for a while.

Gina: 'Excuse me, is there a bus to Hawes?'
Older lady: 'Yes, love.'
Gina: 'Great! When?'
Older lady: 'Once a week.'

You see why people don't want to live in the country? So we go and sit in the pub for hours and take the last train.

Our friend Fabrice Fleurot has joined us for three days to enjoy the walk. He's a nuclear physicist and a member of the Cheshire search and rescue team, so a handy chap to have around if you lose an atom bomb in Altringham. He's also a gifted photographer, so it's interesting to see what catches his eye. On the next day's walk we see some moles hanging in a line on a wire fence – a gamekeeper's gibbet – and Fabrice spends a great deal of time snapping. It's unclear to me why gamekeepers hang up trapped moles. If it's to discourage the other moles it can't be very effective as, a) moles can't see very well, and b) they're underground anyway.

Moles don't seem very harmful to gamekeepers and I've never quite understood why they trap them. Perhaps molehills are unsightly on lawns, or perhaps they think a horse might step into a burrow. Scottish Jacobites used to toast 'the little gentleman in velvet' in reference to William III who died in spring 1702 of pneumonia after complications caused by a broken bone. This happened after his horse, Sorrel, stumbled on a molehill and threw him off.

Moles don't eat plant roots, they are primarily earthworm and insect eaters. Their burrows are actually worm-traps and aren't really for going anywhere in particular. When a worm falls into the burrow the mole runs along and bites it. The mole's saliva contains a toxin which paralyses earthworms, so Mr Mole can store still-living food in his larder. Over a thousand worms have been found in these stores. When it's time to eat the mole squeezes the worm between his paws to extrude the soil from its gut. Less gritty, you see.

We cross the roaring A66 and I note that it was built over long sections of Roman road, now lost forever. Then our footpath takes us along an un-built-on section of the old Roman way and once again it is clear to see that when houses or roads are built on countryside it's gone for good. In Long Marton, the next village, there's a supernaturally tidy farm, completely deserted. The cows are oddly friendly and the village is immaculate and utterly empty of people. There is one of those odd atmospheres here, not unpleasant, but I could imagine farms and villages of the future like this after humans have disappeared into a digital haze. There would be a couple of robot tractors around and . . . no one.

Fabrice has just carefully measured the distance we walked yesterday on the map with a special digital wheeli-thing. It turns out it was 9.5 miles, when we thought it was only 6.5. Fabrice, whose legs seem to be aching, looks slightly relieved. He's been doing twice the mileage that we are, dashing around behind us taking pictures, then hurrying to catch up. It makes us wonder if we're going to be walking further than we thought: a total of 500 miles instead of the 360 miles I had calculated. That's about a million steps for me and a few more for Gina. No wonder our legs are bulging with extra muscles.

We join the River Eden again to find that it has become a wide, luxuriant river. Fabrice says it reminds him of the French river Dordogne in its upper reaches. The bedrock has now switched from limestone to a deep red sandstone. I wonder how many people in England realise what a wonderful riverscape we have up here in Cumbria? Just a little down-stream another river joins the Eden from the west, the River Eamont. Its source is Ullswater in the Lake District, and we had already decided to rent a cottage up there to find out about William Wordsworth's daffodils and Arthur Ransome's *Swallows and Amazons*. We'll shift from our campsite in Settle to the cottage base-camp at Ullswater and continue to walk down the Eden Valley every day, using car and train to get back to the Lake District each evening.

A bit further on we come to Long Meg and Her Daughters stone circle. It was built in the Bronze Age and consists of about sixty stones set in a huge circle. Long Meg herself stands in the centre and she's made of the local red sandstone. She has megalithic symbols engraved into her flanks, including a cup and ring mark. No one has managed to decipher what these represent: they occur all over Europe and consist of a shallow depression carved out of the stone surrounded by concentric circles, sometimes with a kind of straight gutter leading out of the centre. To me they look rather like an aerial map of the Avebury Stone Circle. It's galling to think that we can't go back in time for just ten seconds and shout at the ancient carver: 'What the hell's that?' and he would no doubt say something like 'It's a picture of a tree, idiot,' or 'It's a power-point for my spacecraft, earthling.'

We walk past a grand National Trust house, Acorn Bank,

and admire the savannah-like parkland. There was gypsum mining here. Further on and once again we see a stoat running ahead of us with a rabbit in its mouth.

I'm walking ahead of Gina and Fabrice on a deserted country lane and hear the unlikely strains of an electric guitar twanging through the trees. Rounding the corner, we see an ice-cream van with the owner picking out a tune on his guitar in the driving seat. It turns out his name is Steve Richardson and he thought he had found somewhere quiet to practise. He claims to have just started to learn the guitar, but to us he sounds pretty good. Gina recognises the song as Eric Clapton's 'Wonderful Tonight' and he blushes with pleasure. He gives us another rendition for free, then three ice creams and a 99, which is more than Eric would have done.

The poppies are out in Langwathby, and it's so warm and sunny that a woman is sitting outside her door and painting the doorframe green. Her garden is at eye level, so we stop to talk to her and her border terrier, Scrumpy. Spring is the time for painting the house, she said, and she's also been spring-cleaning. I notice with interest that she has accidentally stuck her hair, which is quite long, onto the frame. I once managed to stick my head to the bottom of my boat. I was upside down in the hull, with my head and shoulders in the sewage tank, slapping on a layer of epoxy resin to the interior in a vain attempt to stop the toilet water ending up in the fuel tank. At the end of the day I attempted to reverse upwards, only to find that my head was firmly stuck to the bottom of the tank. It was getting dark, and only my feet were visible, sticking up into the sky. I tried a few tentative shouts for help, with no response. The only solution in the end was a rather painful self-scalping process. I shouldn't really be allowed out on my own.

CHAPTER TEN

The Lake District – the Wordsworths – a host of golden daffodils –
we take a sailing dinghy across a lake – The Prelude *– Swallows*
and Amazons – a Great Northern Diver? – waterfowl – River
Eden and the Borders – otters – what does spring mean to us in the
way we live now? – Hadrian's Wall – the border – the longest day –
the Arctic sea at night – a conclusion

W e're in Ullswater and we've decided to do some Wordsworth research. Fabrice is going home, limping slightly, and Julian Champkin is returning tomorrow for more punishment, this time to stay at the cottage 'Galena' with us, along with his wife Mary and their two children, Rose and Peter. We have advertised this to them as an idyllic spring holiday in the Lake District. It doesn't quite turn out that way.

Today, though, we're going on a walk to look for daffodils. Just along the lake shore from our cottage is Glencoyne Bay, where William Wordsworth and his sister Dorothy saw something on 15 April 1802 which resulted in his famous poem 'I wandered lonely as a cloud'.

William Wordsworth was a rather serious chap. Said an acquaintance: 'He looks like a man that one must not speak to unless one has some sensible thing to say.' He was the son of the land agent of a wealthy local family, and he sometimes had a beady eye on property values.

The daffodils in question were seen by the sister and the brother and they led to two very different pieces of writing, one in verse and one in prose.

'When we were in the woods beyond Gowbarrow Park,' wrote his sister Dorothy in her *Grasmere Journal* on the day in question, 'we saw a few daffodils close to the water side. We fancied that the lake had floated the seed ashore and that the little colony had so sprung up. But as we went along there were more and more and at last under the boughs of the trees, we saw that there was a long belt of them along the shore, about the breadth of a country turnpike road.

'I never saw daffodils so beautiful, they grew among the mossy stones about and about them, some rested their heads upon these stones as on a pillow for weariness and the rest tossed and reeled and danced and seemed as if they verily laughed with the wind that blew upon them over the lake, they looked so gay ever dancing ever changing.

'This wind blew directly over the lake to them. There was here and there a little knot and a few stragglers a few yards higher up but they were so few as not to disturb the simplicity and unity and life of that one busy highway. We rested again and again. The Bays were stormy, and we heard the waves at different distances and in the middle of the water like the sea.'[1]

Dorothy Wordsworth was herself an excellent writer and frankly her prose description evokes the lake shore on that day rather better than her brother's poem:

> I wandered lonely as a cloud
> That floats on high o'er vales and hills,
> When all at once I saw a crowd,

---

[1] Dorothy Wordsworth, *Grasmere Journal*, 15 April 1802

A host, of golden daffodils;
>   Beside the lake, beneath the trees,
>   Fluttering and dancing in the breeze.

>   Continuous as the stars that shine
>   And twinkle on the milky way,
>   They stretched in never-ending line
>   Along the margin of a bay:
>   Ten thousand saw I at a glance,
>   Tossing their heads in sprightly dance.

>   The waves beside them danced; but they
>   Out-did the sparkling waves in glee:
>   A poet could not but be gay,
>   In such a jocund company:
>   I gazed – and gazed – but little thought
>   What wealth the show to me had brought:

>   For oft, when on my couch I lie
>   In vacant or in pensive mood,
>   They flash upon that inward eye
>   Which is the bliss of solitude;
>   And then my heart with pleasure fills,
>   And dances with the daffodils.[1]

Wordsworth removed Dorothy's presence from the poem, even though he was inspired by her journal, and only his name was on his and Coleridge's joint work, *Lyrical Ballads* (1798), even though it included Coleridge's 'Ancient Mariner' and 'The Nightingale'. He and his friend Coleridge had achieved

---

[1] William Wordsworth, *Poems in Two Volumes* (1807)

considerable fame with their joint work and became known as the Lake Poets. What they did was to simplify poetic language and move away from the high-flown verse of the previous century. Their Romantic poetry recorded powerful emotions 'recollected in tranquillity' which is just what the writer is doing in the last stanza. Whereas Wordsworth was lauded and eventually was made Poet Laureate, Coleridge (in my opinion) was a far more interesting poet and character.

Byron loathed Wordsworth's poem, describing his language as 'not simple but puerile'. In this case he's probably not far wrong: it just cannot compare with, say, 'Kubla Khan', a poem fed by Coleridge's immense background reading and inventive imagination.

The *Guardian* reveals that Wordsworth was an astute property developer. When faced with eviction from a rented house he bought a field next to it and threatened to build on it, blocking the view. He even paid an architect to draw up a design. The eviction was dropped, and he planted the field with daffodils.

On the plus side he objected to the railways being built through his beloved lakes and wrote a sonnet to the planners which begins: 'Is then no nook of English ground secure From rash assault?' The chief consulting engineer replied in kind with 'WE won our way – through rocks – o'er waters grand, Opening, (we trust) the beauties of the land.'

The *Guardian* also repeats the scurrilous story that William's first line of 'Daffodils' originally read 'I wandered lonely as a cow', and that Dorothy had firmly snapped 'William, you simply cannot put that.'[1]

---

[1] www.theguardian.com/uk/the-northerner/2012/mar/20/william-wordsworth-daffodils-rydal-mount-national-trust

Perhaps we have been a little unfair to William Wordsworth, after all, he did help to launch Romanticism in English literature, a vigorous reaction to the crass materialism of the Industrial Revolution, adding shock and awe to poetry. For example, in his *Prelude* he describes stealing a 'Shepherd's Boat' from a 'Cavern' as a schoolboy and rowing across this lake, Ullswater, at night. Facing backwards as he rows, a mountain peak rears up against the night sky:

> I struck and struck again,
> And growing still in stature the grim Shape
> Towered up between me and the stars, and still,
> For so it seemed, with purpose of its own
> And measured motion like a living Thing,
> Strode after me.

The guilty and terrified boy, 'chastened and subdued', paddles the boat back. He now has an animal relationship with nature that sustains him throughout his life.

I want to replicate this experience as far as I can, to get In Touch with William, so we hire a 'traditional' fibreglass sailing boat from the Glenridding Sailing Centre in Ullswater for a few days. These sort of vessels are usually called *Lady Eleanor of Trumpington* or *Fanny of Cowes*, but thankfully this thing came without any discernable name. The type of boat is a Lune Whammel, but, just as my own boat is a Derbyshire Crabber, I have no idea what that can possibly mean. All I know is that it has red sails, fake planks and is made almost entirely of petro-chemicals. It looks lovely, though.

We are not allowed to steal the boat, sail at night or indeed try to row it, so my attempts to find out what the young Wordsworth was up to fail somewhat. However, by sailing the same track as the poet, Gina and I spot a couple of things not mentioned by the literary critics: the mountain that reared up its head is almost certainly Helvellyn, and so he wasn't quite where he said he was. The Wordsworths were wealthy and influential guests at Side Farm, on the south-east side of the lake, and so to see Helvellyn rise up behind him he would have had to be going the other way. I could find no cavern big enough to house a shepherd's boat on that side of the lake, and what was a shepherd doing with a boat anyway? This is not to detract from a poet's licence to invent, but it's interesting to deconstruct a real event and see which parts the writer changes to make their patterns of meaning.

Daffodils are a welcome herald of spring, and are the most visible flower at the beginning of the season. When travelling south in England in February or March it's very obvious that the southern counties are well ahead of the north simply by the numbers of these lovely yellow flowers dancing in the wind. This observation led to the writing of this book: as a child I was told that the spring would travel north at the speed of a walk. Because daffodils grow from bulbs they're easy for children to plant the previous autumn. They look particularly fine on lawns around deciduous trees, or on turf. To make them look natural the trick is to scatter the bulbs around randomly and then plant them where they lie. Just bury them to a depth three times the length of the bulb and wait until spring.

We have great fun in the Lune Whammel. We both agree it's a nice-looking boat and very reminiscent of Arthur Ransome's *Swallows and Amazons* books. We tack to and fro across the wind, reflecting that sailing is one of those activities that involves a disproportionate amount of expense and effort compared to the claimed activity. The wind almost always comes from the direction of travel, so you either have to zig-zag for hours to go that way, or put the engine on. So it should be called motoring, not sailing. But we don't have an engine, so we zigzag. The same goes for horse-riding: if you have a horse it is nearly always lame or ill. You need six of them to have any hope of actually riding anywhere. Skiing is the same: you spend thousands of euros to stand in long queues and then sit on a freezing chair. Then follows a couple of minutes of excitement as you slide down the hill on a pair of planks. You could call all this the faff factor: the proportion of time spent on the claimed activity. Walking wins every time: it took me a couple of minutes this morning to put on my boots, followed by hours of walking in the spring. What could be nicer?

Arthur Ransome would perhaps argue that it's the messing around in boats that is the actual activity, and he would have a point. *Swallow*, the boat used in the 1974 film of the book, lives here at the Glenridding Sailing Centre, and all the varnishing, rigging and mending seems to be half the fun. *Swallows and Amazons* was the first in a series of twelve children's books.

In the spring of 1929 Arthur Ransome had submitted a synopsis and fifty pages of his book *Swallows and Amazons*[1] to

---

[1] Arthur Ransome, *Swallows and Amazons*, Jonathan Cape (1930)

his publishers, Jonathan Cape, who were enthusiastic. Ransome was a most interesting man; he was by turn a writer, a sailor, a sympathetic first-hand observer of the Russian revolution, a British spy with the code name S.76 and then a writer again. Escaping from a loveless marriage, he ended up marrying Trotsky's secretary, Evgenia, in 1924 and took her to the Lake District where he wrote the bestselling series for which he is remembered today. At times MI5 were suspicious of him, but all that has been uncovered is that Evgenia was smuggling diamonds to Paris for the Communist International. After a life like this one might expect Ransome to produce novels like Ian Fleming's *James Bond* series, but no, all he seemed interested in writing about was dinghies crewed by children. Oddly enough, the Japanese seem to have a fascination for Ransome, and had a fanclub before the British did.

It's early summer 1929, and the time seems to belong to an idyllic between-wars era, when the sun always shone and children were always outside. My father and his brother and sister were just this age at just this time and the portrayal is accurate. The action is set on an unidentified lake which seems to be a combination of Coniston Water and Windermere. The Walker children sail their boat *Swallow*, and pretend they are explorers. The Blackett children are pirates, and sail the *Amazon*. Various adventures ensue, but what is interesting is how adults fasten on these stories. They seem to feed a vision of an idealised past which you may just be able to touch if you sail a traditional boat in the Lake District.

Which is what we're doing today. The Champkin family arrive and on the Saturday morning I enthusiastically pile them aboard to show them what a good time they can have as modern-day Swallows and Amazons. It's cold and raining, and we drift off onto the lake, doing the usual zigzagging thing.

We sail past an island and try to imagine it's a hot summer's day in the 1930s. Rose and Peter are patiently tolerating our childish chatter. Daddy Julian quotes the Swallows' father's telegram in response to a request for the children to go sailing alone: 'BETTER DROWNED THAN DUFFERS IF NOT DUFFERS WON'T DROWN'. Julian's own children do not look impressed by this thought.

With my usual sailing ineptitude I steer for the only buoy in sight, and the clunk of the rudder falling off announces that it was marking the only reef within miles. We drift around for a while in the rain. After Captain Graham has half-immersed himself in icy water re-attaching the rudder he catches the sight of the two Champkin children's faces: white with hypothermia, with a somewhat accusing stare. Then the realisation dawns on me: children's books aren't actually for children trying to be adults. They're for adults trying to be children.

Everything improves back at the cottage with a hot fire, tea and cakes. Arthur Ransome had that right at least. Gina cooks a Christmas dinner because it's spring and Mary and the children enjoy a bit of anarchy. The next day, Sunday, we deliver the Champkins, only slightly traumatised, back to the railway station at Penrith.

I can't resist a quick side trip down the A66 to Greta Bridge, which was the subject of a favourite artist, John Sell Cotman. When staying at Rokeby Hall in early summer 1805, using pencil, he sketched the fine bridge thrown over the River Greta near the house. He worked the drawing up into 'the

most perfect example of pure watercolour ever made in
Europe'[1] according to art critic Laurence Binyon. It shows
Cotman's style at its best: using patches of delicate colour he
assembles them into almost geometrical patterns. The manmade bridge and house contrast with the natural shapes of
rocks in the foreground. The river and sky mirror each other
in a classic balanced composition.

I struggle over fences and through deep grass upriver to get
to the same point where Cotman sketched, and turn to look.
And there it is, the view as he saw it. Except it isn't. The
bridge is more real. The riverbanks are far more overgrown.
There are taller trees and more luxuriant undergrowth. This
agrees with the impression that we got as we walked through
England: trees are on their way back. And that's good news.

Another of our friends is joining us to enjoy the spring
walking down the Eden Valley: Charlie Viney, my literary
agent. So we walk from Kirkoswald to Armathwaite with him,
a longish day. We notice that the seeds are forming on the
sycamore trees. I'm still planting an acorn every mile and
Charlie is amused to see me digging holes in the verge every
twenty minutes or so. 'It's like some sort of rite of passage,' he
chuckles. He and Gina walk on ahead and I take some time to
catch up. It occurs to me that walking is a very amicable way
of travelling; we have the time to strike up topics and lengths
of conversation which aren't often possible in the usual rush of

---

[1] Laurence Binyon, *Landscape in English Art and Poetry*, p.132 (1931)

daily life. When there is a clear two-mile stretch of footpath ahead there is time to explore a topic at a more natural length. It's another one of the unexpected pleasures of walking long distances with people: you can get to know each other. Maybe that's one of the joys of golf. We spot a deer bounding through a pine forest, then we drop down to the river where there is a natural weir plunging over a dolerite rock sill intruded into the sandstone.

We arrive at the Fox and Pheasant pub in Armathwaite and relax into a welcome pint. Then we try to get a taxi back to our car, which proves near impossible. None of the Carlisle taxi firms are prepared to come out into the sticks. After listening to me for a while on the pay phone, one of the other customers, a handlebar-moustache-wearing gentleman, speaks up. 'I'll give you a lift. Where are you going?' We explain, and he leads us out to his Mercedes. It turns out that this is 'Chocks', an ex-RAF wing commander. On the way he tells us something of his fascinating life. Once again we have been rescued by the kindness of strangers. Maybe people feel more generous in spring? We wave Chocks away.

Charlie departs the next day, having pounded a few miles of England with us and sailed in Glenridding's Lune Whammel. He did a tough walk in great style. We're on our own now until the Scottish border. There is a report in the *Guardian* today quoting a study which found that English schoolchildren are the least fit they have ever been, and that the reason is their sedentary lifestyles, not an obesity epidemic. It claimed that their level of fitness is declining by 1 per cent annually. Lead researcher Dr Gavin Sandercock said: 'It has got to the stage now that if we took the least-fit child from a class of 30 we tested in 1998, they would be one of the five fittest children in a class of the same age today.' Certainly throughout the country we've seen children ferried everywhere in their parents' cars, and very few out walking. He continued, 'These are the children who had free swimming taken away, these are the children who lived through the demolition of the schools' sports partnerships and they were the ones who lost the five-hour offer of PE.'[1]

Then there's been the scandal of schools being forced to sell their playing fields to developers. The *Telegraph* reports that 10,000 school playing fields were sold off under the 1979 to 1997 Conservative governments. Their Labour successors sold off an average of twenty a year. Shame on the politicians! We are richer than ever in this country, and yet we give in to greed and self-interest and ruin our children's health. The *Telegraph* continued, 'Education secretary Michael Gove . . . also greatly weakened provisions for the minimum outdoor space provided for pupils for team games, and dropped requirements that all schoolchildren should take part in two hours of sport a week: a *Telegraph* survey suggested last year that the proportion doing so had dropped from 90 to 43 per cent.'[2] Our reward will be generations of obesity, diabetes, the consequent collapse of the National Health Service and a great deal of unhappiness all round. And all for a sea of cheap, yellow-brick housing.

In the tree-covered slopes above the River Eden I disturb

---

[1] www.theguardian.com/education/2015/jun/18/england-pupils-the-least-fit-they-have-ever-been

[2] www.telegraph.co.uk/sport/othersports/schoolsports/11092344/Is-it-game-over-for-school-playing-fields.html

another deer. It seems surprisingly large and crashes through
the bracken. I wonder how many English children will have
the excitement of seeing a large wild animal in its natural
habitat. They are becoming disconnected from nature. In the
United States there is still a frontier culture: pick-up trucks,
guns, hunting. Americans are not quite at the top of the food
chain: bears can kill you in the States. Here in England nature
is marginalised. There is no wild animal that could kill us.
And we never see the animal die whose meat we eat. Meat is a
portion in a white polystyrene tray. If we do see a dead
animal, it seems nauseating. So we don't feel the old way
about animals. So there is a disconnect between man and
nature, particularly here in England.

We have only two days left to get to Scotland: we have to
walk from Armathwaite to Carlisle today, then from Carlisle
to Gretna Green tomorrow. And I haven't figured out the
route for tomorrow, it looks awful on the map: walking
alongside the M6 motorway. We continue down the River
Eden, which is getting wider and wider as its affluents or
tributary streams join it. It's now flowing in a deep valley
cut into red sandstone with woods and fine houses in them.
We are in the parish of Wetheral, which was part of the
Scottish kingdom of Strathclyde until the Normans arrived
in 1092. When a railway was built from Newcastle on the
way to Carlisle it crossed the river here and Wetheral
became a desirable place to live, with local industrialists
building large mansions around the village green and along

the river. It's good to have this, my favourite English river, at the end of our journey.

There's a swirl of water near the weir just across the river from where we're walking, and then a sleek, black, humped shape briefly appears: a very rare sighting of an otter. It disappears quickly: we've been spotted.

These beautiful creatures have come back to the Eden after nearly dying out in the 1980s. There are very few rivers left in industrialised England that haven't been turned into pseudo-canals or had their banks straightened and cleared. Otters need natural riverbanks, filled with holes for their holts (dens). They need overgrown vegetation on the banks and in the water, and riverbanks such as these on the Eden with willow, alder and brambles are ideal. People, with their pleasure boats, tractors, dredgers and diggers, are generally bad for otters. They were fairly numerous until the 1950s, when disaster happened. Pesticides such as Dieldrin and other organo-phosphates were introduced throughout England in the 1950s, and farmers applied them indiscriminately, looking for bumper profits.

These poisons ran off the land into the rivers and accumulated in fish. Otters, being at the top of the food chain, received large doses in their livers. But that may not have actually killed them directly. Aquatic plants died off in English rivers, bacteria rotted the dead plants down and the resulting lack of oxygen forced fish to move elsewhere. As a result otters very nearly became extinct in England in the early 1980s.

This is a story of successful conservation, though. As we saw, Rachel Carson's *Silent Spring* helped to start a movement which banned those poisons and the rivers slowly recovered their health. Some of the Scottish population of otters on the Solway moved back in, and the River Eden is now colonised in all the habitats that were formerly occupied. It has been good news in the rest of England, too: in 2011 otters were again reported in Kent, which means that they are now back in all the English, Scottish and Welsh counties. Their numbers have recovered so fast that they are becoming a nuisance to some fisheries.

They are still hard to observe in the wild. You may see their footprints or spraints (droppings) around weirs where fish congregate or where streams join rivers. They have five toes, so their spoor can be distinguished from cats or dogs, those having only four. The toes are webbed, but this doesn't tend to show up in footprints. The spraints are about three inches long (7.5 centimetres) and half an inch in diameter (1 centimetre) and are made up of fish scales and bones. They are dark when fresh, then they dry to look like a cigar ash (the old name for them was coke, like a piece of coke ash, I suppose).

Down in the estuary these otters will hunt on the rocky shores and occasionally out to sea, but they are not a proper sea-otter. The males will travel up to 20 miles (30 kilometres), but females rarely as much as 4 miles (6 kilometres), which means that males are usually the otters killed on the road.

If we hadn't been spotted by this otter the following *might* have happened: it's late spring in *Tarka the Otter*, just this time of year, and the young pup Tarka is following his mother and his sisters:

The brook swirled fast by the farther bank; under the sycamore it moved fast and deep. From the water a nose had appeared and the sight of it has alarmed the wagtail. Two dark eyes and a small brown head fierce with whiskers rose up and looked around. Seeing no enemy, the otter swam to the shore and walked out on the sand, her rudder dripping wet behind her. She stopped, sniffing and listening, before running forward and examining all entrances under the bared roots of the sycamore tree in the steep bank. The otter knew the holt, for she had slept there during her own cubhood, when her mother had left the river and followed the brook to get to the White Clay Pits. The wagtail was still watching when the otter came out of the holt again. It flew away as she whistled. Two heads moved across the pool and a third behind, slightly larger, for Tarka followed his sisters. The cubs crawled into the holt, leaving seals, or marks of five pads and running pad, in the sand with the prints of the wagtail.[1]

Henry Williamson was another of our tortured nature writers. He had a Kent countryside childhood and fell in love with nature. He then took part in the First World War and like so many of his generation was traumatised by the experience. He became disgusted by the greed and hatred that had caused the conflict, and was determined that Britain and Germany should never go to war again. He was invalided out twice, the second time after he was gassed.

He then decided to take up full-time writing after reading Richard Jefferies' *The Story of My Heart*. He was another writer who was inspired by that wonderful naturalist. Unfortunately for Williamson's later reputation he then became enamoured of right-wing politics. He took up with Oswald Mosley and joined the British Union of Fascists. He visited Germany and was impressed by the Hitler Youth movement, and he was an apologist for Hitler, an opinion which is still unpopular amongst literary critics today. Despite that, author Will Self

---

[1] Henry Williamson, *Tarka the Otter*, G.P. Putnam's Sons (1927)

became a writer largely, he said, because of the effect that Williamson's *Dandelion Days* had upon him as a youth.

Does any of this matter? Does a writer's political opinion affect the quality of the work? The political climate was different in the 1930s, and one family might contain Communists and Fascists. I suspect Williamson's political judgement was skewed by his experiences of the First World War, but it does make me wonder if certain naturalists lean towards different political ideologies. Perhaps beekeepers would see the advantages of socialism? And maybe an admirer of a top predator, such as an otter, would have right-wing tendencies?

I lived next to an otter sanctuary for years and became familiar with these playful little murderers. The Chestnut Centre in the Peak District is still run by Roger and Carol Heap, and when we walked through the area I went round there for a refresher. The first thing I learned from Carol is that she and Roger were inspired by Henry Williamson's *Tarka the Otter*. He, as we have seen, was inspired in turn by Richard Jefferies, and it's interesting to see how these interests are handed down through the generations. Gavin Maxwell's *Ring of Bright Water* was another influence, and another book that has inspired a generation of naturalists.

Now the Chestnut Centre has many animals and birds, and we walked through a herd of fifty fallow deer on the way down to the otters. 'The first sign of spring for us is the lime trees greening,' Carol said, 'and these deer are pretty skinny by March.' The males drop their antlers in April and May, and the does eat them for the calcium. The males then grow new ones with velvet on them: the fur-like covering with a blood supply which enables the bone to grow. Spring is a tough time for birds, and quite a few end up here, being cared for at the Chestnut Centre hospital.

There are several species of otter here, including a giant otter that likes to eat piranhas (apparently they're careful to eat the head first). Otters are all mustelids, and the giant otter is the biggest of this family at 5 feet 7 inches (1.7m) in length. Then in another pen I spot a sleek sinuous shape swimming in the pool: a Eurasian otter, the sort we're used to in England. It's good to be able to study one close-up for a while. They are between two and three feet long (57 to 95cm) with a tail of 14 to 18 inches (35–45cm). They have a broad head and small round ears, and have an active manner and a whickering call. I was surprised to learn that they can breed at any time of year, not just in spring, and that the female does all the rearing of the pups. They have whiskers on their elbows so that they can feel vibrations in the water when hunting prey. Another surprise: it's now thought that they can smell under water.

Tarka the Otter was filmed in 1977, and it's odd to note that Henry Williamson died while the crew was filming the death scene of Tarka.

It feels like high summer today beside the River Eden. We're walking quietly in forest with thick leaf cover and so we are likely to see interesting creatures, and yes, suddenly we see a black grouse to our left. He's all black with a red wattle on his head and white stripes on his wings. He's waddling along really close to us, next to the footpath but just up in the field at eye level. We get a good look at him. I've only ever seen them on whisky bottles before, but sadly he's a rare sight now, endangered at red status. It's the same old story: loss of habitat.

We also meet some friendly lambs when we walk through a farmyard. They mob us and are so tame we think they must have been bottle-fed. Lambs are great fun but then they turn into middle-aged sheep. Bit like people, really. A bit further on, near Wetheral priory, we see manmade caves carved in the sandstone banks, at least 40 feet above the water. Apparently they were used by the monks as places of refuge during border warfare. There are similar monkish caves in Mustang, Nepal, in similar cliffs, excavated for similar reasons. This whole area was the scene of continual border raiding by the Scots upon the English, and by the English upon the Scots.

I'm feeling anxious again about reaching the border by tomorrow afternoon, so we press on. We've now left the River Eden and are heading directly for Carlisle across open fields. Gina sets a cracking pace and we do 4¾ miles in an hour and ten minutes; about 4.3 mph. We plunge into the city, feeling out of place in the streets.

This city of Carlisle, bizarrely, claims to be the largest city in England – by area. There are only 108,000 people here, fewer than Cheltenham, but the local government area is 402 square miles (1,039.97 square kilometres). There's a large amount of rural Carlisle, though. That's the kind of city I like. The accent has changed again: we can detect a trace of Scottish.

Running into the train station with rucksacks flouncing we arrive at the end of the Settle to Carlisle line and just catch the 18.14 back to Armathwaite, and as I sit back in the train I think about the absurdity of this whole trip: walking all day and then taking a train back to where we started, then driving a car past the point we walked to, staying the night and eventually driving back home down the length of England. We must have covered about 2,000 miles in total, but this style of

travel has meant that we have walked light and fast, just
carrying day-packs and enjoying the spring. I've done quite
enough of carrying tent, sleeping bags, food and stove in the
past and it's not particularly enjoyable. Plus it would be impossible to find a campsite every night at exactly the right spot.
An even better way to do this would be to have a loving
motor-caravan driver meet you at the end of each day, but you
can't have everything in this world.

It's the last day of spring. We've moved to Carlisle to give us a
full day of walking, and I've figured out a better route on the
map. We'll cross the River Eden by bridge then head for the
Scottish border along the Cumbria Coastal Way, which follows
the true right bank of the river.

We are walking through Carlisle beside a busy main road
and as we cross a bridge I happen to glance over the parapet.
And I see something that seems very significant, but I can't
quite put my finger on it. I see the River Eden flowing past for
the last time, and a little way downstream there is a grey
heron at the end of a tail of shingle. He is hunched over,
utterly still and utterly intent. His back is turned to mankind
with our roar and progress. The river, the heron, the blue
sky . . . it all seems to represent the English spring that is just
passing. And yet the scene is as old as time. My attention
switches back to the crowded pavement and the moment is
gone. But that heron – he meant something.

We have a delightful last day's walk. Once again the weather
is good and we walk on deserted country B roads rather than

alongside the motorway. We arrive at the well-named village of Rockcliffe, although the name actually translates from the Norse and English as 'red cliff': there are sandstone bluffs standing above the river. There's a game of cricket going on here: a delightful English summer scene. We're near the sea, and we see around 100 seagulls standing in a huge ring in a field. I remember my parliament of magpies and wonder if they are having a similar discussion.

The road is dead straight, running alongside a plantation of conifers, and we spot a UFO: a bright silver object floating through the sky at about 2,000 feet (600 metres) with no jet-stream or contrail. Gina describes it as an origami swan, all angles and folds, which makes me think of some kind of radar reflector. There's no attached balloon and no obvious explanation, but it's almost certainly not piloted by aliens. I think about the heron again, and try to grasp the meaning of the moment. The natural scene this morning felt completely indifferent to humanity.

Nature, of course, doesn't care about us in the slightest. Jacques Monod, the biologist/philosopher, wrote: 'Man at last knows that he is alone in the unfeeling immensity of the universe, out of which he emerged only by chance. His destiny is nowhere spelled out, nor is his duty. The kingdom above or the darkness below; it is for him to choose.' We are a uniquely privileged species, we alone know that our existence is due to chance, and we can take some control of our destiny. Monod was a member of the French Resistance and rose to become their chief of staff, a Nobel Prize winner and holder of Légion d'Honneur. It seems that the French value their intellectuals, whereas the English pretend not to understand them.

So what will happen to the English countryside in future? For centuries English yeomen farmers were the backbone of the English economy, which was reasonably sustainable by the countryside we've walked through. The human population was tied to the productivity of the land: when starvation stalked the land our numbers fell. Then Parliament came along in 1604 and destroyed the old property rights through a series of Enclosure Acts, which privatised common land and formed the great landed estates which led to agrarian capitalism. This in turn led to the extraordinary productivity of industrial capitalism and everything that came from that: the Victorians, Americans and now the immense dragon of Chinese capitalism. But this growth cannot continue forever.

In *False Dawn: The Delusions of Global Capitalism*[1] political philosopher John Grey presents us with an apocalyptic future. Global capitalism, he writes, is now endangering liberal civilisation and, crucially, '. . . the present international economic system contains no effective institutions for conserving the wealth of the natural environment'.

Sovereign states will be drawn into wars over resources such as water and land. All of this, he asserts, is because of the never ending rise in human numbers. With two hundred competing sovereign states on the planet, environmentally sustainable policies just aren't possible: someone will always want to build another coal-fired power station. He rejects the Green Utopianism of communes and whirling wind generators: 'Renewable energy cannot support a world of nine billion humans (and we have already seen this predicted figure increased to eleven billion), there is no Green energy mix that can sustain industrialization in a world of high and rising human numbers.'

---

[1] John Grey, *False Dawn: The Delusions of Global Capitalism*, Granta Books (1998)

Grey suggests that the only solution is a staged withdrawal: 'In these circumstances the task for humankind is not to promote sustainable development. It is to work out how to make a sustainable retreat, and here technology will be crucial . . . high-tech solutions, including technologies that most Greens most oppose, such as nuclear power, genetically modified food and cleaner coal – will be indispensable in negotiating the environmental chaos that is now unavoidable.'

Having given everyone a good kicking: his erstwhile right-wing supporters, the Left, the religious fundamentalists, the Russians, Chinese and the Greens, Grey can't expect to be very popular. But his message needs to be heard: 'Humans are like any other plague animal. They cannot destroy the Earth, but they can easily wreck the environment that sustains them'[1] (*Straw Dogs*, 2002). There are far too many of us, but technology can help us out of the mess.

This has been a long walk through England where nothing really happened. But everything happened to me. This journey has changed my outlook in a fundamental way. Having no children, I didn't like militant environmentalists telling me I should buy a greener car to safeguard future generations. Like the merchant bankers during the great crash of 2007 I thought 'I'll be on the beach' when the final reckoning was due. Relaxing into a contented *Telegraph-* and *Guardian*-reading

---

[1] John Grey, *Straw Dogs: Thoughts on Humans and Other Animals*, Granta Books (2002)

middle age I've been jolted into an uncomfortable realisation that we're heading for problems.

I've become much more aware of the need to cherish what we have on this Earth, and above all, to reduce the numbers of our species. If we don't do it on our terms, then it will be done to us by starvation, plague and war. As long as we don't exterminate every other species, Nature will return when we're gone.

We crossed over the River Esk and walked parallel to the roaring M6 motorway on a quiet country road. The drivers in their fleeting cars didn't turn their eyes to the great estuary to the west, nor did they see a couple of walkers trudging along the verge. We turned off towards the true border, the bridge over the little River Sark, and I bent to plant the last acorn. I looked to our right into the last field of England and, in what seemed to us a parting gift, a great winged creature slowly lifted off and flew north. Good God, a golden eagle.

And so at last we stood on that little stone bridge, the border between the two countries, the English spring behind us, now finished, and the Scottish summer ahead, still to come.

'Shall we go on, then?' Gina asked.

'Yes,' I said.

And so we did.

POSTSCRIPT

It's two in the morning on 2 October, in the Arctic Ocean somewhere south of Spitsbergen and north of Bear Island, and I'm on watch on board the yacht *Northabout*. The waning moon casts a great shining track ahead of us, the Vikings' Whale Road, and above stand the Northern Lights – a great, green, shimmering curtain of icy fire hanging down through space. Thousands of feet beneath us on the seabed lie the crumpled hulks of British ships, sunk by the U-boats which preyed on the wartime convoys to Russia. Alone in the yacht's cockpit, now huddled in whirling snow, I try to remember this spring's walk through the English countryside. It already seems a distant dream of green meadows and sunny days. And now I feel that sense of loss that our nature writers struggled to express; the conviction that something precious is about to be lost. Although we saw again and again on our walk that small-scale conservation efforts work, there are forces gathering to destroy our green and pleasant land. Pressures to build over the Green Belt are rising with population pressure. Men will fix price tags to wildflowers and birdsong and other men will throw money down and call in the bulldozers. Unless all of us who really value our countryside rise up and fight it will be lost and gone forever.

Later that night, off watch and lying in my bunk, I have an uneasy dream. I see the ghostly procession of sunken ships

passing under our keel, each with a ghostly crew. Their thin
reproachful lament rises up with the clang of ships' bells:

> 'We drowned to save our country …'
> *'Turn the glass, strike the bell …'*
> 'We drowned to save our country …'
> *'Turn the glass, strike the bell …'*
> 'We drowned to save our country …'
> *'Turn the glass, strike the bell …'*

Someone is shouting, and jabbing me in the ribs. I wake
from one nightmare and enter another. The yacht is crashing
and banging over the waves and the wind has risen. A sail has
to be taken in. I have to go on deck and steer.

As I sit on the bunk pulling on my oilskins in the dark I
have a revelation. *'It was the heron.'* The heron I saw from the
bridge in Carlisle. He is hunched over his beak at the tail of
the river-island, intent on the fish. The fish are living their
lives of terrifying intensity. The river, the valley, the trees, the
sky – they are all part of a great oneness. I am in it, too. We
are all part of the great Ubiquity: *we are all part of Pan.*

ACKNOWLEDGEMENTS

No one reads the acknowledgements, do they? Only the people you've forgotten, so it's an opportunity for me to have a little private fun. Writers practise the art of immortality and time travel, so I can thank everyone alive or dead equally.

So, step forward Denys Watkins-Pitchford, 'BB' to your readers, thank you for filling my childhood with magic. Edward Thomas, Richard Jefferies and Ted Hughes: thanks for your careful observations and descriptions. Bill Shakespeare, you single-handedly keep the economy of Stratford-upon-Avon afloat. And if you did write all that stuff, it's the best writing in English. Keep it up. William Cobbett, thank you for your humanity to the poor people of rural England. And William Morris, try to share the champagne around a bit, would you mate?

Thanks to my neighbours John and Myra Hearnshaw for explaining how spring arrives in their Peak District farm and garden, neighbour Bryan McGee for giving lifts and endless cuttings from the newspapers, neighbour Sheila Ranson of Longendale Nursery, for explaining to a non-gardener how plants experience spring, and Carol and Roger Heap for introducing us to their otters. Caroline, Countess of Harrowby kindly showed me round Burnt Norton and gave me her book of the same name, Charlie Hobson cooked us bacon and eggs and explained farming in Wiltshire, David Hempleman Adams put us up for the night and gave me several trips on his yacht *Northabout*, and has been a steady friend for years. Simon Calder, another long-time friend, fed us with travel solutions and enthusiastic encouragement, as ever. General Sir Peter de la Billière gave me his particular insight into long-distance walking and sailing, and his son Ed provided endless support and help with the project when Scotland seemed a long way off.

Julian Champkin, the man who really does know everything, walked and sailed with us beyond the call of duty, as did his family – Mary, Rose and Peter. Sorry about the hypothermia. Charlie Viney walked with us manfully and explained the arcane world of publishing. There can't be many literary agents prepared to travel with their writers. Fabrice Fleurot walked twice the mileage we did in taking photographs of our walk and provided many of these beautiful images. Thanks, too, to Henri Lloyd for our sailing gear and Berghaus for our jackets, salopettes and rucksacks. Our Garmin GPS equipment navigated us through England by land and around the world by sea. And thank you, Myles Archibald, my editor whose love of English nature and books exceeds even mine.

The Three Lions at Fordingbridge, a restaurant with rooms, gave us a night's accommodation and I can't recommend them more highly if you want to walk in the area, eat a lovely dinner and fall into bed. An old climbing friend, Steve Berry, picked us up and gave us a night's stay at Hawkesbury. Thanks to you and Seraphina. And thanks to John and Gillian who let us leave a large, yellow, tent-shaped patch on their lawn and drove us all over Yorkshire.

I have huge gratitude for the planners and conservationists, particularly the volunteers. You really are the thin green line that defends the garden of England from urban sprawl.

Then there is the kindness of strangers, some whose names we learned and some we didn't: the Army guy who turned round to give us a lift to Sheffield, 'Chocks' in the Fox and Pheasant who gave us a lift, and the man who offered a lift which we had to refuse in Edale.

I had to write this book in less than four months and read over eighty books about spring to research it. I am bound to have forgotten someone or omitted a reference: I am sorry and beg your forebearance.

Finally, thank you to Gina, who supported me, encouraged me, and insisted that we should walk every single step of the way otherwise 'it isn't proper'. You planned the route, fed us and booked every night's stay and every train and bus trip. I really couldn't have done it without you. Thank you, darling.

BIBLIOGRAPHY

Page 19: Optimum Population Trust, 26th August 2009 Gaia
    Scientist to be OPT Patron.
    www.optimumpopulation.org/releases/opt.release26Aug09.
    htm
'Research on the assessment of risks & opportunities for
    species in England as a result of climate change
    (NECR175)' *Natural England*, 22 July 2015
UK Biodiversity Action Plan; Priority Habitat Descriptions.
    BRIG, ed. Ant Maddock (2008).
Horace, *Epistles* I.X.24
UN population study: www.un.org/en/development/desa/popu-
    lation/events/other/10/index.shtml
www.dailymail.co.uk/news/article-1059780/Black-farmer-
    quizzed-police-THREE-times-suspicion-stealing-field.html
Guardian Handsworth editorial:www.nytimes.com/1985/09/15/
    weekinreview/getting-at-the-causes-of-britain-s-latest-
    black-eye.html

BIBLIOGRAPHY

CHAPTER 1

John Dryden, *Palamon and Arcite, Book III* (1700)

Seamus Heaney, *The Names of the Hare* (1982)

Kit Williams, *Masquerade*, Jonathan Cape (1979)

William Cobbett, *Rural Rides* (1830)

Roger Deakin, *Wildwood*, Penguin (2008)

Lewis Carroll, *Alice's Adventures in Wonderland*, Macmillan (1865)

John Lewis-Stempel, *Meadowland: the private life of an English field* (2014)

Hugh Warwick, *A Prickly Affair*, Penguin (2010)

Beatrix Potter, *The Tale of Mrs Tiggy-Winkle*, Warne & Co. (1905)

William Golding, *The Spire*, Faber & Faber (1964)

Kevin Cahill, *Who Owns Britain*, Canongate (2002)

Roald Dahl, *Danny: the Champion of the World*, Jonathan Cape (1975)

Graham Hoyland, *Last Hours on Everest*, HarperCollins (2013)

CHAPTER 2

Edward Thomas, *In Pursuit of Spring* (1914)

Robert Macfarlane, *The Old Ways*, Hamish Hamilton (2012)

Robert Macfarlane, *Mountains of the Mind*, Granta (2003)

Robert Macfarlane, *The Wild Places*, Granta (2007)

Simon Winchester, *The Map that Changed the World*, HarperCollins (2001)

Jane Austen, *Persuasion* (1817)

William Henry Hudson, *Birds and Man* (1901)

Cormack, W.E., *Account of a Journey Across the Island of Newfoundland*, Constable (1824)

W.G. Sebald, *A Natural History of Destruction*, Carl Hanser Verlag (1999)

W.G. Sebald, *The Rings of Saturn*, Eichborn (1995)

Richard Jefferies, *Bevis*, Longmans, Green & Co. (1882)

Richard Jefferies, *Wood Magic*, Longmans, Green & Co. (1881)

Richard Jefferies, *After London*, Longmans, Green & Co. (1885)

Richard Jefferies, *Field and Hedgerow; Being the Last Essays of Richard Jefferies*, Longmans, Green & Co. (1889)

Richard Jefferies, *The Story of My Heart: An Autobiography*, Longmans, Green & Co. (1883)

CHAPTER 3

J.B. Priestley, *English Journey*, Victor Gollancz (1934)

Oliver Rackham, *The Last Forest*, J.M. Dent & Sons Ltd (1989)

Laurie Lee, *Cider with Rosie*, Hogarth Press (1959)

Alec Clifton-Taylor, *English Parish Churches as Works of Art* (1974)

Gerard Manley Hopkins, 'The Windhover' (1877)

Dylan Thomas, *Under Milk Wood* (1954)

Joseph Conrad, *Heart of Darkness*, Blackwood's Magazine (1899)

Arthur Conan Doyle, *The Adventure of the Copper Beeches*, The Strand Magazine (June 1892)

CHAPTER 4

Bill Bryson, *A Walk in the Woods*, Broadway Books (1998)
William R. Forstchen, *One Second After* (2009)
Alan Weisman. *The World Without Us*, St. Martin's Thomas
    Dunne Books (2009)
T.S. Eliot, *Burnt Norton*, Faber (1941)
Gilbert White, *The Natural History and Antiquities of Selbourne*
    (1789)
Richard Mabey, *Gilbert White*, Profile Books (2006)
Bill Bryson, *The Road to Little Dribbling* (2015)
Bill Bryson, *Notes from a Small Island* (1995)
John Moore, *The Seasons of the Year*, Collins (1954)
Nick Davies, *Cuckoo: Cheating by Nature*, Bloomsbury (2015)

CHAPTER 5

'BB' Denys Watkins-Pitchford, *The Little Grey Men*, Eyre &
    Spottiswoode (1942)
'BB' Denys Watkins-Pitchford, *Down the Bright Stream*, Eyre &
    Spottiswoode (1948)
'BB' Denys Watkins-Pitchford, *Wild Lone: The Story of a
    Pytchley Fox*, Eyre & Spottiswoode (1938)
J.R.R. Tolkien, *The Hobbit*, Stanley Unwin (1937)
J.R.R. Tolkien, *The Lord of the Rings*, Stanley Unwin (1954–1955)

CHAPTER 6

'BB' Denys Watkins-Pitchford, *Manka, the Sky Gypsy: The Story
    of a Wild Goose*, Eyre & Spottiswoode (1939)
Antoine de Saint-Exupéry, *Wind, Sand and Stars*, Reynal &
    Hitchcock (1939)

Kenneth Grahame, *The Wind in the Willows*, Methuen (1908)

Rachel Carson, *Silent Spring*, 'Houghton Mifflin (1962)

James Lovelock, *A Rough Ride to the Future*, Allen Lane (2014)

John Moore, *The Year of the Pigeons*, Collins (1963)

CHAPTER 7

John Clare, 'The Ragwort' (1832)

Izaak Walton, *The Compleat Angler* (1653)

Ted Hughes, 'Swifts', *Collected Poems for Children*, Faber (2008)

CHAPTER 8

Michael Hoyland, *The Bright Way In*, Free Man's Press (1984)

Ted Hughes, 'The Thought Fox', *The Hawk in the Rain* (1957)

CHAPTER 9

Emily Brontë, *Wuthering Heights* (1847)

Bill Bryson, *The Road to Little Dribbling*, Doubleday (2015)

Jan Bondeson, *Greyfriars Bobby: The Most Faithful Dog in the World*, Amberley (2011)

Michael Shermer, *How We Believe: The Search for God in an Age of Science*, Times (2000)

CHAPTER 10

Dorothy Wordsworth, *Grasmere Journal*, 15 April 1802

William Wordsworth, *Poems in Two Volumes* (1807)

Arthur Ransome, *Swallows and Amazons*, Jonathan Cape (1930)

Laurence Binyon, *Landscape in English Art and Poetry* (1931)

Henry Williamson, *Tarka the Otter*, G.P. Putnam's Sons (1927)

Gavin Maxwell, *Ring of Bright Water*, Penguin (1960)

John Grey, *False Dawn: The Delusions of Global Capitalism*, Granta Books (1998)

John Grey, *Straw Dogs: Thoughts on Humans and Other Animals*, Granta Books (2002)

INDEX